# The Masks of War

*God has given you one face,*
*and you make yourselves another.*

—Shakespeare, *Hamlet*

# The Masks of War

*American Military Styles
in Strategy and Analysis*

*Carl H. Builder*

*Foreword by Sam Nunn*

*A RAND Corporation Research Study*

The Johns Hopkins University Press
Baltimore and London

Originally published in hardcover and paperback, 1989
04 03 02 01 00 99 98 97 96 95    7 6 5 4 3

The Johns Hopkins University Press
2715 North Charles Street
Baltimore, Maryland 21218-4319

The Johns Hopkins Press Ltd., London

*Library of Congress Cataloging-in-Publication Data*

Builder, Carl H.
   The masks of war.

   (A RAND Corporation research study)
   Bibliography: p.
   Includes index.
   1. United States—Military policy.   2. United States—Armed
Forces.   3. Military planning—United States.   4. Strategy.
I. Title.   II. Series.
UA23.B7855      1989      355'.0335'73      88-13517
ISBN 0-8018-3775-8 (alk. paper)
ISBN 0-8018-3776-6 (pbk. : alk. paper)

A catalog record for this book is available from the British Library.

*To Gabriele,*
*Who shared in the joy of discovering the keys*
*and opening the doors*

# CONTENTS

Foreword                                                    ix
Preface                                                      xi

**Part I   Personalities**                                   1

  1   The Masks of War                                        3
  2   Five Faces of the Service Personalities                17
  3   The Service Identities and Behavior                    31

**Part II   Strategy**                                      45

  4   What Is Strategy?                                      47
  5   Service Strategies                                     57
  6   The Air Strategy                                       67
  7   The Navy and Strategy                                  74
  8   The Army and Strategy                                  86

**Part III   Analysis**                                    93

  9   What Is Analysis?                                      95
 10   Service Styles toward Analysis                        104
 11   Images of Conflict                                    115

**Part IV   Implications**                                125

 12   The Service Concepts of War                           127
 13   Military Commitments to Combat                        143
 14   Implications for Military Planning                    154
 15   Implications for Regional Security                    168

**Part V   Prospects**                                                183

    16   The Army's Identity Crisis                          185
    17   Implications for the Future                         194

Notes                                                                207
Bibliography                                                         231
Index                                                                235

# FOREWORD

Today America faces significant technological, economic, political, and social challenges in the national security environment. Our twin trade and budget deficits, unless addressed quickly, will jeopardize our ability to fund national security needs. Dramatic events in the Soviet Union—with their implications for arms control, the character of the Soviet military threat, and the unleashing of centrifugal forces in the Soviet empire—indicate that we are moving to new, uncharted, and, possibly, unstable ground in superpower relations.

Adapting our military planning to this new environment will place great demands upon all of our national security institutions, including the Congress, the Defense Department and the military services, and the intelligence community. Changes in our nation's military needs and the allocation of resources will require careful thought, negotiations, and, most of all, understanding by the participants—not just of national security issues, but also of the institutions and people involved.

Carl Builder provides us with a better understanding of some of these key national security institutions—the American military services. This book is devoted to analyzing and explaining why the United States Army, Navy, and Air Force behave the way they do. The author believes that an understanding of this behavior can be gained by observing the unique styles of the military services in their approaches to strategy and analysis. Rather than trying to expose what the military services have done wrong or failed to do, this book attempts, by stripping away their "masks of war," to understand how they think and what they are likely to do in the future.

Few of us will agree with everything in this provocative book. All of us, however, will benefit from the author's invitation to look beyond what the stategists, analysts, and even the military services themselves say they are doing in the name of military planning and national security in an effort to understand why the military services act as they do.

*—Sam Nunn*
*U.S. Senate*
*Washington, D.C.*

# PREFACE

Early in 1985, I accepted an invitation from E. B. (Van) Vandiver III, director of the U.S. Army Concepts Analysis Agency (CAA), to spend a year with his agency in Bethesda, Maryland, playing gadfly. I welcomed the invitation because I had found Van to be one of those rare government officials who are both bureaucratically effective and intellectually lively. Besides, a year in Bethesda matched my preferred operating cycle at RAND in Santa Monica—one year away for every two years on the beach. We agreed that I would do some individual research while there.

It was July before we could clear away all the necessary arrangements and I had a desk in Bethesda. Van was away for my first week there, giving me time to settle in and find the coffeepot. On Monday afternoon, 22 July, fresh from a Pentagon staff meeting, Van swept into my office and, by way of greeting, said: "I know what I want you to do while you are here. Why don't you find out why the Army does so poorly in strategic planning? We do a terrible job as compared to the Navy or Air Force. Look into strategic planning as it is done in the United States—the whole thing, from the top right on down, the Army's role in that process, and how CAA might contribute to that process—all with a view toward our doing it better than we do now."

Those words, that minute, was the clear beginning of a straight line of actions that has led to this book. Van's original request led to a year-long study of the Army in the strategic planning process that resulted in reports published by both CAA and RAND.[1] That study was mostly about strategy and the strategic planning challenge that faced the Army.

But even as I briefed that study in its early stages, it became obvious that of greatest interest to most audiences was my comparison of the three services and their unique attitudes toward various things. Therefore, when I was asked to be the banquet speaker at the Army's Operations Research Symposium, I resorted to that same theme as the centerpiece for a talk on the Army's style in analysis.[2] The comments on those publications, briefings, and talks indicated widespread interest in the comparative analysis of the institutional personalities of the American military services. It was a short intellectual step from there to this book, even though the writing and publication involved much more from others in the way of encouragement and support.

Behind any speculative piece of research and writing, such as this, there are always to be found inspired instigators and enlightened sponsors. The inspired instigator, of course, was E. B. Vandiver III, who not only posed the initiating question but also pressed for its publication as a book. The enlightened sponsors were to be found both in the Army and in the Army's Arroyo Center at RAND. In the Army, it was Major General Jack O. Bradshaw, then director of Strategy Plans and Policy for the Army staff, who saw the early research pointing toward a comparative analysis of the military services and, given the opportunity to turn it off then and there, had the courage to say, "Go ahead." At RAND, it was Stephen M. Drezner, vice president for the Army Research Division and director of the Arroyo Center, who was the first to alert me to the different analytic styles of the services, and who later stood up as sponsor of this book.

Along the way, I had the opportunity to stand upon the shoulders of several competent researchers who have preceded me in my examination of the behavior of the military services. Perry McCoy Smith, in his devastating analysis *The Air Force Plans for Peace*,[3] codified much of what I had always suspected about institutional incentives in military planning. I was led to Smith's book by James Lacy, who wrote the complementary analysis of Navy postwar planning, *Within Bounds*.[4] A colleague at RAND, David Kassing, upon hearing of this research, put me onto Lacy's trail. Army Major Peter Kinney suggested Admiral J. C. Wylie's fine treatise *Military Strategy*.[5] And while browsing through the CAA library shelves, I discovered the work of another RAND colleague, Arnold Kanter's *Defense Politics*.[6] These four texts stand as pillars of research to support this book.

Arthur Hadley's fine institutional analysis of America's armed forces, *The Straw Giant*,[7] differs in several important respects from what I have attempted here. From his vantage point as a reporter, Hadley has used his broad perspective of the American military establishment to suggest reforms that would "replace straw with steel." By contrast, as a strategist and analyst, I have looked at the military services more narrowly, with the purpose of understanding them: who they are, where they are coming from, what they seem to be about, and where they may aspire to go.

To convert my various writings into a published book, Constance Greaser, head of RAND's publications department, took me firmly by the hand and confidently guided me at every step along the path.

My greatest debt accumulated in this enterprise is to the United States Army. This book was born and nurtured in Army sponsored research; and Army people—uniformed and civilian—gave hearty encouragement to its publication all along the way. My professional associations with the Army are more recent than those with the Air Force and Navy, but the Army has certainly won my admiration and gratitude as the most open and straightforward of the American military institutions. I believe that the Army, alone among the services, has the security and humility to tolerate, even encourage, what has been attempted here.

# Part I
# Personalities

# 1

---

# THE MASKS OF WAR

This book advances three simple arguments:

1.  Institutions, while composed of many, ever-changing individuals, have distinct and enduring personalities of their own that govern much of their behavior.
2.  The most powerful institutions in the American national security arena are the military services—the Army, Navy, and Air Force—not the Department of Defense or Congress or even their commander in chief, the president.
3.  To understand the distinct and enduring personalities of the Army, Navy, and Air Force is to understand much that has happened and much that will happen in the American military and national security arenas.

To grasp these three arguments is to master the book's message. While advancing these arguments is no great leap, making them credible and vivid, so they result in empathetic understanding and a reliable basis for action, is a much more extensive undertaking. And it is that larger undertaking, rather than the arguments themselves, that justifies the many words and pages that follow.

An empathetic understanding of the American military institutions, as personalities, requires spending time with them, wrestling with their problems, interests, and aspirations—or at least trying to stand in their shoes as they deal with these things. Perhaps nothing is more self-revealing about the problems, interests, and aspirations of the American military institutions than their approaches to military strategy, planning, and analysis. It is here, on these matters, that they write and, therefore, leave some durable, analyzable

**3**

record of their thinking. And it is here that we can look for evidence of their personalities.

## The Roots of American Military Strategies

Most contemporary texts on military strategy treat the subject as an artful exercise in logic, one that can be mastered by careful study of its immutable principles. Yet anyone who tries to follow the current debates over the maritime or NATO strategies, or the concepts of assured destruction or "Star Wars," must be struck by the great diversity of answers that seem to flow from, or are often justified by, those immutable principles of strategy.

The explanation, of course, is that strategies, and the concepts or conclusions that are drawn from them, come from much more than science or analysis or axioms. Their sources are deeply embedded in the interests of the people or institutions that advocate them. Though the words and arguments used to support or attack strategies and concepts may be referenced to classic strategic principles, the motivations toward or away from a strategic theory often lie hidden even from its proponent.

The roots of modern American military strategies lie buried in the country's three most powerful institutions: the Army, Navy, and Air Force. Though many people outside the military institutions, including academics and presidents, may propose military strategies and concepts, these can be implemented only if and when military institutions accept and pursue them. To understand the American military institutions, then—who they are and what they are about—is to understand almost everything of enduring significance in the national debates over military issues.

The roots of modern American military strategies can be unearthed by digging down into the institutional personalities of American military services, by looking at their history and behavior instead of the words they may use to mask or explain themselves. When those institutional personalities are compared, much of the unique behavior attributed to each of the services suddenly pops into focus. The evidence is not new, only newly perceived as a part of a larger and consistent pattern that fits the recognizable personality of a particular service. Everything observed here about the service personalities has been seen before—somewhere, by someone, perhaps by many, so often as to become an invisible part of the background to the national security arena. When the fragments are assembled into the patterns of a recognizable personality, then the behavior suddenly becomes coherent rather than chaotic or quixotic. Historical behavior can be explained; and future behavior can be predicted with greater confidence. The personality differences of the three American military services are profound, pervasive, and persistent.

Since these personalities are deeply embedded inside large military institutions, they will persist despite changes in administrations, the Department of Defense, the Joint Chiefs, and the joint or specified commands. They will even persist through the trauma of war. They affect how the services, in peacetime, perceive war and then plan and buy and train forces. To understand the American military styles is to understand what is going on and much of what is likely to happen in the national security arena—from Star Wars to the Persian Gulf.

## The Traditional View of Military Planning

The traditional view of military planning presumes that military forces are acquired and deployed as the military means, alongside economic and diplomatic means, for the pursuit of political ends. For the United States, in peacetime, those political ends are generally assumed to be the promotion of international stability, prosperity, and security. Thus, it follows that peacetime military forces can and should be derived as appropriate military means to ensure international political objectives in the face of perceived threats.

Of course, such logic is not so neatly applied. Military forces are the products of much more complex processes. Powerful people and institutions, and their combining or conflicting interests, intrude. Nevertheless, in any formal discussion of military planning, the semblance of the logic is assiduously maintained. The military planning catechism goes something like this:

- These are the agreed-upon national objectives;
- Those are threats to these objectives;
- To secure these objectives in the face of those threats, that is the adopted strategy;
- This is the set of military capabilities needed to underwrite that strategy;
- And, thus, the following military forces are required to provide this set of capabilities.

The elements are laid out in this way because it is a rational, logical approach to security problems, not because it is really how we arrive at military forces; it is how we explain them.[1]

Despite the logical wrappings of defense planning, there is considerable evidence that the qualities of the U.S. military forces are determined more by cultural and institutional preferences for certain kinds of military forces than by the "threat." There are many ways to interpret a threat; there are many ways to deal with any particular interpretation of a threat. There is, after all, an American style about military forces, just as there is about business and life. It is people, not threats, who argue for and against the acquisition and maintenance of specific military forces. The advocates for a particular kind of military instrument can hardly be faulted (at least in peacetime) if their interpretations of the threat—and the effectiveness of a particular military system to counter it—reflects the interests of their institutions and the importance of their chosen careers. And, since these incentives derive more from human nature than ideology, we may reasonably assume that much the same is true for other military institutions, including those of the Soviet Union.

Is the arcane logic of military planning then only a sham, a deliberately contrived cover to mask the parochial ambitions of the military services? It is no more a sham than the logic that most of us use to explain to friends the purchase of our new automobile. Or the logic that both sides to an *offensive* arms race may use to explain their *defensive* motives: "So central is the concept of defense to the security debate that it would now be surprising for an accretion of military power to be justified by anything other than defensive motives—a response to the apparently more offensive orientation of the potential adversary. As a result it is quite normal for two opponents each to claim defensiveness and to charge the other with offensiveness."[2]

Even if military forces are only partly driven by institutional and cultural preferences, it may still be useful to explore the implications of those preferential engines at the extreme: What if military forces were not what we pretend them to be—the military means to political ends—but were, instead, institutional ends in themselves that may or may not serve the larger interests of the nations that support them? If that hyperbole is entertained as an intellectual device for thinking about military forces, then the qualities of those forces are likely to be more important (and revealing) than their quantities. The size of forces may be determined by national allocations of resources—by the Congress or Politburo or Parliament—but the character of those forces—the types of weapons chosen—are typically decided or promoted by the military institutions.

If we understand the American military institutions and their interests not simply as faceless, mindless bureaucracies doing their "thing" but as unique characters or personalities, like ourselves, we can begin to see a rationality in what they are doing, and have been doing for so long. It is asserted here that such an understanding explains their behavior much better than all the elaborate logic and language that have been developed around the traditional descriptions of military planning.

## Analysis as Language

Over the past forty years, certain kinds of military analysis have become an integral part of the vocabulary for debating strategy, military planning, forces, and weapons. Though arcane concepts such as "counterforce" and "flexible response" and "assured destruction" have meanings apart from analysis, many of them had their origin in, and are most vividly defined by, analyses. Thus, to understand the military services and their different attitudes toward strategies and forces, it may be helpful, here, to provide some understanding of the language of analysis used to debate these subjects. Though our treatment of analysis need not be exhaustive, a few contrasting examples of military analysis are provided later to illustrate the art form and its application.

Moreover, the services' attitudes toward analysis are quite different and reflect important aspects of their institutional personalities. Therefore, the American military styles of analysis serve as a two-way mirror: They certainly reflect the character or personality of the services; but they also allow us to look into and understand the nature and the issues of the debates among them.

## Institutions as Personalities

Like all individuals and durable groups, the military services have acquired personalities of their own that are shaped by their experiences and that, in turn, shape their behavior. And like individuals, the service personalities are likely to be significantly marked by the circumstances attending their early formation and their most recent traumas.

But treating institutions as if they were individuals with a personality raises several troublesome issues. Even for individuals, personality sketches can be misdrawn; the discernment of personality remains an art, not a science. Institutions, made up of large numbers of individuals, are more than the sum of those complex human individuals;[3] and complexity alone would seem to increase the risks of misdrawing their personalities. On the other hand, one's access to information on an institution, its behavior and words, is likely to be much greater than that for any individual.

Nevertheless, the complexity of institutions when examined closely—approaching the resolution of its individual members— requires that sketches of their personalities be made from a distance and with a very broad brush. To emphasize the differences among the services, their positions or attitudes on some aspects take the form of caricatures, with all that the word implies about exaggeration and loss of detail. The complex has been made simple; the great diversity of views within each of the services has been transformed into a monolithic voice speaking for the service.[4] The purpose in these obvious distortions is not ridicule, but discernment—to bring that which has become so familiar as to be hidden from view back into focus in order to understand the past, present, and future behavior of the services.

Despite that purpose, many will still object: Individual members of an institution that has been turned into a caricature will deny that the caricature speaks for their views or values or that it exhibits their own behavior or motivations. That is, they do not recognize themselves in the caricature of their institution; and they are, after all, loyal, mainstream members of that institution and ought to be able to find themselves in the caricature. The problem, of course, is attributing a "personality" to any body made up of individuals. The variance among individuals may be enormous, yet the institution may take on a distinctive personality. Few, perhaps none, of the individuals will have the same personality as the institution; but, collectively, they take on a recognizable personality. Thus, to attribute a personality to a military service is not to say that any individual member—regardless of loyalty, longevity, or position—could be found with the views, values, behavior, or motivations attributed to that service. Arthur Hadley wrestled with the same difficulties in *The Straw Giant*: "Such broad generalizations are always open to challenge. . . . How can a service that includes carrier pilots and submariners have an integrated personality? How can one that includes missile engineers and fighter jocks? Yet they most certainly do, though there are important subsets of attitudes within each service."[5]

Personality characterizations are like analytical models: They cannot be perfect precisely because they are models. If they were perfect, they would not be models; they would be the modeled object itself. The utility of the model is not its perfection of the object but the capturing of essential or important features in something simpler than the object. The utility of personality characterizations of the services is not their accuracy or completeness but the capture of some important aspects of the service behavior in something far less complex than the service itself, something we can hold in our minds and easily manipulate to project future behavior.

Institutional personalities do not account for everything; they are not the only aspect that needs to be considered in understanding the debates of military issues. But they may be simultaneously one of the most useful and most neglected aspects deserving consideration. Their value is that they reveal or explain so much, yet take so little effort to grasp and remember.

Each of the services can suffer or, in turn, shine by comparison with its sisters on one or more facets of their personalities. Those most loyal to one of the services may take exception to (or pride in) the way their service has been portrayed here. But the proper tests for these comparisons is whether they capture recognizable differences among the services and are substantially correct in direction and color, even if not always in degree or detail. If they are to be useful for their purposes here, these comparisons must be compelling on the basis of what one already knows; their general truth must be self-evident, for they rely on recognition more than revelation.

Finally, the service comparisons have been limited to the Army, Navy, and Air Force. What about the Marine Corps and the Coast Guard? They certainly have distinctive, even colorful, institutional personalities. However, neither the Marine Corps nor the Coast Guard enters the defense planning arena as an independent institutional actor with a significant voice in the national approach to strategy or military force planning. This is partly because of their institutional subordination,[6] partly because of their relative size, and, perhaps, partly because of their own institutional personalities or styles.[7]

Characterizing institutions as personalities can be amusing (or painful), but that, of course, is not the reason for doing so here. Turning institutions into personalities is a way of converting something amorphous and hard to grasp into a vivid picture that can be easily recalled and recognized again. The extraordinary human ability to recognize human faces is well known. Having once seen a face, most of us are able to recognize it again, even though it has changed in expression, age, and context. Giving institutions a personality is a way of giving them a "face" that can be remembered, recalled, and applied in evaluating future behavior or circumstances. As with the police artist's sketch, it need not be photographic in its details; the essential features, even if exaggerated somewhat, are the keys to recognition.

## Institutional Motivations

It is one step to attribute a personality to an institution; it is an even larger step to imbue that personality with motives. Attributing motivations to a person or an institution has great potential for mischief. Motivations are likely to be both more complex and more revealing than either their owner or their observer can admit. There is always more than meets the eye, yet what does show may be too much or too little at the same time, depending on the viewpoint. If one attributes another's action to greed, there may be much more to it than that, yet greed may be the one motivation its owner would most like to deny.

The problem is illustrated by the situation of the firemen for steam locomotives when the railroads began their transition to diesel engines. The new engines did not need anyone to tend the boiler fire; but the firemen argued for retention of the second person in the locomotive cab, a second set of eyes looking down the track, someone to take over if necessary. Their argument and implied motivation was about safety. A much less charitable view attributed the motivation to featherbedding, the retention of an easy job and its income. But it was not simply one or the other. The firemen were not thinking only of safety; nor were they thinking only of their pocketbooks. But it was much more comfortable for the firemen to couch their arguments on the former (which was altruistic) rather than the latter (which was self-serving). The motivations were more complex than safety or income; they also included the firemen's sense of their personal worth and contribution—a legitimate and common concern, but one that is not easily presented or argued. Indeed, one can conjecture that a fireman must truly believe in the safety argument in order to have respect for himself and his worth to other human beings.

A modern example is the case of flight engineers on commercial aircraft. With the latest generation of jet transports and their microelectronic instrumentation, both the aircraft designers and operators challenged the need for a "third seat" in the cockpit. The arguments from the flight engineers echoed those of the railroad firemen forty years earlier. They presented their motivations as concerns for safety, whereas, if truth be knowable, they were about much more.

The arguments get distorted because all the motivations do not get tabled. Some are too deep to be perceived, others are ignored or avoided because they do not seem admirable. If the motivations are avoided, others are likely to pick them up and attribute them, whether they are admirable or not, possibly driving the arguments into all-or-nothing corners. To say that the firemen's concern was motivated less by safety and more by self-interests (self-worth, esteem, job security, income, etc.) is not the same as saying that they really did not care about the safety of others, only about keeping money in their own pockets. By the same logic, to say that the motivation behind a service's strategy is less about national security than the service's institutional interests is not the same as saying that the service does not give a hoot about national defense, that it just wants to keep its empire alive and is willing to fabricate a strategy in order to do so.[8]

Institutional and personal interests are not intrinsically bad; but they may be made so if they are always cloaked in altruism and not acknowledged as legitimate interests. Has self-esteem become an unworthy (or unmentionable) motive? It is the (perhaps unconscious) perversion of legitimate institutional or personal interests in the guise of noble altruism that sets off the alarms in the minds of suspicious critics.

When I attribute motivations here to the American military services, I recognize:

- No individual member of that institution may have that motivation.
- Motivations are complex and seldom all-or-nothing in their character.
- Institutional motivations toward institutional survival, sovereignty, and well-being are legitimate enough, they just are not necessarily the same as those, say, of the country.

- Institutions are not necessarily free from some motivations sometimes found in individuals, even though they may not be universally admired or socially accepted.

Here, it will be most useful to say things about the services that are widely perceived as being so, but are usually not said in polite or respectful company. Indeed, these are things that the services generally will not say about one another even behind backs, perhaps because of a shared professional respect or because they know that they are all too vulnerable to some equivalent observation about their own service. These things are said here not to insult or impugn, but to get past some of the pompous nonsense and pretensions that have accumulated around strategy and analysis in American military planning. If, in trying to get past these barriers to visibility, the words have been unnecessarily unkind, unfair, or dead wrong, then apologies are due and will be rendered on demand.

The American military institutions are arguably the most powerful such institutions ever created. Two of them possess independent capabilities for waging global conflict on a scale never seen before and difficult, if not impossible, to imagine. All of them pervade almost every aspect of American life, yet they remain largely hidden behind the masks of security and the esoterics of military planning. Their critics, like pygmies surrounding an elephant, jab them with accusations of ineptness, hoping, it would seem, to change their course on this or that aspect. The purpose here is not to criticize the American military services but to understand them better—to see past the masks they hold up in front of themselves to screen some of their motives or self-interests: the masks of war.

## Warriors and Institutions

To imply that the American military institutions hold up masks of war to hide, from themselves as well as from outsiders, some of their less noble institutional interests is not to deny the individual or collective courage, dedication, or skill of the warriors within. The institutional self-interests are most evident in peacetime and among the senior officers of the services. It is the "fathers" of the institution who must look after their institution's well-being, for they have been entrusted with its care; the junior members of the institution will look to them to ensure the future of a healthy and nationally important institution. The warriors, as ever, are most evident among the younger members of the institutions; and they generally leave it to the institutional fathers to look to the institution's future while they hone their warrior skills for today.

When I talk with the young people who have committed themselves to one of the military institutions, I always come away impressed with how many are proud of, and dedicated to, their military crafts and duties. I could relate many examples, but one will illustrate the point. I remember visiting an Air Force base in the 1970s where a squadron of KC-135 aerial tankers of the Strategic Air Command stood alert, ready to refuel the bombers in flight if war came. Four of the tankers, brimmed with fuel, stood side by side on their hardstands, ready to go, next to the runway. Rifle-armed sentries standing in the planes' shadows made it clear that these four tankers were an important asset if war came that day. Less than fifty yards away was a bunker where the flight crews for the four planes lived for the several days they stood their alert duty.

As a civilian visitor, I was introduced to the flight crews in the bunker; we talked about their airplanes and the need for certain improvements in their performance, particularly about more power for takeoff. As I talked with one of the pilots, a young Air Force captain in his twenties, I noticed behind him, on the wall, a signboard with current information pertinent to the aircraft just outside the bunker. Among other things, it announced that the takeoff distance for the planes, as presently loaded, was 11,111 feet. The number was memorable not just for its repetition: I knew that the runway at that particular air base was only 10,000 feet long. So I asked the pilot whether or not the signboard was correct. He assured me that it was. When he did not elaborate, I protested that the runway was not that long. He simply nodded and said, "That's right, sir."

His level look said that it was up to me to press the issue: "What will you do, then, when you get to the end of the runway?"

"When I hit the overrun strip, I'll just pull back on the stick and hope that it flies. My main concern is that I'll be able to slide around or between some trees that are out there past the end of the runway."

I watched his eyes to see whether or not he was putting me on. They were blue and steady. Maybe he knew something I did not—that he had done it before and knew he could make it. So I probed further: "Do you practice these conditions?"

"No, sir, it's considered too dangerous."

"But those planes will have to be flown for training."

"Yes, sir. But when we take them off alert, we will offload some of the fuel into trucks so that they are safer to fly."

While there were, undoubtedly, some safety margins (for temperature and obstacles) built into the calculated takeoff distances for those heavily loaded airplanes, the discrepancy between the required and available runway was significant; the variables were many, untested, and not without consequences. Yet, whatever doubt there might be about the safety of the situation, there could be no doubt that those pilots were ready to fly those four airplanes when the horn sounded.

In my experience, that kind of dedication and courage is the norm, not the exception, in our armed forces. The warriors are there, everywhere. It is the institution that holds up the mask of war to cover the pursuit of its self-interests, not the warriors within it. The warriors need no masks to hide behind; it is they who face the prospect of war or its consequences every day.

## Do the Masks Ever Drop?

Do the American military services ever drop their masks of war and admit to their institutional self-interests? Rarely, I think, and then only within earshot of their own family.

The first time I saw an open admission of self-interest by a military institution was in a 1982 White Paper on the British decision to modernize their submarine-launched ballistic missiles (SLBMs) by exchanging the Polaris missiles for the new Trident.[9] For Britain and the British defense establishment, this was a difficult and contentious decision. For the United States, the Trident program was simply another step in the continuing evolution of its submarine-launched ballistic missile force—from Polaris to Poseidon to Trident—which, in turn, was only a part of a broader program of modernization for the U.S. strategic forces. But the change from Polaris to Trident represented an enormous investment for the British, one that would both bulge their defense budget and cut into the budget slices for other forces and services.

The opposition in Britain to the Trident modernization was substantial; it found voice in both the public and various segments of the British armed forces. In the face of this opposition, the Ministry of Defense took pains to explain the need for modernizing the SLBMs in a White Paper. Most of the paper was devoted to the typical military planning arguments—Britain's strategic objectives, the threat to those objectives, the strategy being pursued, and so on. Perhaps the strongest possible argument for modernizing the SLBMs—that they were wearing out—was missing because the government had earlier been forced to admit that the old Polaris missiles were good for at least another ten years.

Then, toward the end of the paper, almost as an afterthought, was a remarkable argument that can be paraphrased as follows: "Besides, if we don't modernize the Polaris, we won't be able to continue to attract and retain the very best people for our strategic nuclear forces, and that is the place where we want our very best." That, I would submit, is a very real and important concern of institutions about their future. Whether or not it is considered a valid or appropriate argument for modernizing Britain's strategic nuclear forces or for spending billions of pounds sterling, it reflects the understandable concern of an institution that has been made responsible for those forces. It is not the concern that is remarkable; it is its explicit expression.

Central to most institutions and their future is the ability to attract and retain good people. When I told a colleague[10] about the British using that concern as an argument for modernizing their SLBM force, he recalled one of his experiences with the American Strategic Air Command (SAC):

In the mid-1960s, the Air Force wanted to replace its B-52 bombers with a bomber that would be recognized today as the B-1, only then it was called the AMSA—the advanced manned strategic aircraft. But it was not successful in convincing the administration or Congress of the need; and Secretary of Defense Robert McNamara was pushing the Air Force to accept a strategic bomber adapted from his controversial TFX program—the FB-111. It would be an understatement to say that none of the services was enthusiastic about the TFX or its variants; it simply was not their airplane; it was McNamara's child.

The then fathers of SAC, who at the time were also essentially the fathers of the Air Force, met in the SAC "board room" to decide what to do about the next bomber they wanted so badly for the institution, since they would probably never fly it. My colleague was a "strap hanger" in the back rows and shadows around the main conference table. It was unlikely that they would be able to get the bomber they wanted, the AMSA, for another ten years. But they could get the bomber they did not want—the small,

short-legged FB-111—if they would go along with Secretary Mc-
Namara.

My colleague remembers what he thought to be a telling argument made during the deliberations that day. Someone pointed
out that even though the FB-111 was not the right airplane for
SAC, it did offer some glamour with its supersonic speed and,
therefore, would attract young pilots into SAC. It was those young
pilots SAC needed to ensure its institutional future now; the right
bomber could come later. And that is pretty much what happened:
SAC, as an institution, never loved the FB-111; but a new generation of SAC pilots teethed on it; and SAC finally did get the plane
it wanted, the B-1.

If the institutional fathers ultimately make such fateful decisions
about forces and weapons, how can they avoid looking out for the
future of the institution that has been entrusted to them? The
choices for war are seldom clear or unambiguous, despite all the
military planning and analysis rhetoric; but the choices for the
institution are almost always urgent and painfully apparent. And,
thus, the masks of war cover what the institution must do.

# 2

---

# FIVE FACES OF THE SERVICE PERSONALITIES

By comparing the services on five aspects, or "faces," I initially sketch here some basic outlines or features of the service personalities. In the next chapter, these fragmented sketches are more fully developed into institutional "identities," each with its easily recognized behavior patterns. I originally considered more than two dozen aspects in a search for attitudes, questions, behavior, and concerns that might distinguish the services from one another. Some differences, like uniforms and insignia, while substantial, did not appear to shed any light on service approaches to strategy or analysis. Others, like critical command progressions for officer advancement, seem to show only minor differences among the services. And still others, such as the differences in their public images (as portrayed, for example, in motion pictures), were rich in color but difficult to relate to service self-images and behavior toward strategy or analysis.[1]

The five faces used here for the initial sketches of the service personalities have been deliberately chosen to reveal differences rather than similarities among the services: (1) altars for worship, (2) concerns with self-measurement, (3) preoccupation with toys versus the arts, (4) degrees and extent of intraservice (or branch) distinctions, and (5) insecurities about service legitimacy and relevancy. Their order is one that seems naturally to unfold the distinctions in service identities or personalities. Each of these faces invites a fresh comparison of the three services, comparisons intended to draw out important differences among them, progressively capturing sufficient features to "recognize" the personality that seems to be lurking inside the institution.[2]

## Altars for Worship

What do the services revere most as a principle or cherish as an ideal? How do the services differ in the altars at which they choose to worship?[3] The question concerns the ideas or concepts that serve as inspirations and aspirations. For the knights of old, the altar might be the code of chivalry. For the hippies or "flower children" of the 1960s, it might be "love." Altars worshiped are revealing about how the worshipers see themselves and their values.

Tradition has always been an important part of military life, but the Navy, much more than any of the other services, has cherished and clung to tradition. The U.S. Navy was born and bravely fought its way out from under the massive shadow of the British Royal Navy and its rich traditions. Some who served in the new Navy had served (perhaps involuntarily) in the Royal Navy, and the extraordinary success of that Navy, with its traditions, frequently served as an institutional model of professionalism for the U.S. Navy.[4] This reverence for tradition in the U.S. Navy has continued right to the present, not just in pomp or display, but in the Navy's approach to almost every action from eating to fighting—from tooth to fang. In tradition, the Navy finds a secure anchor for the institution against the dangers it must face. If in doubt, or if confronted with a changing environment, the Navy looks to its traditions to keep it safe.

If tradition is the altar at which the Navy worships, then one of the icons on that altar is the concept of independent command at sea, which, like the Holy Grail, is to be sought and honored by every true naval officer. The reference to religious concepts in describing the Navy is not new: "As Secretary Stimson once remarked, the admirals were wrapped up in a 'peculiar psychology' in which 'Neptune was God, Mahan his prophet, and the United States Navy the only true Church.'"[5] Independent command of ships at sea is a unique, godlike responsibility unlike that afforded to commanding officers in the other services. Until the advent of telecommunications, a ship "over the horizon" was a world unto itself, with its captain absolutely responsible for every soul and consequence that fell under his command.

The idealization of independent command at sea is probably well captured by the exploits of Commodore Matthew Perry in opening up Japan to Western trade in the 1850s. Perry, halfway around the globe and months away from Washington, acted as presidential emissary, ambassador, commander in chief, secretary of state, and trade commissioner, all under the guns of his ships, as he threatened war and negotiated treaties with feudal Japan. The nearest examples of such autonomy and power being vested in military officers on land are the early expeditions to the new world and the American West. On land, military officers were brought under scrutiny and supervision by means of the telegraph in the middle of the nineteenth century. But naval officers, once their ship was "hull down, over the horizon," remained beyond the pesky grasp of the telegraph. Until the advent of reliable, worldwide radio communications in the middle of this century, the responsibility and opportunity of the independent command at sea remained unique to naval officers. It is not surprising, therefore, to find the Navy as the most disgruntled of the services over the encroachment of Washington into the details of its command and control.[6] The broad authority to engage and retaliate against provocations, granted to the Sixth Fleet commander during that fleet's maneuvers off the Libyan coast in spring 1986, comes close to the naval ideal of independent command at sea.

The Air Force could be said to worship at the altar of technology. The airplane was the instrument that gave birth to independent air forces; the airplane has, from its inception, been an expression of the miracles of technology. The very knowledge of how to fly came from technical devices and experiments, and fliers have been the major instigators and beneficiaries of technological advances in everything from structural materials to microelectronics.

If flight is a gift of technology, and if the expansion of technology poses the only limits on the freedoms of that gift, then it is to be expected that the fountain of technology will be worshiped by fliers and the Air Force. If the Air Force is to have a future of expanding horizons, it will come only from understanding, nurturing, and applying technology. There is a circle of faith here: If the Air Force fosters technology, then that inexhaustible fountain of technology will ensure an open-ended future for flight (in airplanes or spacecraft); that, in turn, will ensure the future of the Air Force. The critical element of this faith, of course, is the continued expansion of flight-related technologies, which is at least arguable as the air and space technologies mature.[7]

The altar at which the Army worships is less apparent than the altars for the other two services. That may be because its ideals are more diffuse or variable or subtle. Several consistent themes surface, however, when the Army talks about itself: They have to do with the depth of its roots in the citizenry,[8] its long and intimate history of service to the nation, and its utter devotion to country. For example:

> Although each of our armed services is unique and different, the U.S. Army holds a special position of significance and trust. Its ranks come from the people, the country's roots, and it is closest to the people.[9]

> Out of the Army's long and varied service to our nation, tested and tempered through 200 years of peace and war, have emerged certain fundamental roles, principles and precepts. . . . They constitute the Army's anchor in history, law and custom, suggesting the sources of its present strength and the trust and confidence of the nation in the essential role of the Army.[10]

> [T]he Army ethic must strive to set the institution of the Army and its purpose in proper context—that of service to the larger institution of the nation, and fully responsive to the needs of its people.[11]

These ideas are sufficiently altruistic and patriotic that they could be ratified with little modification by any of the military services. What makes them unique to the Army is that they really are important to the Army as matters of belief and expression. They represent, at a level that is probably deep and difficult to express, who the Army thinks it is and what it believes in. Of all the military services, the Army is the most loyal servant and progeny of this nation, of its institutions and people.

If the Army worships at an altar, the object worshiped is the country; and the means of worship are service.

## Measuring Themselves

Each of the military services measures itself against some institutional standard of health:

> It is a well-known fact that service Chiefs who advocate in their respective budgets 17 divisions, 27 tactical fighter wings, or 15 aircraft carriers are unlikely . . . to advocate less. Those who hope each year that they will, hope against impossible odds.[12]

> For the military services, the size of their budgets—both absolutely and relative to those of the other services—is a measure of organizational success.[13]

The question here is not how the services choose to measure themselves but how important those measurements are to them. How concerned or preoccupied are they with taking or meeting those measurements?

The Navy has been the most consistently concerned of the three services about its size, which it measures first in the number of its capital ships and then, so they may be adequately backed up, in the numbers of other ships, by category, and, more recently, in the aggregate.[14] The Navy's peacetime demand for capital ships has remained essentially unchanged since before World War I, even though the kind of capital ship has changed from dreadnought to battleship to carrier to supercarrier; the perceived enemy and geographical orientation of the Navy have changed as many times. The Navy demand for 100 submarines goes back before World War II, despite dramatic changes in submarines, their role, and the threat.[15] It would be difficult not to notice that the size and composition of the required fleet have been remarkably constant despite the changes wrought by several wars, the fall and rise of empires, dramatic technological advances, new enemies, and even an altered sense of national purpose.

The Navy's concern about meeting these measurements is acute: Being one capital ship down is to be "a quart low," with ominous consequences if not corrected soon. Part of that concern is justified in the long lead times required to produce a capital ship and in the impact of even one key ship on the rotation schedules for forward deployments. Quick to question its ability to "make do" when it is short a capital ship, the Navy is equally quick to rebuff any questioning of the need for the forward deployments that drive its requirements. The Navy is the hypochondriac of the services, constantly taking its own temperature or pulse, finding it inadequate, caught up in an anxiety largely of its own making.

The Air Force has, from time to time, argued strongly for its size in terms of the number of wings of bombers or fighters needed or desired.[16] But the Air Force appetite for newer and more technologically advanced aircraft, with their attendant higher cost, has tempered its demands when the choice came to more of the old or fewer of the new. For the Air Force, the aerodynamic performance and technological quality of its aircraft have always been a higher priority than the number. Thus, in measuring itself, the Air Force is likely to speak first of the kind or quality of its aircraft (speed, altitude, maneuverability, range, armament) and then the numbers.

Evidence for this emphasis on quality over quantity is easily observed: The Air Force does not lament the size of its bomber force so much as it does the age of its B-52s. It considers the necessity of fathers and sons' flying the same bomber as a national disgrace. The trade of larger quantities of arguably less capable F-16s for F-15s was never attractive to the Air Force. Confronted with a mix of the new B-1 bomber and an even newer advanced technology bomber (the B-2), the Air Force favors more of the B-2s. The Air Force concern about self-measurement becomes acute only if its qualitative superiority is threatened. New aircraft developments by the Soviets are of much greater concern if they reflect new flight envelopes than if they are being produced in large quantities. To be outnumbered may be tolerable, but to be out-flown is not. The way to get the American flier's attention is to confront him with a superior machine; that has not happened very often or for very long in the relatively short history of aviation.

The Army appears to be the most phlegmatic of the three services about measuring itself. Although division flags are one indication of its current status, the Army has been accustomed to growing and shrinking with the nation's demands for its services. At least until recently, the Army has consisted mostly of people, and over thirty of the last forty years, conscripted from the citizenry. To the extent that the Army publicly expresses concern about its health, it is likely to be about the "end strength" (number of people) of its "active component" (not counting Guard and Reserve units). That is the salient measure of its readiness to fight or to expand, as may be demanded of it.[17]

Thus, when the Army does talk about its size, it tends to be in terms of people, not equipment. The Army may refer to the number of active divisions, to its state of modernization or readiness, as percentages of the whole, but the basic measure remains the number of people. And the Army is accustomed to that number varying, depending upon the commitment of society and the government to defined causes.

## Toys versus the Arts

How do the services differ in their devotion, possessiveness, or pride toward their equipment and skills? With what do people in military service tend to identify themselves? The things that attract and hold the attention of service professionals at the individual level provide an insight into the preoccupations of the service that go deeper than the assertions of the institution itself.

The Air Force is, by far, the most attached of the services to toys.[18] Air Force pilots often identify themselves with an airplane: "I'm a 141 driver." "I flew buffs." Sometimes this identification goes right down to a particular model of an airplane: "I fly F-4Cs."[19] The pride of association is with a machine, even before the institution. One could speculate that, if the machines were, somehow, moved en masse to another institution, the loyalty would be to the airplanes (or missiles).

Air Force pilots delight in showing visitors their toys. It is not hard to get an invitation to sit in the cockpit, to share its owner's excitement with the power and freedom of flight. The cockpit visitor will probably find it easier to engage the owner in a discussion of the difficulties and restrictions associated with weather and airspace in peacetime than the relationship of the man and machine to war. This is not to denigrate the great skill and courage of those who are prepared to fly and fight but simply to note that flying and flying machines are nearest to their hearts. The prospect of combat is not the essential draw; it is simply the justification for having and flying these splendid machines.[20]

The history of American airmen flying for foreign governments shows just how strong the draw has been. The Lafayette Escadrille, Chennault's Flying Tigers, the Eagle Squadron, the migration of fliers to the Royal Canadian Air Force in the early 1940s, all attest to the overriding love of flying and flying machines. When America did not possess the planes or the reasons to fly them, the pilots (or would-be pilots) followed the airplanes, even if that meant serving in other nations' military services and wars. To be sure, the pilots rationalized their extranational services sometimes in terms of helping with noble wartime causes, seldom just for money, but almost always, upon reflection, by their love of flight. They rejoined American units when that option became available, but flying came first.[21]

The Navy is far less toy oriented, even though it has a more diverse set of toys to play with and a love for both ships and the sea. But the true lover of the sea and ships can be just as attracted to yachts or working at sea as to the modern fighting ship or the Navy. Whereas the things the Navy owns and operates are clearly a source of interest and pride for those who serve in them, Navy personnel are more likely to associate themselves with the Navy as an institution.  This loyalty to institution appears to extend even to Navy fliers:

> Whereas the Army aviators under General Billy Mitchell had continually agitated following World War I for a new aviation service separate from the Army, the Navy fliers had always been Navy officers first and aviators second.[22]

> These seagoing aviators, unlike their Army counterparts, had always had a stronger affection for their service than for their aviation units.[23]

Army people have historically taken greater pride in the basic skills of soldiering than in their equipment.  Until the last few decades, the Army was notorious for its reluctance to embrace new technologies or methods.  The Army took great pride in the marksmanship of the citizen soldier and clung to a marksman's rifle (the M-14) whereas the Air Force, as might be expected, quickly embraced the high-technology, volume-of-fire approach embodied in the Stoner AR-15 (later known as the M-16) rifle.

If one engages, say, an Army artilleryman in conversation about his business, it is soon apparent that his pride is in the art of laying a battery of guns for accurate fire.  The kind of gun—155mm, 8-inch, or even a captured gun—is incidental; the power and satisfaction are in the knowledge and skills required to do something that is both important and general to warfare.  Conversations with infantry and armored officers reveal a similar pride of skills—a thorough grounding in the basic arts of employing infantry or tanks effectively in battle.

Of late, however, the Army seems to be moving toward the other services in an attachment to machines.  The Abrams tank and the Bradley fighting vehicle have some of the color of institutional toys. That shift may be a necessary response to the technology changes now confronting the Army, or it may be seen as a better way for the Army to compete for budget slices in a toy-oriented defense program.  In any event, there are signs the Army is getting "hooked" on toys too.

## Intraservice Distinctions

> For no service was intraservice competition ever equal in importance to competition among the services.  The organizational and administrative ties which bind a service together preclude intraservice controversy from becoming as intense as interservice controversy.[24]

Interservice cleavages ordinarily will dominate intraservice distinctions. . . . Each of the services, however, is itself a complex organization composed of numerous subsidiary units and components. . . . Moreover, these differences are important to the members of each service. In particular, promotions to higher rank typically are reported (albeit unofficially) in terms of a variety of intraservice distinctions.[25]

All three services make intraservice distinctions among their people, particularly their officers, on the basis of their specialties or skills. They differ, however, in how these distinctions are made and used. Therefore, these distinctions are a useful clue to differences among the services on what they think is important and what they are about.

The Navy is the most elaborate in its distinctions among, and the relative ranking of, its various components, branches, or activities. The implicit intraservice distinctions within the Navy provide an extensive, fine-structured, hierarchical pecking order from top to bottom. At the pinnacle of this structure, since World War II, has been carrier-based fighter aviation.[26] At (or very near) the bottom is mine warfare. Submarine and surface warfare specialties, in that order, lie in between. But the distinctions go further. Among aviators, carrier (tail-hook) pilots are above land-based fliers. Within the tail-hookers, attack aviation is not so high as fighters, but above antisubmarine warfare aviation. Among submariners, attack submarines are, without any doubt, preferable over ballistic missile launchers. Nearer the bottom of the heap are amphibious warfare and land-based patrol (VP) aviation. The captain of a carrier with origins in fighter aviation clearly has credentials. The greater the diversity of experience, the better, but it cannot compensate for good bloodlines acquired somewhere in carrier aviation and surface warfare. Career devotion to the VP squadrons or the "boomers" (SSBNs) is deadly; similar devotion to carrier aviation or attack submarines is not.

It is apparent from this hierarchy that the distinctions are made on the basis of what the Navy calls "platforms," the machines in which the men serve, and their basing. These distinctions usually divide careers at their beginning; the blending (if any) usually comes at the 06 level (captain); in between, few cross over from one career (platform) path to another. The Navy supports the notion that every new line officer is a potential candidate for the Navy's top job, the Chief of Naval Operations (CNO). Therefore, the hierarchy in career specializations can be associated with the experience relevant to the management of the total Navy: The

SSBNs are too isolated from the mainstream of naval operations; carrier aviation is at the heart. Curiously enough, despite these strong and important discriminations, naval officers see themselves, first, as naval officers, and only secondarily as specialists (e.g., as fighter pilots or submariners).[27]

The Air Force and Army are quite similar in their intraservice distinctions, perhaps because the Air Force has been separate from the Army for only forty years. Both have divided their officers into two groups that stand on different levels—in effect, a two-plateau or two-caste system of status. In the Air Force, the division is between pilots and all others. Whereas there has always been a healthy rivalry among pilots of different types of aircraft (not only among the categories of aircraft flown, but even down to models of the same category), pilots are collectively on a plateau quite far removed from all others, including flight crew members and ballistic missile officers.[28] Pilots are likely to identify themselves with a specific model of aircraft and to see themselves as pilots even more than as Air Force officers.

Although the ownership of the Air Force is clearly in the hands of pilots, the rivalry between fighter and bomber pilots still manifests itself in swings of ruling power between the Strategic and Tactical Air Commands (SAC and TAC). Currently, the Air Force is dominated by TAC. Although the major commands tend to capture and put their marks upon officers throughout their careers, crossovers and mavericks are more evident in the Air Force than in the Navy.

In the Army, the basic division is between the traditional combat arms (e.g., infantry, artillery, and armor) and all others, who are seen in (and fully accept) support roles to the combat arms.[29] The branch distinctions are a source of pride and banter, but their effect upon promotion and power within the Army is not so clear as it is with the Navy and Air Force. Kanter argues that the Army is the least differentiated of the services, noting: "It is perhaps symptomatic of the relatively low salience of intra-Army cleavages that, when Army officers are promoted to flag grade, they remove their branch insignia from their uniforms."[30]

Nevertheless, Army officers are more likely to offer up their specialty when identifying themselves than are officers in either of the other two services. Whereas Navy and Air Force officers, as authors, may be content to be identified by their service alone, Army officers almost always append their specialty (e.g., artillery or infantry). This identifying probably has less to do with status than it does with pride or candor in the officer's qualifications. When an Army officer identifies himself with the Army Engineers, it is evident that he is saying much more about his background and qualifications than he is about his status in the Army, since his branch is not one of the traditional combat arms.

Despite self-identification by branch within the Army, the branches have a brotherhood not evident among the specialties in the other services. To a degree significantly beyond that exhibited by the Navy and Air Force, the Army branches acknowledge their interdependency and pay tribute to their siblings. Whereas the Navy submariners and fliers and the Air Force TAC and SAC pilots may privately think that they could get the job done largely on their own, the Army branches of infantry, artillery, and armor each see themselves as inextricably dependent upon their brother branches if they are to wage war effectively. That dependency is longstanding, comfortable, and almost eagerly acknowledged. While each branch is proud of its unique skills and contribution, there is seldom any hint of dominance over, or independence from, its brothers.[31]

## Institutional Legitimacy and Relevancy

If institutional concerns about the legitimacy and relevancy of a military service were plotted as orthogonal vectors, the three services would be found widely separated at three of the four corners. Here, institutional legitimacy refers to the confidence of the service in its rightful independent status, and relevancy refers to the pertinence of its missions and capabilities. The substantial differences among the three services in their concerns about legitimacy and relevancy are important because they mark the behavior of the institutions in their approaches to strategy, analysis, and military planning.

The Air Force, as the newest of the three services and the one whose separation from the others had to be justified within living memories, has always been most sensitive to defending or guarding its legitimacy as an independent institution. The fight for autonomy by the Air Force was long and hard; and the victory was not total: The Navy retained control of its aviation, and the Army has periodically threatened encroachments. If aviation in support of naval operations is controlled by the Navy, why should not aviation in support of ground operations be controlled by the Army? If the Air Force is not a decisive and independent instrument of warfare, the reasons for having a separate service to wield aerospace power evaporate.

> [T]he doctrine and the decisiveness of strategic bombardment in future warfare were inextricably tied to the AAF case for autonomy. If strategic bombardment could not be decisive in warfare, and if victory could be obtained only by having an army actually meet and defeat the enemy on the battlefield, then it would be difficult to refute the case for maintaining with the United States Army the Army Air Corps (with its missions of close support of ground troops and interdiction of lines of communication) in order to support the majority of this nation's forces.[32]

Even though the Air Force has broadened its purview beyond strategic bombardment, particularly in the last half of its forty-year life, to include tactical air warfare, its legitimacy as an independent, autonomous institution still rests on the decisive and independent nature of the air war. Support of the ground troops and interdiction of the lines of communication may be the ultimate ends, but the means to those ends is success in waging the air war; and that is the true business of the Air Force.

At the same time, the Air Force is supremely confident about its relevance, about the decisiveness of air power as an instrument of war, whether that instrument is wielded for strategic or tactical objectives. Indeed, the Air Force arguments for its autonomy and legitimacy are rooted in the very same theory that provides its confidence about its relevancy and pertinence. With such vital institutional interests vested in a single theory, the institution can no longer question the validity of that theory:

> Making all due allowances for the difficulties and the genuine accomplishments of our strategists, it should, nevertheless, be perfectly clear that every salient belief of prewar American air doctrine was either overthrown or drastically modified by the experience of war.[33]

> The one great, determining factor which shaped the course of the Second [World] War was not, as is so often said and so generally believed, independent air power. It was the mechanization of the ground battlefield with automatic transport, with the "tactical" airplane and above all with the tank. Airpower in its independent form was, in sober fact, relatively ineffective. It was the teaming of the internal combustion engine in the air and on the surface, in order to take the traditional objectives of surface warfare which, together with the

remarkable development of electronic communications, really determined the history of the Second World War.[34]

Instead of making the common mistake of planning to fight the next war with weapons and techniques that had been effective in the last, the Air Corps planners were laying plans to conduct the next war using weapons and techniques that had been proven largely ineffective in the present war. The reason is quite obvious: the planners were not making detailed plans for fighting the next war but rather *were planning for a force that could provide the justification for autonomy.*[35]

In exactly the opposite corner is the Navy. The Navy is supremely confident of its legitimacy as an independent institution, but with the advent of long-range aviation, and again with nuclear weapons, its relevancy has come into question.

After 1945, U.S. naval power ceased to be something explainable in its own right and assessable in its own terms. . . .

. . . Advocates of strategic air power argued that World War II had proven decisively that there would never again be a war like it, and that armies and navies were now virtually obsolete. . . .

. . . The Navy's position in this regard was by no means curious; in a unified Department of Defense, it saw grave threats to its institutional identity, and with some justification. The Navy had long viewed itself as possessed of a peculiar strategic mission and faced with peculiar strategic and technical problems beyond the ken of the other services. In the establishment of a higher central control lay risks that the Army and the Air Force would dominate both strategic planning and resource allocation, leaving the Navy in the perennial position of poor step-sister.[36]

The institutional Navy has been buffeted by technology since the advent of steam power, through iron-cladding, rifled guns, airplanes, the atomic bomb, ballistic missiles, space surveillance, and antiship missiles. It was the airplane and atomic bomb, in the hands of the air-power enthusiasts, that brought the relevance of the Navy explicitly into question. The threat posed by the airplane was ultimately co-opted by transferring the capital ship mantle from the battleship to the carrier;[37] but the Navy has dealt with the threat of nuclear weapons to its relevance by its dismissal of nuclear war as being much less likely than a protracted conventional war.[38] The ballistic missile was adapted to the submarine, but it has never been close to the heart of the Navy, despite the envy of the Air Force and the affection of the arms control community.

The Army has always been the most secure of the three services on both counts. Although the Air Force seriously challenged the relevancy and necessity of both the Army and Navy after World War II, the Army was secure in the absolute necessity of its purpose and continued existence. The Army could console itself in the view that modern warfare, as demonstrated in Korea, the Middle East, and Vietnam, was ultimately decided on the ground. There might be air campaigns and support from the sea, but in the end, someone had to take and hold the ground. To be sure, the Army's size might be whittled down to a shadow because of new strategic theories, but the Army had suffered drastic expansion and reduction before; its job was fundamental and remained, even if its popularity and support might vary over time and circumstances.

This Army sense of security has been evident throughout the forty years of efforts to unify the U.S. armed services. If the Navy has been the most resistant of the three services to accepting the constraints of unification and "jointness," the Army has been cooperative to the point of taking the initiative, with the Air Force falling in between. A good example is provided by the Army's pursuit of the Air Force in the evolution of the AirLand Battle doctrine. Though such joint planning is obviously appropriate, the Army appears to be the more enthusiastic of the two services for the venture.

# 3

## THE SERVICE IDENTITIES AND BEHAVIOR

Comparisons of five faces of the three services are sufficient to sketch their unique personalities—who they are and what they are about. The purpose of the sketches is to capture the salient characteristics of each service that seem to bear upon its approaches to strategy and analysis. The sketches are deliberately brief and vivid so they can be held easily in the mind; their order of introduction is intended to contrast their differences.

### The Navy

The Navy, more than any of the other services and over anything else, is an institution. That institution is marked by two strong senses of itself: its independence and stature.

> The . . . Navy argument [in the Woodrum Committee hearing of April 1944] was the principle that each service should be assigned a broad general mission and then left free to obtain whatever forces and equipment, within budgetary limitations, that it needed to carry out this mission.[1]

> "The Department of the Navy," General David Jones volunteered, "is the most strategically independent of the services—it has its own army, navy and air force. It is least dependent on others. It would prefer to be given a mission, retain complete control over all the assets, and be left alone."[2]

The Navy's stature as an independent institution is on a level with that of the U.S. government (which the Navy must sometimes suffer):

"Let us remember," warned [Admiral Bradley A.] Fiske, "that the naval defense of our country is our profession, not that of Congress." The naval profession . . . must have room to work out its own "rules of strategy, tactics, and discipline."[3]

So fierce had been the Navy's opposition to service unification, that even Truman was intrigued with one exasperated Army unification proposal which suggested that "the only way to overcome the Navy's resistance would be to do away with the War Department, transfer all of its elements to the Navy, and redesignate that organization as the Department of Defense."[4]

Who is the Navy? It is the supranational institution that has inherited the British Navy's throne to naval supremacy. What is it about? It is about preserving and wielding sea power as the most important and flexible kind of military power for America as a maritime nation. The means to those ends are the institution and its traditions, both of which provide for a permanence beyond the people who serve them.

## The Air Force

The Air Force, conceived by the theorists of air power as an independent and decisive instrument of warfare, sees itself as the embodiment of an idea, a concept of warfare, a strategy made possible and sustained by modern technology. The bond is not an institution, but the love of flying machines and flight.

The coincidence of opinion within the Air Corps on the supreme importance of autonomy can be explained by years of frustrated efforts, the common bond of the joy of aviation, and the crusading attitude of these men. At last the tenuous theoretical arguments of Douhet and Mitchell had been justified in the eyes of the Air Corps leaders and the years of frustration were over. The great joy and overstatement in the period immediately following the successful explosion of the two atomic bombs was well recorded in the press and in the congressional hearings of 1945 and 1946. Airpower would defend this nation; air power would guarantee the success of a new international security organization; air power would punish aggression wherever it might manifest itself; air power would save the world. Salvation had come; all America and the world needed to do was to maintain and support a strong United States Air Force—a simple, reliable formula. The airplane was not considered just another weapon; it was the ultimate weapon for universal peace-keeping.

Objectivity about this weapon was absent within Air Corps circles for many reasons. Perhaps the foremost reason was the psychological attachment of the airman to his machine. To him the airplane was not just a new and exciting weapon; it was what carried him miles behind enemy lines and brought him back; it was a personal possession which was given a personal, usually feminine, name, kissed upon return from a mission, and painted with a symbol for each enemy plane shot down or bombing mission completed. The affinity of pilot for airplane has its parallel in the history in the cavalry soldier and his horse. The airman, like the cavalryman of the past, was not known for his modesty, or his objectivity, when it came to the employment of his chosen steed.[5]

Who is the Air Force? It is the keeper and wielder of the decisive instruments of war—the technological marvels of flight that have been adapted to war. What is it about? It is about ensuring the independence of those who fly and launch these machines to have and use them for what they are—the ultimate means for both the freedom of flight and the destruction of war.

## The Army

The Army sees itself, ultimately, as the essential artisans of war, still divided into their traditional combat arms—the infantry, artillery, and cavalry (armor)—but forged by history and the nature of war into a mutually supportive brotherhood of guilds. Both words, *brotherhood* and *guilds*, are significant here. The combat arms or branches of the Army are guilds—associations of craftsmen who take the greatest pride in their skills, as opposed to their possessions or positions. The guilds are joined in a brotherhood because, like brothers, they have a common family bond (the Army) and a recognition of their dependency upon each other in combat.

What is the Army? It is, first and foremost, the nation's obedient and loyal military servant. It takes pride in being the keeper of the essential skills of war that must be infused into the citizenry when they are called upon to fight. "Traditionally, the American Army has considered itself the neutral instrument of state policy. It exists to carry out the government's orders and when ordered into action does not ask 'Why?' or 'What for?'"[6]

What is it about? It is about keeping itself prepared to meet the varied demands the American people have historically asked of it, but especially prepared to forge America's citizenry into an expeditionary force to defeat America's enemies overseas. And in this latter role, the Army accepts (with understandable unease) its utter dependence upon its sister services for air and sea transport and firepower.

## Behavioral Patterns

Can these identities be observed in the behavior of the services? If the sketches capture the essence of the services, then we should be able to see those personalities again and again in many of their actions and positions. The evidence is not hard to find. A few examples are provided here, but those who have dealt with the services will probably be able to provide their own.

Should not the three service academies reflect the personalities of their parent institution? The academy mottos should capture who the service is and what it is about. Indeed, the mottos are splendid and, in the light of the personality profiles that have been drawn, need no identification or further explanation:

- *Ex scientia tridens*: From knowledge, sea power.
- Man's flight through life is sustained by the power of his knowledge.[7]
- Duty, honor, country.[8]

The ultimate objects of affection or aspiration are obvious in each case. Even the singular use of Latin among the three is somehow fitting.

The service academy chapels also exhibit their institutional personalities. All of them, of course, reflect the time and place of their construction and fit in with the architecture of their surroundings. The Air Force Academy chapel is the most dramatic of the three, inside and out. From the outside, it resembles seventeen B-49 bombers[9] standing on their swept-back wingtips, prepared to bolt for the sky. Inside, it is a surprisingly small cavern of softly colored light and aluminum strutting, giving the impression of being inside an airplane that has had half of its skin panels replaced with stained glass.

The chapel at West Point would not be out of place in a Scottish glen: small, dark, solidly built of stone. As compared to the chapels of its sister service academies, it is remarkable for its provincial character, its lack of display or attempts to awe. This is a quiet place for simple ceremonies with people who are close to each other and to the land that has brought them up.

The Naval Academy chapel is the largest of the three. With vaulting dome, light marble stonework, and huge stained glass windows throughout, it could be a Christopher Wren church in the West End of London. Everywhere the eye is given a feast of architectural or decorative detail. A stained glass window showing Farragut damning the torpedoes in Mobile Bay gives away its American heritage; but it is a chapel fit for nineteenth-century royalty and ceremonies.

The halls of the Pentagon provide a striking reflection of the service personalities as sketched here.[10] Each service has a corridor devoted to its chief of staff (all of them in the "E" or outside ring of the Pentagon). Each corridor is elegantly decorated in a motif that reflects how the services see themselves (or would like others to see them).

The Navy's corridor is rich in dark wainscoting and brass door hardware. Stern faces in gilded frames stare from the wall at all who pass here. Along the walls are low glass cases with exquisitely detailed ship models. Change the ship models from steel and steam to wood and sail, and one could easily imagine being in the British Admiralty offices of the ninetenth century. The whole effect is one of a stuffy British men's club somewhere in the Mayfair or Haymarket districts of London. Truly, one gets the message that it is an institution with stability, with a history and a rich set of traditions. It is a place for gentlemen, properly attired, to meet and decide the fate of empires.

The Army's corridor is much warmer, with the bright colors of its division and command flags set off against light walnut paneling along one wall, all in their standards, attesting to the loyalty of the men who have fought under them. Many of those flags show their roots in the citizenry (e.g., the "Yankee" division). A cavalry officer of the old American West, with boots and spurs and a dusty hat, would not be out of place here if you met him "ching-chinging" in the opposite direction. This is a proper setting for weary, dedicated soldiers to draw strength from those who have served before as they set about to learn what task the nation is laying on their shoulders today.

Until recently, the Air Force's corridor was bright with chrome, glass, and fluorescent lights, yet it had a churchlike quality, perhaps because of a wide stairwell leading up to its centerpiece: Six tall, modern, lighted, museum exhibit cases displayed the instruments of flight—models of airplanes, past and present.[11] The Collier Trophy, as modern and cold as the hub of an airplane propeller, had a place of honor on the edge of the stairwell. It was a place not for people so much as for things—like a museum or church where people sometimes go to talk in hushed tones while they look at things that inspire pride or wonder.

With a recent renovation, however, the Air Force corridor has taken on the look of the modern corporation. Portraits of past corporate executives mounted on designer wall panels line a hall that might well lead from the board room to the CEO's office in any "Fortune 500 executive suite." The image is of corporate taste, stability, and, above all, power. If these corridors are harbingers of the future, then the Air Force may be changing from an adventure to a business.

## The Power of Identity

From the analysis of high-performing groups—groups of people who have performed well above expectations or the norm—one of the most consistent attributes is a shared sense of identity and purpose.[12]

> *[T]he definition and clarification of purposes is . . . a prominent feature of every high-performing system* [HPS] *I have ever investigated.*
>
> . . . HPSs are clear on their broad purposes and on nearer-term objectives for fulfilling these purposes. They know why they exist and what they are trying to do. Members have pictures in their heads that are strikingly congruent.
>
> Motivation is "peculiar" in the literal sense of that word: "Belonging exclusively to one person or group; special; distinctive; different."[13]

Thus, a collective, shared sense of identity and interests is a hallmark of the most successful institutions. The cause and effect, between the hallmark and success, can be deduced. A clear, shared sense of identity and purpose may lead to high performance because it facilitates decision making that would otherwise be difficult, perhaps so difficult as to be deferred, to the group's detriment.

Of the American military services, the Navy currently has the clearest sense of its identity and interests. Whether or not one admires the Navy's identity or agrees with its interests, the clarity of its identity and interests in Navy decision making is remarkable. The Navy knows what it wants and knows its priorities. Even though the Navy, like the other services, must deal with diverse interests within the institution, there is little doubt of, or challenge to, the exquisite and well-established hierarchy of those interests.[14] The salutory significance of this hierarchy is that everyone knows where one stands in the Navy and what the Navy priorities will be. Thus, the Navy is less likely than its sister services to have difficulty in making decisions, even painful decisions. The Navy may resist cuts in its budgets, but if forced to take them, it immediately knows how and where to proceed for the interests of the Navy. If higher authorities—outside the institutional Navy—override the Navy's decisions, then they have made a direct assault on the Navy's sense of itself as an independent arm of the nation. More than once, such an insult has prompted the Navy to respond with an insult of its own: resignation of its leadership.[15]

The Navy may very well face tough times in the years to come, but it will not be burdened by a lack of clarity about who it is, what it is about, or what it wants to be. Those things are embodied in the clear vision the Navy has of itself. There may be troubles lurking in the validity of the Navy's vision, but not in any lack of clarity or confidence in how it sees itself. It will find its decisions easy to make, even though outsiders may criticize, dispute, or overturn them.

Why is that sense of self so clear in the Navy and less so in the Air Force and Army? And how, then, does any institution come to a clear sense of its identity and interests? Institutions are made up of people. Some people come early and easily to a sense of identity and purpose; others struggle to achieve that sense throughout their lives. And of those who do achieve it, some have realistic and constructive self-visions, whereas others do not. Still others develop a distorted sense of identity as a result of "heady" experiences.

Institutions display similar variety. The Navy came early and easily to its sense of identity. The Navy sees itself, first and foremost, as an institution. The Air Force identifies itself with flying and things that fly; the institution is secondary, it is a means to those things. A brave band of intrepid aviators, bonded primarily in the love of flight and flying machines, may have a clear sense of themselves, but it is not so much an institutional as it is an individual sense of self. And it is not focused so much on who they are as it is on what they want to do.

Of the three services, it appears that the Army is currently suffering the most with its sense of identity and interests. Though many would point to the traumatizing effects of the debacle in Vietnam, I see a longer-term problem: The Army's identity as the nation's "handyman" or loyal military servant is a fair characterization of most of its history. But something happened to the Army in its passage through World War II that it liked; and it has not been able to free itself from the sweet memories of the Army that liberated France and swept victoriously into Germany. That heady experience has marked the Army with an image of itself that is distinctly different from that which it had before and, more important, from its experiences since.[16] Thus, the Army finds itself dealing with something like a "split personality." Part of the Army is trying to revert to its traditional, historical role; and part is hanging on to an image of the Army at its finest year, the last year of World War II.

## Future Behavior

Because these sketches of the service identities are based on historical behavior, they do not necessarily portray how the services will behave in the future. There is evidence that all three services are changing:

- The submariners (or more generally, the nuclear power community) are rising relative to the aviators and surface warfare officers in the Navy.
- The fighter pilots have superseded the bomber pilots in control of the Air Force.
- The Army increasingly emphasizes high-cost toys.

But much more is constant. The personalities of the services, like those of individuals, are hard to change quickly or deliberately. They are the products of the culture and acculturation of hundreds of thousands of people, whose leadership requires decades of institutional experience, and whose behavior is continuously reinforced by social and professional incentives.[17] A strong, radical leader, such as Admiral Elmo Zumwalt, may disturb the identity of a service while in command, but reactionary, restoring forces are likely to form quickly and persist longer. Since people are more likely to associate themselves with an institution for positive rather than negative reasons, a large reservoir of restorative attitudes always maintains those values which originally attracted the institution's membership.

Many who choose a particular military institution and dedicate their lives to it make their choice because there is something about the service—who it is or what it is about—that appeals to them. They see something in that service attractive or admirable and make an implicit contract with that service to serve in exchange for the associative benefit they perceive.[18] If impending changes in their service then threaten that which they found attractive, they will exert a restoring or stabilizing pressure. With tens or hundreds of thousands of such implicit contracts outstanding, the potential for voluntarily changing the institution is very small. Significant, rapid change is almost certain to be imposed from the outside and vigorously resisted from the inside.

Thus, barring a catastrophe that decimates one or more of the services,[19] the unique service identities (whether they have been portrayed here correctly or not) are likely to persist for a very long time. Indeed, the service identities or personalities are likely to be one of the most stable aspects of the nation's future security prospects.

## The Engines for Stability

The engines for stability in institutions are visible when one looks not only at the whole but also at any level of detail, right down to the individuals who compose the institution. Like fractals, the pattern appears to be the same no matter what magnification one uses to examine it. Though the ballistic missile has never enjoyed the status of the airplane in the Air Force, the history of the MX missile illustrates the stability and persistence of eddies or side currents off the mainstream of the institution. In 1965, the blueprints for the last of the Minuteman missile series, the Minuteman III, were finished and being rolled up from the drawing boards. Fresh sheets of paper were then rolled out on those same boards, and the designers began to lay out the lines of the next missile—the follower to the Minuteman III. The missile that took shape there would be instantly recognized today, more than twenty years later: the MX, the Peacekeeper, in all of its essential features—a large, solid propellant, highly MIRVed, silo-based ICBM.

For the next twenty years, the Air Force tried vainly to bring that missile, under various program names, into the world. Each time it tried to go ahead with development of the new missile, Congress or the Department of Defense (DoD) or the White House would push it back up its birth canal. And each time, the Air Force and its contractors went back to the drawing boards, made some changes (more in the basing, which they did not care about, than in the "bird," which was what they really coveted), and tried again a few years later. After twenty years of watching this natal pushing and shoving, any logical observer would be impelled to ask, "What is going on here? Do these people really want or need a new missile?" The arguments were about land-based missile basing and its vulnerability; but the shoving match looked as if it was about the missile itself.

After twenty years, and over considerable objection, a few of these missiles were allowed to enter the world, where they were put into the same cribs as the Minuteman missiles that had preceded them. One could reasonably infer this compromise: The Air Force got its new bird, with unexpressed hopes that it might be able to get more of them, while its opponents felt assured that they had firmly limited the size of that unwanted flock (or clutch).

But the troubling residual of this history was the source of the continuous, sustained pressure to develop a new ICBM. After the new ICBM was rejected the first time, why did not the effort stop there and then? The pressure to continue did not come from any urgent concern about the existing missiles wearing out and needing to be replaced; the life of the Minuteman missile was greater than expected. It did not come from an accepted need for a bigger missile, because the Scowcroft Commission immediately recommended the development of a smaller missile. Was it—one hesitates even to suggest—simply an example of Eisenhower's warning about the evils of the "military-industrial complex"?

> This conjunction of an immense military establishment and a large arms industry is new in the American experience. The total influence—economic, political, even spiritual—is felt in every city, every State house, every office of the Federal government. We recognize the imperative need for this development. Yet we must not fail to comprehend its grave implications. *Our toil, resources and livelihood are all involved; so is the very structure of our society.*
>
> In the councils of government, we must guard against the acquisition of unwarranted influence, whether sought or unsought, by the military-industrial complex. The potential for the disastrous rise of misplaced power exists and will persist.[20]

It would be easy to attribute the twenty-year sustained pressure for a new ICBM to the Air Force and its contractors in their pursuit of power and profit. But if one carefully watched and listened to the people who were most committed to the birth of a new ICBM, power and profit were not their motives. They argued effectively and ardently, in national security terms, about why America needed a new ICBM and what would happen if it did not develop one. If someone suggested that the country did not need a new ICBM, they could only shake their heads in disbelief. Such suggestions were either Soviet-inspired or rooted in wishful thinking. They really believed (then and now) in what they were trying to do.

At some abstract level, perhaps power and greed came into play, as we sometimes suppose they do when nations choose to go to war. But those who are on the front lines are not there for those reasons. The ardent advocates of the new ICBM were committed to that cause because they could not be otherwise. They had devoted their professional lives to those machines. Their own personal worth and the worth of ICBMs had become intertwined in a way that could not be easily separated. To consider that development of new ICBMs might no longer be necessary or worthwhile was equivalent to considering whether they, themselves, were any longer necessary or worthwhile. And for their sense of personal worth, people will fight hard and long.

The fight over the MX was not a test between good and evil, right and wrong, or simply the predations of a military-industrial complex. Eisenhower had touched upon the very core of the problem in the words emphasized above: "Our toil, resources and livelihood are all involved; so is the very structure of our society." We have a society in which people identify themselves with their toils and, thence, with things. As with railroad firemen, their livelihood and self-worth are involved. Though the debates about the MX were carried out in the esoterica of the nuclear age—first strike, throw weight, window of vulnerability, deterrence, counterforce, and so on, they were really very much about people, what they have devoted their lives to, and the worth of their contribution to community, society, and country.

The engines for stability in the American military services are evident not only in the subinstitutional pressures to continue the development of a weapon, such as the ICBM, but in the institutional resistance to the introduction of new weapons, such as the cruise missile. Cruise missile technology and its implications for weaponry became widely recognized in the late 1970s, when the DoD instigated the serious development of modern cruise missiles in a joint Navy–Air Force program, and when the potential of cruise missiles for good or evil was the subject of much public debate.

But the technology for modern cruise missiles had been lying fallow for more than ten years, ignored or dismissed by the services, because it offered little for, or even threatened, their institutional interests. The critical technology components of the modern cruise missile were small, efficient turbofan engines to propel them and terrain-following and matching radars to guide them at low altitude. Both these developments had been carried into the flight testing stage by the mid-1960s; their potential combination in cruise missiles of revolutionary capabilities were immediately evident to the few who were aware of the developments. They imagined such small missiles being built by the thousands, being carried by the dozens in airplanes, ships, trucks, and submarines, and capable of saturating any defenses against them by their sheer numbers.

Alas, those few visionaries had not reckoned with the affected institutions. The Air Force certainly had no love for a small, unmanned aerial torpedo flying hundreds of miles into enemy territory to attack the target—that was precisely the job of big, manned airplanes. When the cruise missile advocates suggested to the Air Force that the new missiles might be carried by big, manned airplanes to a safe point outside the enemy's defenses and then launched toward their targets, one SAC colonel reminded them that SAC was not about to abandon its intention to fly over the targets, open the bomb-bay doors, and watch the bombs fall until they detonated. The imagery of World War II was alive and well— twenty years later.

Nor did the prospect of such cruise missiles offer much to a Navy dominated by carrier aviators, except as another potential threat to the carriers themselves. The attack submariners might have become advocates if the new missiles could be stuffed into a torpedo tube, if they had more of a voice in the Navy, or if they had been aware of the technology; but all these things would have to wait for another ten years. The only advocates were the technologists and analysts; and they had little effect inside or outside the services. The cruise missile had no home in the technology laboratories that had been organized around airplanes and ballistic missiles. The cruise missile was neither an airplane nor a ballistic missile, so it was a technological orphan and, therefore, an institutional orphan.

Hence, for the next ten years after their conception and the demonstration of their critical technologies, cruise missiles became back-burner developments for both the Air Force and Navy. Then, in the late 1970s, when the DoD was confronted with rising claims by the services for resources, the cruise missile surfaced again, this time as a cheaper alternative to some big ticket items, like the Air Force B-1 bomber. When the DoD set up a joint program office to coordinate the development of cruise missiles and put a naval officer in charge, things began to move much more quickly. Today, a decade later, modern cruise missiles are an accepted (if not universally loved) weapon carried by airplanes, ships, submarines, and trucks in the Navy and Air Force. But, if the DoD had not forced the issue upon those two services, cruise missiles might still be simmering slowly as experimental programs, being deferred by more urgent expenditures for new airplanes or another carrier and its entourage.

Thus, the engines for stability within the American military institutions tend to continue those activities that have established a significant constituency within their ranks and, at the same time, tend to reject any new activities that might encroach upon those already established. The effect of those engines is sufficiently powerful and predictable as to be a good guide to institutional actions in the future on new and old issues.

# Part II
# Strategy

# 4

## WHAT IS STRATEGY?

Military strategies provide the rationale for military actions: they explain why we undertake certain military operations or acquire certain military forces. Strategies explain. To understand a strategy is to understand why—or at least to understand the reasons the military give for the actions they take, or want to take.

But to say what strategies do for us—explain actions—does not tell us *what* they are. How does one recognize a strategy? If one met a strategy in a dark corridor of the Pentagon, or over coffee mugs on a map table, how would one know for sure that it was a strategy and not a doctrine or a tactic? What, then, is strategy? For most of those involved or interested in military planning, the question is trivial or the answer is obvious: Everyone knows what strategy is. It is the part of the process that tells us *how* we intend to achieve our goals or objectives.

When "everyone knows," it is time to slow down and be careful. If strategies explain actions, particularly military actions, they are much too important to be casually defined. And the more one examines the word, the deeper the abyss. There are many different kinds of strategy, even within the realm of national security— grand, coalition, regional, national, military, theater, service, and so on. Are the selection and ranking of goals separate from, or a part of, strategy? What are its essential ingredients? Where do strategy and tactics and doctrine divide? Where does strategy come from? Who is responsible for making it? These kinds of questions suggest that strategy can be a minefield for confusion and argument, particularly if the formulation and application of strategy are made the central basis for explaining military actions. These considerations argue for going back to the fundamentals and approaching strategy anew, without the baggage of implied definitions and assumptions that have accumulated around military planning and planners.

## Definitions

The first step is one of definition. The dictionary definitions of strategy confuse more than they clarify. Consider, for example, these four:

> *Webster:* The science and art of employing the political, economic, psychological, and military forces of a nation or group of nations to afford the maximum support to adopted policies in peace or war.

> *Random House:* The science or art of planning and directing large military movements and operations.

> *American Heritage:* The science and art of military command as applied to the overall planning and conduct of large-scale combat operations.

> *Joint Chiefs of Staff (JCS) Pub. 1:* The art and science of developing and using political, economic, psychological, and military forces as necessary during peace and war, to afford the maximum support to policies, in order to increase the probabilities and favorable consequences of victory and to lessen the chances of defeat.[1]

According to these definitions it is unclear whether or not strategy is limited to combat or even to military operations, or whether strategy is about employment, command, or planning, or all three.[2] Strategy can also be defined in another sense—that of a plan—but that definition is consistent only in a tautology: a strategy is a plan resulting from the practice of the science and art of strategy.

Part of the definitional problem with strategy, of course, is that it is a slippery word. Like "systems analysis," it has become such a widely and broadly used term as to become blurred in its meanings:

> There are probably more kinds of strategy, and more definitions of it, than there are varieties and definitions of economics or politics. It is a loose sort of word.[3]

> Strategy, like policy, is an accordian word.[4]

But the dictionary definitions probably suffer more from overdefining than underdefining its meaning. Simpler and more general notions of strategy are not hard to find:

The essential notion of strategy is captured in the relationship of means to ends.[5]

In its most fundamental sense, military strategy consists of an objective and a course of action to achieve that objective.[6]

A plan of action designed in order to achieve some end. . . .[7]

By *strategy*, I mean a definable path toward goals.[8]

These simpler notions of strategy are more appropriate here because military planning encompasses many different kinds of strategy and their ganglia. Any of these simple notions are probably adequate, but it will be helpful to pick one and remain consistent in the use of words. The definition of strategy to be used here is:

*A strategy is a concept for relating means to ends.*

Thus the essential ingredients of strategy are means, ends, and some concept of how those means and ends can be related. The essence of strategy is in the relational concept; but finding that concept may hinge upon the means or ends—in their judicious selection or in the setting of priorities among them.

Note that means and ends are plural, while the concept that links them is singular. A strategy is a single concept that relates one or more means to one or more ends. The choice or ranking of multiple means or ends may be an important creative step in finding a relational concept between means and ends. Strategies (plural), then, are several such relational concepts between means and ends. Obviously, strategies carry with them costs (mostly about their means) and uncertainties or risks (mostly about their ends).

This definition of strategy may seem so broad as to deny the separation of strategy from any number of things, including tactics, doctrine, plans, designs, and even proposals. But the distinctions between strategy and these other things, or among various kinds of strategy, ought to come from *the kinds of means and ends that are being related.* Concepts for relating grand ends and means are properly in the domain of grand strategy. Strategy can be dynamic or static, depending upon the stability of the means or ends. Strategy may change if new means become available or if different ends appear to be preferable. Means and ends concerned with the deployment or employment of a particular weapon system will probably be recognized as tactics rather than strategy; but the precise boundary between the two need not be sharply defined: One person's tactics can be another's strategy. And institutionally adopted rules for relating means to ends have the smell of doctrine.[9]

The idea of using the nature of means and ends to classify strategy leads to the temptation to define and, thereby, to distinguish more precisely between means and ends; but it is a temptation that probably ought to be resisted. "Courses of action (means) and outcomes (ends) are relative concepts. All outcomes that have consequences can be considered to be means to those consequences; and every course of action has some satisfaction or dissatisfaction associated with its use that is independent of its outcome, hence can be considered to be an end."[10] It is probably sufficient here to recognize that ends include interests, goals, objectives, aims, and purposes, and means include devices, tools, power, forces, and pressures for achieving them. Strategy is the concept, design, scheme, plan, or idea that relates one as being appropriate, effective, efficient, optimum, or adequate with respect to the other.

Note further that strategy, by this definition, implies some choice in (a concept for) the relationship between means and ends. If both the means and ends are fixed, and there is only one way to relate the two, then there is no strategy—only a situation. The formulation of strategy is the creative act of choosing a means, an end, a way to relate a means to an end, or any combination of those three. In the absence of some choice about means, ends, or their relationship, there is no strategy. And if that choice is obvious or dictated by circumstance, then strategy is trivial. Thus, for the Secretary of Defense to declare: "In a word, our basic defense strategy is deterrence"[11] begs several questions:

- Is deterrence the means or the end or the relationship between the means and the ends?
- Whichever it is, what is the alternative to deterrence?

If there is no obvious or viable alternative to deterrence, then the strategy of deterrence is trivial.[12] Strategy becomes more significant as the dilemma of choice deepens; but the formulation of strategy becomes most inspired in the discernment or perception of the decisive choices and their consequences.

## Historical Examples of Strategy

But strategy, however defined, tends toward the abstract. Some familiar historical examples may be more helpful (and concrete) in clarifying the meaning of the word as it is used here.[13]

- President Franklin Roosevelt's Europe-first strategy[14] at the beginning of World War II shaped priorities in the acquisition and deployment of military capabilities (means) to prosecute quickly the war against Germany as the most virulent of the Axis powers to be defeated (end). MacArthur's island-hopping strategy in the Pacific can be viewed as a responsive adaptation either to the consequences of Roosevelt's Europe-first strategy or, less charitably, to the three separate wars fought by the Army, Navy, and Army air forces in the Pacific—against the Japanese and each other.[15]
- Less ambiguous in their devotion to service interests DeSeversky's vision of victory through air power[16] and John Lehman's maritime strategy,[17] both of which represent concepts for relating the military capabilities of one service or component (means) to its arguable perceptions of the national purposes of military capabilities (ends).
- Churchill gave his regional concerns about postwar political arrangements as the motivation for his World War II proposals to strike into the soft underbelly of Europe, a concept for relating the growing offensive capabilities of the Allies (means) to the political purpose of blocking Soviet expansion into Europe (end). Huntington's proposed strategy of a retaliatory offensive posture for NATO is a concept of offensive military capabilities (means) to deter a Soviet invasion (end) by threatening a counterinvasion rather than a successful defense.[18]
- General Bernard Rogers's proposals for dealing with follow-on echelons of Soviet forces in central Europe and President Reagan's strategic defense initiative both represent controversial concepts for relating new military means afforded by technology to ends provoked by the principal military threat each of them faced, that is, to avoid being overwhelmed or annihilated.[19]
- Budgetary concerns were behind Robert McNamara's concept of assured destruction, which was originally intended as a criterion for sizing—or more precisely, capping the de-

mands for—strategic nuclear forces.[20] But it also had the color of strategy and, for many, became a concept for relating the rationale for nuclear forces (means) to the deterrence of nuclear war (end).

- George Kennan's broad concept of the containment of communism[21] after World War II could properly be classified as grand strategy,[22] yet it still lies within the specific sense of strategy used here because its end—the eventual mellowing or collapse of the Soviet regime—did shape military capabilities as one of the several contributing means. Indeed, John Foster Dulles's declaratory strategy of massive retaliation could be considered a contributing military component of Kennan's strategy of containment. On the other hand, the Marshall Plan, also a contributing component of the containment strategy, was a concept for using economic rather than military means for its political end of strengthening the Western European nations against both internal and external Communist pressures.[23]

## Looking behind Strategies

These examples reveal much about strategies that is both subtle and important:

1. Strategy takes on historical stature only when the choice of means and ends—the very essence of strategy—becomes nontrivial, that is, when a conundrum or a dilemma forces tough or inspired choices and decisions. Much articulated strategy in the bureaucratic planning processes (i.e., the Planning, Programming, Budgeting System and the Joint Strategic Planning System) lacks this tension and has more the flavor of doctrine or simple preference.

2. In real strategies, the means and ends are usually quite obvious and so sometimes (not surprisingly) are the underlying motives.

3. The attribution of strategies to individuals or their proponents does much to reveal the means, ends, motivations, and dilemma embedded in a strategy. The who and why of strategy may be even more informative than the what or how of strategy.

These three observations can be swept up into a general principle[24] about strategy that does much to explain the elusiveness of strategy when dealt with as an abstract art or science:

*Strategy takes on meaning mostly in the context of the identity and interests of its formulator.*

This principle suggests that, to understand a strategy fully, its formulation and application, one should first know its formulator—who the individual is and what that individual is about.[25] If one knows the who and why of a strategy, the what and how are likely to become obvious or secondary. The what and how of Churchill's strategy for attacking the soft underbelly of Europe become obvious or relatively unimportant upon an appreciation of Churchill's situation and his world view.

At the same time, the what and how of a strategy, divorced from the who and why of its proponent, are much more likely to make the strategy seem opaque, ambiguous, and contentious. If the identity of its formulator is blurred (as it often is in a coalition) or if interests are diffuse (as they frequently are in pluralistic democracies), then the formulation of strategies is likely to be difficult:

Of the current world's great and near-great powers, the United States has a particularly difficult time in producing and following through on national policies and strategies, especially those with global reach and long-term horizons. This difficulty is not necessarily because of a lack of intellectual acumen or the relatively short national election cycle as often asserted. It is more probably because of the heterogeneity, pluralism and diversified constituency of the electorate and of the many interest groups in US society.[26]

And those strategies that do evolve from diffuse interests are likely to be ambiguous.[27]

In sum, strategy is a concept for relating means to ends. In peacetime military planning, strategy takes two forms:

- In war or contingency plans, the means are existing military forces and the ends are those military objectives which political leaderships might authorize in the event of a conflict.
- In force planning, the means are taken to be future military forces and the ends are the expected purposes for which those military capabilities are to be acquired.

But the key to understanding both forms of strategy is to be found in knowing who its formulator is and what that formulator is about, because institutional interests in means can affect the setting or posing of ends.

## The Relevance of Strategy

At the outset, several negative views concerning strategy must be addressed lest they shadow every aspect of its treatment here:

1. *Strategy is abstract nonsense.* A few are so bold as to assert that strategy is mostly the hot air of academics and theoreticians who like to talk in abstractions.[28] They hold that academic debates over strategy have little to do with anything important or real; strategies can never substitute for military capabilities, the basis of real power. Strategies may come and go like fashions; military might prevails.[29] Strategies, if necessary at all, do not come from the pipesmoke of seminar rooms; they are the expedient plans that commanders generate on the spot when confronted with real situations involving the use of military force.

2. *The United States cannot formulate strategy.* There are several arguments that support this assertion. One is that democracies, as pluralistic societies, usually cannot agree on either their identity (who they are) or their interests (what they are about), so they are unable to agree on strategy except in extremis.[30] Another argument is that open societies, such as the United States, cannot publicly acknowledge all of their motives or purposes. Though lofty and noble objectives are easily claimed, they do not always suffice to cover the actual purposes and interests at work in the acquisition and employment of military forces.[31]

3. *Strategy does not drive the forces.* There is a view that strategy does not drive the acquisition or the planning of military capabilities; these are driven by the threat or by service preferences, or both. This perspective sees strategy as the intellectual rationale that follows after and attempts to explain the forces sought or in being for other unspoken or unspeakable reasons.

4. *The services do not make strategy.* Despite the services' pursuit of strategies, such as their maritime and air strategies, there are opposing views:

- There can be no such thing as a ground or air or sea (or even space) strategy today—ground, air, and sea are media for war, not means or ends;
- The services, as institutions providing specialized force capabilities, are not the makers of strategy; or
- The nation makes strategy; the services must execute it.

According to these views the services are the means and not the makers of strategy.

Each of these four positions is an independent show stopper in the sense that any one of them, by itself, if accepted as absolutely correct, argues against trying to understand either strategy or the services' role in its development. In effect, they say:

- Even if there is such a thing as strategy, it is not important;
- Even if it is important, the United States cannot formulate one;
- Even if it could be formulated, it is not really used; and
- Even if it is used, the services are not the place to make it.

All four positions, of course, contain some elements of truth or they would not be voiced. Some, perhaps much, of what is written about strategy and its use is probably nonsense, including even the revered works of Karl von Clausewitz. But the history of real strategies offers ample evidence of their important effects upon thinking, the design of forces, and the waging of war. The contemporary claims for (and the hand-wringing over) strategy in the literature may, indeed, be overblown; but strategies have—for good and bad—had an impact. Making or changing strategy can and does influence the perceived purposes of military forces and the kinds of forces acquired to fulfill those purposes.

To be sure, democratic and open societies do have difficulties in formulating and declaring strategies. But despite the difficulties, they have successfully done so, and not all the resulting strategies have been bland or ambiguous.[32] The difficulties are not so much with strategy as with coming to grips with the ends (rather than the means) of strategy. To the extent that the strategic planning process forces clarification of ends, the anguishing over strategy is something to be embraced rather than avoided. If the formulation of strategy in the United States is too often contentious, it is probably because the debates pass too quickly over the matter of ends (as being self-evident) in order to promote the means (where the vested interests lie): "Pessimists and optimists often differ less on what American forces *can* do than on what they should be *asked* to do. In short, although the issues one hears debated most often are about specific weapons, force deployment, and resource allocations, the hidden agenda of the defense debate is a dispute about strategy."[33] If strategy is defined, as it is here, as a concept for relating means to ends, then the dispute is about the ends more than the means.

Strategy, of course, is not the only determinant of the purposes and kinds of military force. Institutional preferences, technological developments, opposing forces, and so forth can be detected as influences on the acquisition of military capabilities. But strategy is supposed to sweep up all these externalities in its formulation and application. If strategy does not adequately take into account or allow for service predilections or differing interpretations of the threat, the military forces will be driven to some degree by factors omitted from strategy. Strategy should drive the forces; if it does not, it may reflect the inadequacies[34] of a particular strategy rather than the proper role of strategy.

# 5

## SERVICE STRATEGIES

### The Services and Strategy

In their peacetime planning, the U.S. military services encounter at least four different kinds of strategy that relate military means to military and political objectives:

1. *National security strategy*—the collection of concepts relating the national means (e.g., political, military, economic, moral) to the various security ends of the nation (e.g., survival, sovereignty, well-being),[1] as promulgated by the National Security Council through memoranda to or from the president.

2. *Commanders in chiefs' (CINCs') strategies*—concepts for relating the JCS-assigned means to JCS-approved ends, the latter presumably consistent with the national security strategy.[2] These strategies are probably more reflected than stated by the force or regional commanders in their actual war plans.

3. *Defense strategy*—a component of the national security strategy, it is interpreted and restated by the DoD, the JCS, and each of the services in their program planning guidance. The services are obliged to use (or to conform to) defense strategy in the formal planning, programming, and budgeting processes required by the JCS and DoD.[3]

4. *Service strategies*—ideally components of the defense strategy, but more likely proposed alternatives to, or reinterpretations of, the defense strategy. The services then use these strategies for setting their own institutional agendas, ra-

tionalizing their requirements, and arguing for a larger or protected slice of the budget.[4]

Of these four, the last appears to have the greatest effect upon the kinds of forces sought by the services and upon concepts for their use.

The national security strategy is fragmented among separate policies to deal with specific security problems, such as those raised by arms control, access to Middle East oil, Central America, and so forth. These policies are typically reviewed and revised only when a problem becomes salient; they are far from providing a complete or coherent strategy for national security. When a fragment of national security strategy does manifest itself, it is likely to emphasize, appropriately enough, ends more than means.

The CINCs' strategies, at least up to now, have little to do with the planning of future military forces. They are mostly about how to fight (apply) the assigned forces, sometimes (implicitly) about the need to assign more of the available forces (currently assigned somewhere else), and seldom about the planning of future military forces. Although the CINCs' strategies should logically flow directly from the national security strategy, the latter is usually so fragmented or incomplete that the CINCs have considerable latitude for their own interpretations. Thus, it might be more correct to say that the CINCs' strategies are generally not inconsistent with a reasonable interpretation of the national security strategy. Faced with insufficient means to achieve the ends expected of them by orthodox approaches, several of the CINCs have resorted to novel approaches, thereby at least drawing attention to, if not solving, their plights.[5]

The defense strategy, as manifested in the defense guidance, is not really strategy as it has been defined here—a concept for relating means and ends. Rather, it is a statement of general (mostly political) ends and a prescription of specific military means to be acquired and maintained. The relationships between those means and ends are often missing or only implied. From time to time, new defense concepts arise and may modify either the general political ends or the specific military means found in the defense guidance.[6] The political ends (e.g., deterrence, reassurance of allies) are consistent with the fragmented national security strategy, but since the tenure of Robert S. McNamara as secretary of defense, they have seldom been converted or transcribed into specific military criteria for their achievement.

While the defense strategy may, indeed, have an effect in defining (rather than rationalizing) the amount of forces acquired and supported, the heart of the strategic planning process—in which ideas define the purposes and kinds of forces—is probably more influenced by the service strategies. The services (particularly the Air Force and Navy) have their own concepts of the military purposes (ends) to which military force ought to be applied and of the kinds of forces (means) best suited to these purposes. These important relational concepts are embedded in the service strategies and not in the defense strategy found in the program planning guidance.[7]

## The Purposes of Service Strategies

Whether or not the services should formulate and apply strategies for their particular brand of military power is obviously a question much in dispute at the present. And it is a question that is very near to the point of this book.

It is not enough to argue that the services do not (or should not) make strategy. If that proscription is meant to apply to national or military levels of strategy, then it is quite correct, at least to the extent that the military services are not the ultimate arbiters of strategy at such levels. But that observation leaves open the question of whether the services can and should participate in the formulation as well as the application (including execution) of national and military strategies. Certainly the services, as executors of the strategies, have some interest in their formulation and application. To say they should not participate is to suggest that it is an inappropriate activity for them because they are incapable (by their limited perspectives), incompetent (by their biases), or untrustworthy (because of the potential political corruption of military power). All these suggestions are insulting and ought to be dismissed as such.

Whether there are (or should be) service strategies is a more complex question. If service strategies are proposed as substitutes or replacements for national military strategy,[8] then there may or may not be merit to their consideration in the process of formulating military strategy at the national level, depending upon the perceived soundness (or acceptability) of the existing national strategy or the service theories being advanced. But such service proposals are bound to cause heated debate, whatever their merits or lack thereof, because they imply a dominance or priority of one service over the others, with all that it implies for encroachment upon the other services' roles, stature, and claims to resources.

The service strategies may have purposes beyond contributing to the national formulation of military strategy. If they are concepts for the service's independent use of (and justification for) its own forces, then they are almost certainly not in the national interest so much as they are in pursuit of service interests. If, however, they are concepts to orient and motivate the internal organization and decisions of a service,[9] they may be more inspirational than predatory in their purpose: "A Navy still requires a theory of a Navy. Whether stated explicitly or discernible only through after-the-fact examination, there must exist something in addition to a fleet—a policy, a strategy, a plan, some sort of expectation of the conditions and anticipation of consequences—which, if not the source of inspiration, at least provides a fair means for explanation."[10]

The reality of service strategies is that they can and have been simultaneously used for all three purposes:

1. as proposals for the dominant element of national military strategy;
2. as declarations of the independence of service missions, operations, and forces; and
3. as a conceptual focus to bring coherence to the internal decision making of the service.

It is the first two uses of service strategies, not the third, that cause heated debate. The third use of service strategies has more the flavor of doctrine than strategy; it is a vision of the service and its role in the larger scheme of things—how it would like to employ its resources in those particular conflicts which make its contributions most relevant. The Navy talks about protracted conventional wars and the Strategic Air Command talks about spasm nuclear wars because those are the only kinds of wars that fully justify their unique capabilities. Such visions of war (and the institution's role in it) do provide a clear goal for institutional efforts and can be a source of institutional pride and enthusiasm for those efforts. But to the extent that such visions promote myopia about war and are used as springboards for institutional independence and dominance, they are at least contentious, if not counterproductive, to national security.

## The Uses of Service Strategies

The need for the services to have some concept of operations is as
old as the services themselves; but, historically, such concepts have
been expressed in the form of service doctrines rather than national
security strategies. The collision of service doctrines is more recent
and can be associated with the appearances of air forces and
theories about air power. Before the advent of aircraft, the boundary between land warfare and sea warfare was relatively sharp, with
only subordinate elements of the Navy and Army—the Marines
and Coast Defense Artillery—operating at their interface. The
mainstream doctrinal interests of the Army and Navy, therefore,
overlapped only at the margin until airplanes, based on land or sea,
demonstrated the ability to reach deeply and importantly across the
shoreline. Then, what originally passed for service doctrine quickly
escalated to competing national strategies:

> Prior to the 1930s, doctrine was reasonably well developed in the Navy,
> somewhat less so in the Army. The rise of airpower, however, was a
> powerful stimulant to the military quest for ideology. Lacking secure
> organizational existence or general acceptance during the 1920s and
> 1930s, the supporters of airpower—like any new, crusading group—
> needed to develop an intellectual rationale. The existence of the surface
> forces might be taken for granted; the need for an air force had to be
> demonstrated. Moreover, no longer was it possible for a service to elab-
> orate a doctrine defining its importance to the nation and its relation to
> national policy without explicitly, and not just inferentially, defining the
> position of the other services also. Mahan had constructed a doctrine of
> seapower without specifically denigrating landpower. For the supporters
> of airpower, however, the attack on the surface forces was unavoidable.
> Once the Air Force was established, the intensity of their doctrinal con-
> cern perhaps moderated somewhat, but by this time the other services
> had felt compelled to reply in kind.[11]

Indeed, the establishment of an independent Air Force, based
upon a strategic theory for the decisive use of air power, set the
stage for interservice battles in various forms and across many
issues, right down to the present:

> In the choice of a federated rather than a genuinely unified service sys-
> tem after the war, issues about weapons, functions and forces were also
> and inescapably clashes between powerful service interests, orientations
> and instincts for institutional survival, and between these interests and
> the policies of political controllers. The balance of political power
> among the services did not permit any wholesale reallocation of roles

and missions—regardless of how changed the external environment—but this simply meant that the issue was either finessed administratively or argued in other terms: in debates about the character of war, the efficacies of alternative strategies, the economies and effectiveness of competing weapons, forces and tactics.[12]

Thus, while these interservice battles have been wrapped in the language of war and weapons and strategies, they were, at the core, about organizational and institutional interests:

> [T]he content of the strategic doctrine promoted by each service was a reflection of the distribution of influence among intraservice groups. Alterations in the intraservice distribution of influence (and corresponding shifts in doctrinal emphasis), in turn, are attributed to changes in the services' environment. [In] the strategic environment, for example, the projected behavior of potential foreign adversaries had only a modest impact on the services' behavior. Rather, the environmental stimuli toward which their strategic planning efforts were directed were overwhelmingly *domestic* in origin and were predominantly defined in *organizational* terms.[13]

Service strategies were not so much the logical responses to threats as they were the drivers of threat interpretation:

> Understandably, each service inclined to conceive of a U.S.-Soviet conflict in terms that were consistent with its own capabilities and theories of warfare. External facts about Soviet military capabilities were subject to any number of interpretations, and each service derived its own meanings and promoted its own particular emphasis.[14]

> Thus, the priorities among roles and missions set by the services themselves, and the policies they were eager to advocate, were conditioned by threats and opportunities they perceived in their organizational environment. Specifically, the *strategic preferences of elected politicians*, and the *allocation of budgetary resources* in a manner consistent with these preferences, were . . . the origins of the changing distribution of influence within the services and the defense policies advocated by them.[15]

Quite apart from the relative merits of the competing service strategies, within their own terms of reference, there is some question as to their import for, or impact on, national security strategy: "To the extent that ambitious strategy and muscular visions of wartime missions make plausible politically the case for certain levels and kinds of forces, they cannot be disregarded, but this hardly means that any administration would actually choose to use U.S.

forces according to these prescriptions in something as serious as an actual war."[16]

But the dangers of having the services pursue their own strategies for national security have been evident for some time:

> The purpose of the NSC [National Security Council], according to Hoopes, was "to bring the separate organizations and traditions of the Military Services under sufficiently central authority to ensure an end to multiple and conflicting strategies for defending the nation and its interests; and to bring the Military Establishment as a whole into close and continuous relations with the State Department, the intelligence agencies, and the economic counselors—for the purpose of planning foreign policy, weighing its military risks, judging the demands on national resources, and coordinating day-to-day operations. . . . The NSC was designed to ensure detailed considerations of all the major factors that bear upon US foreign policy decisions."[17]

That expectation of the National Security Council, however, ignored the peacetime needs of the military services to plan future forces and operations around specific concepts for relating their military means to national ends (i.e., strategies): "There is an inherent contradiction between the military and its civilian leaders on [the setting of objectives]. For both domestic and international political purposes the civilian leaders want maximum flexibility and maneuverability and are hesitant to fix on firm objectives. The military on the other hand need just such a firm objective as early as possible in order to plan and conduct military operations."[18] It is this need to plan against clear objectives that compels the services toward strategy; but it is their concomitant desire for institutional independence and control that attracts them to advance separate service strategies for national security.

Although airplanes were the first instruments to blur the mission and doctrinal boundaries of the services, the successive appearances of nuclear weapons, long-range ballistic missiles, and spacecraft battered down the institutional attempts to define new service boundaries:

> The services thus were confronted with the increasing need to justify their existence in terms of national policy at a time when the possibility of a service's having a distinctive mission or even a clearly defined hierarchy of strategic missions was slowly disappearing.
> . . . The diversification of service activities affected the content of the proliferating doctrine stimulated by interservice competition. No longer could the services be justified in terms of exclusive missions or functions required by national policy. Before the innovation of the

[McNamara-Hitch] functional programs, military doctrine was service doctrine. So long as the significant missions were related to the command of the sea, the conquest of territory, and the control of the air, such doctrines were meaningful in policy terms. The functional requirements of deterrence, however, ended the strategic importance of elemental doctrines. The purpose of doctrine is to relate force to purpose, and airpower or seapower in and of themselves served no distinctive ends of policy. Mahan and Douhet were strategists of seapower and airpower; the Cold War produced strategists of massive retaliation and limited war.[19]

These developments temporarily changed the content of the debates among the services, although the fundamental issues—institutional independence and control—remained:

[The] interservice debate was just as prevalent and intense as it had been previously. The issues at stake in the controversy, however, had changed in character. Strategic questions no longer dominated the discussion. Instead, proprietary issues had become prevalent. Neither the fundamental existence of the services nor fundamental alternatives of national strategy were at issue, but rather marginal gains and losses of resources, forces, and weapons. The question of what should be done was less controversial than the questions of who should do it and how much resources should be allocated to it.[20]

Although the distinctions between the services' missions have become increasingly blurred since World War II, they have remained predominantly separate organizations with substantially unique capabilities: for the vast majority of contingencies, each service continues to be a "monopoly supplier" of military resources and capabilities.[21]

Those services which could establish major interests in higher priority functions had little incentive to bolster their contribution to lower priority functions in which other services had a primary interest. The Army regularly criticized the Air Force for its alleged neglect of tactical aviation and airlift. Both these services criticized the Navy for its alleged neglect of antisubmarine warfare and continental defense.[22]

But the national strategy of deterrence—by the threats of nuclear escalation in conflicts overseas or of retaliation for attacks upon the homeland—has been increasingly questioned on its efficacy, relevance, and morality. And this has created a market for new strategic concepts as candidates for the centerpiece of national strategy. One, advanced by President Reagan in April 1983, is for defensive shields against nuclear attacks. Another is the concept of horizontal escalation,[23] which has been partially captured within the so-called maritime strategy. The Navy has vigorously advanced the maritime strategy in recent years, coincidentally with a preferential buildup of naval forces, arguably at the expense of the other services' budgets. This initiative represents, to some, a renewal of the service strategy debates engendered by the air power advocates of an earlier era.

Whether the maritime strategy signals the services' return to the debate over national strategy, or simply the rationalization of a predisposition to rebuild naval forces, remains to be seen. Among other things, the Navy's apparent success in promoting its maritime strategy has stimulated many in the Army to pose the question (sometimes in the form of a plea): Why doesn't the Army have a ground-power strategy? Latent in that question is the implication that such service strategies are worthwhile for one or more of the following reasons:

- to orient the services' planning of forces or operations,
- to garner more of the defense budget, or
- to enhance national security.

Whether such service strategies have, in fact, been motivated by such purposes or have been (or will be) successful in achieving them is worthy of closer examination. To that end, the air and maritime strategies are scrutinized in some historical and analytical detail in the next chapters. Together, they tell an important story about service strategies and their motivations:

1. The Air Force and Navy initiatives for the formulation and application of strategy in planning future forces are derived mostly from their own service strategies—the air and maritime strategies.
2. Those service strategies, while defended and promoted in terms of national security, are more deeply motivated by the services' interests in institutional autonomy and mission independence.

This is not an indictment of the services per se; they are only doing what institutions (and individuals) almost always do when placed in a competitive environment. The bald fact is that the institutional arrangements for national security in the United States are perceived as encouraging and rewarding competitive behavior of the services for strategies, roles, missions, and budgets. Though one might hope that such interservice competition occurs only in peacetime, there is ample evidence that it is just as prevalent during wartime as well. All wars must end and, even in wartime, institutions must (and do) look ahead to their institutional futures in peacetime.

# 6

# THE AIR STRATEGY

Of the three services, the Air Force is clearly the most comfortable with strategy and things strategic—in thinking, theorizing, and planning. The Air Force was conceived around a strategic theory and midwifed by strategists. Its continuing existence—its justification as an independent institution—rests upon strategic theory. Strategy colors almost every action of the Air Force, from defining roles and justifying missions to the development of doctrine and the acquisition of forces. The Air Force (unlike the Army and Navy) does not assign flag rank responsibility for the development of strategy,[1] possibly because the entire Air Force has been built around a developed, articulated, and understood strategy. Much more important to the Air Force is the development and promulgation of doctrine that will prevent the erosion or undermining of its strategy.

## The Pioneers of the Air Strategy

Giulio Douhet is generally acknowledged to be the first to advance the air strategy in what he called "command of the air."[2] There, he posed the first and central premise of the air strategy as an axiom: "To conquer the command of the air means victory; to be beaten in the air means defeat and acceptance of whatever terms the enemy may be pleased to impose" (p. 28). To this axiom, he added two corollaries:

1. In order to assure an adequate national defense, it is necessary—and sufficient—to be in a position in case of war to conquer the command of the air.

2. All that a nation does to assure her own defense should have as its aim procuring for herself those means which, in case of war, are most effective for the conquest of the command of the air. (p. 28)

Douhet posed the second premise of the air strategy as an affirmation: "The command of the air cannot be conquered except by an adequate aerial force" (p. 29). And from this he concluded: "National defense can be assured only by an Independent Air Force of adequate power" (p. 32).

What Douhet meant by an "Independent Air Force" was somewhat tautological: It was "all those aerial means which, taken together, constitute an aerial force capable of conquering the command of the air" (p. 32).[3]

These same elements are to be found in the modern conception of the air strategy or theory in three tightly linked premises:

1. Air power can be the decisive instrument of war.[4]
2. The decisive use of that instrument requires air superiority.
3. Achieving air superiority requires central control of air power.

Douhet riveted the attention of the armies and navies of the day on his proposal:

For the present I ask only that we give the air arm the importance it deserves—in Italy we are far from doing that—and that during the transition period we adopt the following modest program: *A progressive decrease of land and sea forces, accompanied by a corresponding increase of aerial forces until they are strong enough to conquer the command of the air.* This is a program which will approach nearer and nearer reality as we grow firmer in promoting it.[5]

This proposal for promoting air power at the expense of land and sea forces was the first verbal shot in a fraternal-institutional war that has continued, with varying intensity, down to the present, with no end in sight.

Billy Mitchell became the outspoken American "proponent of an independent air force and of unified control of air power";[6] but the theory of air power did not gain broad public acceptance until World War II. In America, it was the Book-of-the-Month and Disney film *Victory through Air Power* that did much to broaden support for the air strategy.

DeSeversky's book,[7] admiringly dedicated to Mitchell, opens with the first basic premise of the air strategy: "The most significant single fact about the war now in progress is the emergence of aviation as the paramount and decisive factor in warmaking" (p. 3).

The second basic premise of the air strategy comes shortly thereafter: "*We cannot and must not dream of conquering the enemy without first capturing dominance in the air—but once we have a clearcut dominance in the air, all else becomes a secondary subordinate, auxiliary operation*" (p. 26; emphasis in the original).

The third and final premise of the air strategy is taken up as the emancipation of air power in this curiously phrased dictum: "The simple truth is that a separate Air Force is not a wonder-working device to guarantee automatic military ascendancy, but merely the minimal precondition for successful modern warfare" (p. 255).

## The Tests of Fire

During World War II, the AAF leadership acted out the air strategy, accepting its first two basic premises as proven (even as they strove to demonstrate them) and laying the groundwork for the third. The central control of air power in a separate, independent, autonomous Air Force became the implicit objective of almost all AAF actions:

> The focus of attention for the postwar [AAF] planners . . . was planning for Air Force independence from the United States Army. Since Air Force autonomy was the primary concern for the planners, other factors such as doctrine, base requirements, and weapons systems forecasts were secondary considerations which could be modified in the interest of strengthening the AAF aim. The postwar planning for the organizational independence of the Air Force was thorough, detailed, and well-conceived, while that for international contingencies, though considerable, suffered from this concentration on the organizational aspects of the postwar military structure.
>
> . . . What the postwar world situation might hold in the way of threats to American national security was, of course, of considerable concern to the postwar [AAF] planners. What was of greater concern, however, was how the AAF could justify its case for autonomy in the immediate postwar period. There were numerous plans . . . , each based on a different set of specific assumptions, yet all were designed primarily to justify the case for an autonomous Air Force within the national defense structure of the United States.[8]

The theoretical arguments for Air Force autonomy were rooted almost entirely in the air strategy. But the full implications of the Air Force quest for autonomy became increasingly apparent to the Army and Navy:

> In this justification for autonomy there was no evidence of any deviation from the arguments of the 1920's and 1930's. It was when the Air Force leaders expanded upon this with a discussion of the strategic impact of technological developments in aeronautics that the preeminence of airpower in the accomplishment of national defense was hinted at by some and hammered at by others.
>
> Certainly Colonel William Mitchell had claimed that airpower was the first line of defense and offense, but the Air Corps leaders of the 1920's and 1930's had been much more subtle in their arguments for autonomy. As World War II drew to a close, subtlety had largely disappeared and the obsolescence of navies and armies was pointed out by key AAF commanders such as Lieutenant General James Doolittle and General George Kenney. They claimed that they wanted equality with the Army and Navy, but in making their case before Congress and the press their arguments were such that they could justify not equality but supremacy of the Air Force. (p. 15)

The centerpiece of the air strategy and the bid for an independent Air Force was strategic bombardment:

> To the AAF leaders, the strategic bombardment mission for years had been both a means and an end. It was a means by which autonomy might be justified and obtained, but it was also considered by the AAF leaders to be the primary purpose of military aviation. The dual technological breakthrough of very-long-range bombers and atomic weapons made the strategic aviation enthusiasts of the past appear quite prophetic to the American public.
>
> The serious questioning of the decisiveness and importance of strategic bombardment which was beginning to take place as the United States Strategic Bombing Survey reports were being completed never became a significant public issue. No matter how ill-conceived the Combined Bomber Offensive against Germany or the strategic offensive in the Pacific had been, it all became irrelevant to the American public, Congress, and the Air Force. Overnight, strategic bombardment had gone from thousand-plane missions with hundreds of escort fighters to a single bomber dropping a single bomb. Strategic bombardment had won its case, and the ignored lessons of World War II could remain ignored by the public, Congress, the Air Force, and all others except the inquiring scholar or the parochial Army or Navy man. (p. 17)

Thus, the validity of the air strategy was taken to be proven despite the growing wartime evidence to the contrary:

When doctrine becomes dogma, all kinds of counter-dogma signals can be ignored. If the lessons of the Battle of Britain could be ignored, if the high losses in bombardment aircraft whenever they were seriously opposed by German fighters in the early, unescorted daylight raids in 1943 could be discounted, if it took the loss of 60 aircraft on a single mission over Schweinfurt in August 1943 and 60 more over Schweinfurt in October 1943 finally to convince all the Air Corps leaders that unescorted bombardment against defended targets was self-defeating as well as suicidal, then is there any reason to believe that attitudinal changes among the American public and the War Department would have permitted a different Air Force to develop? The answer has to be a tentative no. (p. 112)

Even when the counterevidence was acknowledged, it could be interpreted by the air strategy theorists as anomalous:

The fact that the Germans failed to knock out England from the air decidedly does not mean that knockouts from the air are impossible. It means only that Germany was not properly prepared to do it.[9]

The opponents of the air theory said the Korean experience "proved" that strategic bombers were overrated. The heavy bomber supporters said that this was not so; Korea was the wrong war, in the wrong place, at the wrong time.[10]

The blindness was induced by doctrine, and though the doctrine was built around a theory of air power, it was motivated by the prospect of institutional independence:

The formulation and articulation of the doctrine is ordinarily designed to justify fully the service's attempt to obtain or maintain exclusive control over certain missions. Criticism usually results in an undermining of the case the service has so carefully made for certain roles and missions in national defense. Dissent is therefore discouraged, and breakthroughs in technology which might bring established doctrine into question are often ignored.

. . . Air Corps leaders had reached a doctrinal decision by 1935 as to the efficacy of unescorted long-range strategic bombardment and were unwilling either to question that decision or even to observe technological advances that might cause them to modify this doctrine until 1943 when the whole concept of strategic bombardment was endangered by the horrendous losses over Germany.

To point out the vulnerabilities of strategic bombardment was to jeopardize the Air Corps case for autonomy, for if strategic bombardment was proved ineffective as the element of warfare which alone might prove to be decisive in battle, then its case would be seriously undermined. If flights of bombardment aircraft could be turned back, or if the defensive fighters could inflict unacceptable losses upon the bombing formation, then the whole concept of strategic bombardment would be proved erroneous, and the Air Corps would then be expected to accomplish only close support, air superiority, and interdiction, none of which (nor all in combination) could justify complete autonomy.[11]

The drive for an independent Air Force colored almost everything the AAF planners saw or did:

Since the aim of the postwar planners was to plan for and justify an autonomous Air Force, and since this was the reason that [General] Arnold "tolerated" the planners, it is understandable that they based their plans on theories of war causation, potential enemies, and base requirements which would best justify autonomy. (p. 35)

The planners were an extremely optimistic group, probably because they were convinced that American airpower was winning World War II. The enormous role that the Russians, the British, and the Chinese, as well as the United States Navy, Marines, and Army were playing in the victory was not recognized by the Air Force planners. (p. 49)

The airman's reverence for technology (see chapter 2) also colored the AAF interpretations of national security threats:

The Air Force planners viewed threats to national security largely in terms of technology as it related to airpower. If airpower was the key to national security and national strength, no other state would pose a threat unless it possessed a sophisticated air force.

It was assumed that deficiencies in technological sophistication were the reason the Soviets did not develop a strategic air capability in World War II. (p. 52)

They measured a state's power by heavily weighting technology and by assigning lesser values to natural resources, manpower, and ideology. (p. 39)

To his credit, as an advocate of the air strategy, DeSeversky foresaw the limitations of air power against states that did not measure high by these standards: "Total war from the air against an undeveloped country or region is well-nigh futile; it is one of the curious features of the most modern weapon that it is especially effective against the most modern types of civilization."[12]

Though many, perhaps most, of the air strategy theorists were, and still are, true believers in its three basic premises, the air strategy was never proven before, during, and after World War II; its only demonstrable utility was institutional: the achievement of an independent Air Force. Even there, the victory was partial—the Navy was able to retain its own air power,[13] and eventually the Army reacquired its own air power of a sort. Thus, the real and demonstrable effect of the air strategy was institutional independence; all the rest remains disputed theory even today. But Perry McCoy Smith argued that the theory served its proponents well:

> The end sought was not national security through a properly balanced military defensive and deterrent force but rather an autonomous, powerful United States Air Force which would be the first line of defense, the largest of the three military services, and the recipient of the largest share of the defense budget. Assumptions were drawn not as an initial step in the planning process, which would, in turn, provide the guidance for the structure, size, and deployment of the military forces. Instead, they were drawn in order to lead to the end desired.[14]

The strident claims made for the air strategy have softened over the last several decades, but the basic premises remain even today:

> As a critical element of the interdependent land-naval-aerospace team, *aerospace power can be the decisive force in warfare.*[15]

> Considering the nature of modern war, airpower can dominate not only the air but the land and sea as well. The Air Force *must be able to deny control of the air* to enemy air forces and to provide ground and naval forces the assistance necessary for them to control their environment. (pp. 1–4; emphasis added).

> In sum, since 1943, several fundamental beliefs have remained embedded in Air Force doctrine. Airpower can exploit speed, range, and flexibility *better than land and sea forces,* and therefore, *it must be allowed to operate independently* of these forces. These characteristics are most fully realized when *airpower is controlled centrally* but executed decentrally. (pp. A–6; emphasis added).

# 7

# THE NAVY AND STRATEGY

## The Navy's Search for Strategy

The U.S. Navy is no stranger to strategy. For the first half of the twentieth century, the Navy, thanks to Alfred Thayer Mahan, had a world-class theory of sea power and its use. According to that theory central position and concentration of force were general principles of strategy, equally applicable to continental or insular powers. For an insular nation, like the United States, the central positions were the seas; command of the seas conveyed power, for commerce and in war. Certainly the importance of the seas to an insular (i.e., maritime) nation and the imperative of commanding the seas (i.e., sea control), both of which are to be found in the modern maritime strategy, have their origins in the writings of Mahan.[1]

With Mahan's theories to explain why sea power was necessary for insular nations like the United States, Britain, and Japan, and with great oceans separating the United States from its potential enemies in Europe or Asia, the role of the Navy as "America's first line of defense" became self-evident. It was the Navy that would shield the country from attack; the Navy would meet and presumably defeat any potential enemy on the high seas.

The airplane, as it developed increasing capacities for range and payload, doubly threatened that view of the Navy: Airplanes with bombs could reach across the oceans that had heretofore isolated America from her enemies, bypassing the Navy as the first line of defense. And airplanes, from enemies across the oceans, could find and threaten the survival of naval ships on the high seas. These were the concepts that Billy Mitchell and, later, Frank Andrews

were trying to prove in their highly publicized demonstrations with
bomber aircraft against ships: Mitchell tried to prove that bombs
from aircraft could sink battleships, and Andrews tried to prove
that aircraft could find ships (the Italian passenger liner *Rex*) far
out to sea.[2]

Thus, until the 1920s and the emergence of the air-power
theories of Douhet and Mitchell,

> [t]he Navy thought of itself as the nation's "first line of defense," the
> service which had to remain at all times maximally ready because it was
> the service that would first meet and engage any approaching enemy
> aggressor. The Mitchellite strategic doctrine rejected all this, claiming
> that *all* surface forces—especially naval forces—were obsolete. They
> were obsolete, the Mitchellites said, because they were wholly vulnerable
> to air attack and consequently useless. The fliers asserted that the new
> "first line of defense" was an air offense, the use of long-range aerial
> bombardment to knock out an enemy in quick decisive blows.[3]

> The Navy of the prewar period, to understate the case, was unreceptive to
> radical technological innovations. For fifty years it had been planning to
> fight the next war with battleships and related vessels. An elaborate stra-
> tegic concept as well as a massive body of thinking and planning had been
> erected on the assumption of certain fixed characteristics and capabilities
> of these basic pieces of hardware, and any changes, even if improvements,
> would have destroyed the entire interrelated structure.[4]

> Before [World War II] it was commonplace and congenial to conceive
> of naval strategy as a thing apart: a discrete body of thinking about
> indisputably naval functions and missions, concerned almost entirely
> with "naval" enemies, and engaged-in almost exclusively by naval offi-
> cers. The distinction between land war and sea war was still sharp
> enough (or so it was commonly perceived) to permit individual,
> exclusive strategies for each. So long as the missions of war could be
> defined in traditional terms such as command of the sea, control of the
> air, the conquest or defense of territory, military strategy could be com-
> partmentalized according to the medium in which each service
> operated. National defense was merely an aggregation of separate ser-
> vice strategies.[5]

> The revolution in weaponry and its uses during the Second World War
> made it no longer congenial to articulate strategy wholly in terms of dis-
> tinct mediums (air, land, sea) or to conceive of entire missions and
> functions as within the exclusive purview of one or another military ser-
> vice. Wartime uses of air power had irrevocably shattered the tradi-
> tional boundary—the coastline—that separated land and naval warfare,
> Army and Navy strategies.[6]

But even as World War II proved that ships were vulnerable to attacks by aircraft, the Navy convincingly demonstrated that it, too, could use airplanes, carried on ships, to project power ashore, that is, the bombardment of land targets. Before World War II, the Navy considered shore bombardment as an ancillary mission for naval gunfire. Gunfire, provided by the capital ships (battleships), was intended for sinking other ships in battles on the high seas. Aircraft were ancillary, to be used mostly for scouting and spotting gunfire.

After World War II, the Navy saw power projection as the primary mission of naval forces, one to be carried out principally by carrier-based aircraft. Of course, to carry out that mission would also require control of those sea areas necessary for naval forces to project their power; such action, in turn, would require self-defense for naval forces. In effect, power projection became the mission of the capital ship (the carrier), which then justified the additional, supporting naval forces for sea control and self-defense. Control of the sea lanes or sea lines of communication (as distinct from control of those sea areas needed for the exercise of naval power projection), though still recognized as a naval mission, no longer enjoyed the attention that the Navy now gave to power projection, despite the concern of many, including the Army. The capital ship, the aircraft carrier, and its supporting forces were justified by power projection; sea lane protection called for a different and less interesting Navy. Thus, for the Navy, particularly its aviators, a new role for sea power, beyond that envisaged by Mahan, had emerged.

The theorists of independent air forces, such as DeSeversky, saw power projection from the sea as a temporary or inadequate approach to the use of air power: "Except in limited stretches of ocean as yet beyond the reach of land-based aviation, ship-borne aircraft is a most hazardous substitute for true airpower: first, because it is inferior to the enemy's land-based planes, and second, because the carriers themselves are perfect targets for enemy aviation, being among the most vulnerable ships afloat."[7] DeSeversky's assessment of the relative performance of land- and carrier-based aircraft, though arguably correct at the time, did not fully anticipate the evolution of tactical jet aircraft and aerial refueling, which have made the differences in performance because of land or carrier basing vanishingly small. His assessment of carrier vulnerability, of course, remains disputed even today.

Thus, within twenty years, in the crucible of World War II, the Navy adopted the air offense for itself in the form of the carrier as its primary instrument of naval power. This adaptation was not solely based upon the proven lessons of the war:

*The forthcoming dominance of aviation forces in the postwar Navy was not decided in response to a new strategic concept or to an analysis of the international political situation but rather in response to an institutional threat* [by the Air Force] *to the Navy which originated within the domestic political arena.*[8]

The submariners had as good a case as the aviators or any other Navy group if the matter [of dominance in the postwar Navy] was going to be decided solely on the basis of comparative war records. No less notable figure than Admiral Raymond A. Spruance, one of the most renowned carrier task force commanders in the Pacific (although not himself an aviator), is reported by one reputable Navy historian to have made the flat statement: "The submarine beat Japan."[9]

Nevertheless: "The naval fliers, who had used those few opportunities given them before the war to experiment with carrier operations, were now in control of the Navy. . . . They were not prepared to accept the metaphysical reasoning of the Air Force that all air everywhere was indivisible and that therefore only the Air Force had a right to conduct U.S. military air operations" (p. 228).

But the security afforded by this adaptation was short lived:

The new notion that navies were useful for a far more comprehensive range of actions than naval battles . . . was . . . one of the major lessons that the Navy learned in World War II. But the Navy had been known to ignore important lessons in the past. Why did it learn this particular lesson so thoroughly—and so quickly too . . . ? The first reason . . . was the emergence of Russia as the new enemy. Inasmuch as Russia had only negligible naval strength, the U.S. Navy could not claim a major role in defensive plans against this threat unless it abandoned its old dogma about the chief use of navies. But even more important than this reason were five other closely interrelated developments:

1. The advent of the atomic bomb.

2. The belief . . . that the atomic bomb had made navies obsolete, not only because ships were thought to be too vulnerable to atomic attack but also because no naval force could deliver an atomic weapon.

3. The exploitation of the foregoing views by the Army Air Force, which claimed that atomic bombs had made all forms of warfare outmoded except strategic bombing, that only the Air Force could deliver atomic bombs and, therefore, that a new separate Air Force ought to be

made the dominant component of the postwar U.S. defense establishment.

4. The susceptibility of the Congress to the arguments of the Air Force, believing that emphasis on the atomic bomb would give the U.S. a cheap, painless, and invincible military force that no other nation could match.

5. The growing determination of the Navy, led by its aviators, not to let these developments succeed in reducing the Navy to a secondary component of the U.S. defense establishment. (pp. 189, 190)

Thus, just as the Navy adjusted with pride to its new, proven capabilities in warfare, the advent of atomic bombs suddenly threatened the fundamental need for sea power. If airplanes could reach across the oceans, and if one airplane with one bomb could destroy an entire city (or fleet), why did America need or want a Navy? Within the space of little more than a decade, many of the conceptual foundations of the Navy had been overturned:

- The airplane was no longer an auxiliary or ancillary instrument of naval warfare; it had become the primary strike weapon of fleets.
- The aircraft carrier had replaced the battleship as the Navy's capital ship; the aviators had ascended to the top of the naval hierarchy.
- The Navy could no longer claim to be the nation's first line of defense; but it could project significant power ashore by means of carrier-based aviation.
- The vulnerability of ships (or any other object that could be found) to nuclear weapons could no longer be questioned.

Little wonder, then, that the Navy found itself adrift in strategic theory for more than thirty years after World War II, and at the very time when the Air Force was using its air strategy to lay claim to institutional independence and dominance in service status and budgets.

> The political fight with the War Department and, more particularly, with the Air Force soon dominated the Navy men's every consideration. Their responses to this political struggle—which they sincerely believed to be a fight for the very survival of their service—thus provided the context for all remaining decisions about the postwar Navy. (pp. 155, 156)

For the Navy the struggle was . . . seen as a fight for institutional survival and, concomitantly, a fight to guarantee that the U.S. would continue to have the large degree of seapower that the Navy men were still
convinced that it needed. (p. 226)

The . . . carrier was seen by the Navy as a guarantee of institutional survival, but it was viewed by the Air Force as a threat to its own monopoly of atomic delivery [and] by the Army as a wasteful drain on
resources.[10]

The past forty years have seen the Navy awash in proposals and
arguments for new directions and theories for sea power. These
have included the relative emphasis the Navy should give to:

- the traditional mission of sea control as compared with the
  newly found capabilities for power projection ashore;
- nuclear weapons delivery (and nuclear warfare) as compared
  with conventional warfare missions;
- air, surface, or subsurface warfare capabilities as the dominant naval forces (and, hence, medium) of the future;
- the retention of amphibious and mine warfare capabilities;
  and
- ship quantity versus quality; big versus little carriers.

But the Navy's deeply held reliance upon traditions for safe passage allowed little leeway for actual change beyond what was forced
upon it by the trauma of World War II. Thus, rather than embrac-
ing any radical new theory about sea power or itself, the Navy
creatively waffled:

While the other services tended to become associated with a single
theory and strategy of war, the Navy made a *virtue* of having no such
singular strategic preoccupations [*sic*].[11]

The advantages to a service in not becoming peculiarly identified with
any single strategic mission were well illustrated by the smooth sailing
of the Navy in the interservice conflicts after 1950. The Air Force was
identified primarily with strategic deterrence, the Army with European
defense and then limited war. Traditionally, the Navy argued that it was
not limited to any single medium, that it must include all the air, sea,
and ground forces necessary to accomplish its mission. The Navy also
maintained broadly diversified forces which could be interpreted as supporting one or more functional missions. A carrier task force could be
used for strategic retaliation, European defense, or limited war.
Antisubmarine warfare, similarly, was relevant to continental defense,
European defense, and limited war.[12]

Moreover:

> The size, composition, roles and missions of the Navy have never been determined in a political vacuum or by means of an orderly process in which strategy follows from national objectives, naval strategy from overall military strategy, and naval forces from naval strategy, but always in a real world in which the relationships are much more complicated, and in which naval policy is both a product of and a reaction to the competition, interaction, and ambiguities of broader conceptual, technological, fiscal, political, and organizational factors.[13]

The history of the Navy since World War II has been a search for a strategic concept to justify naval power in the form judged desirable by the Navy as an institution.

> The very general nature of the Navy's postwar strategic thinking— actually, little more than the elaborated conviction that a strong diversified Navy offers the U.S. a versatile fighting force of great value in many varied military situations—plus the obsessive focus on the struggle with the Air Force have led the naval officers to neglect until recently efforts to refine their strategic thinking in the specific context of the emerging new world order. A generally versatile fighting force is certainly a good thing to have, as an axiomatic proposition, but in a defined situation a more precise capability of special nature might be incomparably more valuable than a kit of general-utility tools. (p.269)

> The final [Navy] postulate was the concept of a functionally integrated, strategically independent naval force at sea: self-sustaining and self-replenishing, needing no foreign bases, and self-possessed of all that was required to perform wartime missions. This was the Navy's victory in the interservice struggles of the 1940s: to keep control of the Marine Corps and its own air power. In the ensuing years, the Navy resisted all attempts to alter these facts or their significance. It was also the most persistently resistant of the services to efforts at greater defense centralization and any reallocations of roles and missions. (p. 550)

It is against this background that the maritime strategy emerged. The Navy's affection for strategy, going back to Mahan, is strong; and the major buildup of the Navy, begun in 1981, needed an explanation for sea power that went beyond the available pronouncements. Yet, the Navy's dilemma in declaring a strategic view was real:

> The essence of peacetime strategic decision-making must . . . be to face up to difficult choices between competing conceptions of war when one is no more obviously "correct" than another, and when the defense establishment cannot do everything it would want. Yet, to embrace one

set of answers was to risk all on the wrong choice; to hedge and cover as many bets as possible ran the risk of having a little bit of everything and not enough of anything; to attempt a strategy for every possible contingency was likely to result in a strategy for none. (p. 569)

That painful choice is evident in the maritime strategy the Navy has adopted.

## The Maritime Strategy

The maritime strategy emerged over several years as fragmented concepts or arguments in briefings, testimony, and unpublished papers, so that it came to be debated in the academic journals even before it had been explicitly expressed in the open literature.[14] Uncertainty about just what the maritime strategy was, or ought to be, was apparent in the debates:

What [Ambassador Robert W. Komer] resists is a shift to a "maritime strategy" that would go beyond controlling the seas and would use the seas to project power against the Soviet Union. . . . One use of maritime power under this concept would be attacks by aircraft or missiles from ships directly onto the Soviet homeland. Another use would be "horizontal escalations" or attacks on Soviet interests outside the homeland. . . .

The maritime strategy Mr. Komer describes is not a maritime strategy that would be useful for the United States today or in the future. *Yet, it is easy to see how he could interpret the term in this way.* What he criticizes is, in fact, the direction that the U.S. Navy is moving under the Administration's defense program. Quite simply, *the Navy is asking to do more of what it has done so well ever since World War II,* projecting power onto hostile shores with aircraft based on aircraft carriers.[15]

This public speculation as to what the maritime strategy was finally ended with the publication of *The Maritime Strategy* by the U.S. Naval Institute,[16] as a supplement to its *Proceedings.* It was no tentative or vague offering of a proposed strategic theory as an invitation to debate; it was codified strategy:

Naval strategy has recently received more attention than in any peacetime era since Alfred Thayer Mahan dominated the scene. This unusual prominence stems from the Navy's attempt to think through and spell out a maritime strategy within the national military strategy. Because the best developed and most detailed statements of "The Maritime Strategy" have been available only in classified versions, public debate between its supporters and detractors has often suffered from misinterpretations or exaggerations.

This supplement provides the most definitive and authoritative statements of the Maritime Strategy that are available in unclassified form. They are the nearest thing to a British 'White Paper'—that is, an official statement of policy—that we are likely to encounter in the American political system.[17]

[T]he Maritime Strategy has rationalized, disciplined and focused Navy program development, budgets and procurement to a degree that would have seemed remarkable only five years ago. Since 1982, a formal presentation of the maritime strategy begins each annual naval program development cycle.[18]

The publication of the maritime strategy in the Naval Institute's supplement to the *Proceedings* has stirred considerable comment and discussion on the merits and wisdom of the strategy by its proponents and opponents, but little analysis of its content.[19] The presentation of the maritime strategy requires only seventy-three paragraphs, so its content can be analyzed by simply reducing each of the seventy-three paragraphs to its topic sentence, combining those topic sentences into eleven paragraphs of related ideas, and scanning that condensed statement for assumptions and principles.

What emerges from this reduction and structuring is a barebones sketch of the principal premises and promises of the maritime strategy. It becomes apparent that it is not so much strategy as it is an explanation of (1) how naval forces can contribute to national security at every level of conflict (i.e., a rationale for naval forces), and (2) how the Navy would prefer to employ its forces in combat (i.e., naval doctrine).

The strategy (or perhaps more correctly, the combination of several substrategies) spans the spectrum of conflict from peacetime to global war, a variety of objectives, and every form of naval power. At the extremes of conflict—peace and all-out war—the strategy thins out to a simple claim for the unique contributions of naval forces: from showing the flag to the survivability of submarine-launched ballistic missiles. Several substrategies take form and subside in between those extremes, shifting in their ends and means with the intensity of conflict.

At the lower levels of conflict, the strategy claims that forward naval presence can deter conflict or escalation by the implied threat of direct confrontation or defeat. In the middle, at the threshold of superpower conflict, the strategy calls for aggressive forward deployments of naval forces to present the enemy with the prospect of a protracted and expanded war, preventing the enemy from focusing its efforts in time or space. If the enemy should persist, then strikes on its flanks and rear should dilute and divide its efforts. At the upper levels of conflict, but still with conventional weapons, the strategy seeks to coerce the enemy by threatening to tip the nuclear balance adversely. This threat would take the form of exposing its submarine-based strategic nuclear forces to attrition. The strikes on the flanks and rear of the enemy and the attrition of its submarine-based nuclear forces would, of course, involve the concomitant or prior destruction of the enemy naval forces.

The applications of military force in the maritime strategy can be arranged as shown in table 1. It is apparent that the maritime strategy is intended to apply to all possible levels of conflict, war aims, force types, and uses of naval power. What is less clear is whether the war aims are in consonance with national aims for the use of military force and, if so, whether the proposed uses of naval power are central, relevant, or productive to those aims. But the breadth of application provides the strategy with a robustness: All the Navy specialties—aviation, ships, submarines, Marines—not only have a piece of the action; they have their day in the sun as the principal players. All levels of conflict are included. The Navy plays no matter where the geographical point of conflict, even in a land war in Central Europe.

Thus, the maritime strategy resolves the dilemma today's Navy faces in having a coherent strategy and yet recognizing the traditional roles and missions of its diverse elements. The means of the maritime strategy are all the existing types of naval forces; the ends are all those military objectives which might apply across the spectrum of conflict. The maritime strategy is not a concept for relating means and ends; it is an explanation of how all existing means can be related to all ends.

Nevertheless, three premises about the use of naval forces are evident in the maritime strategy:

1. The presence of naval forces can have a significant effect on deterring the instigation or escalation of local conflicts.
2. Threatening the Soviet flanks and rear with naval strike forces can significantly inhibit the Soviets from concentrating their military efforts in time or space.
3. Threatening the survivability of Soviet ballistic missile-carrying submarines can significantly tip the nuclear balance.

Table 1.   Applications of Military Force in the Maritime Strategy

| Transition | Objective | Force Type* | + Application | = Effect |
|---|---|---|---|---|
| Peace-crisis | Regional stability | Surface | + Presence | = Deterrence |
| Crisis-conflict | Seizing the initiative | All | + Forward deployment | = Defocusing |
| Conflict-war | Expanding, protracting | Air and amphibious | + Strike | = Dilution |
| War-peace | Termination | Subsurface | + Attrition | = Coercion |

*Here, force type refers to the principal (cutting edge) or most effective type of force to be applied in order to achieve the desired effect, recognizing that naval forces are almost always deployed and used in combinations.

The last two premises both rest on implicit assumptions that they:

- are attractive and credible uses of military force in conflicts with the Soviet Union and
- will require the possession or achievement of maritime superiority.

These three premises and two assumptions are the five anchors of the maritime strategy. If any one of them fails or is not accepted, much of the strategy's support for the existing character of the Navy is lost. Thus, whatever the merits of the many arguments or assertions that adhere to the maritime strategy, these five anchors are central to the Navy's institutional stake or interest in that strategy. For example, the assertion that the United States is a maritime nation is not central to the strategy.[20] Whether Europe is more important than Northeast Asia is also not central to the maritime strategy insofar as that strategy supports the Navy's institutional interests.[21]

On the other hand, arguments about whether or not attacks on the Soviet flanks and rear are attractive or credible uses of military force in a conflict with the Soviets over Central Europe[22] go right to the heart of the Navy's justification for its considerable vested interest in carrier air strike forces. A similar relationship exists between attacks upon Soviet ballistic missile-carrying submarines and the Navy's high interest in attack submarines (probably even over its own ballistic missile-carrying submarines).

In sum, an analysis of the content of the maritime strategy suggests that it is a carefully woven fabric of substrategies that more clearly serves the Navy's institutional interests in rationalizing its existing force mix than it does the U.S. national strategy or security interests.

# 8

## THE ARMY AND STRATEGY

The Army as an institution has not shown any particularly strong affinity for strategy. At the same time, however, Army leaders have traditionally been major contributors to the formulation of national strategy. It would seem that the disconnection has to do with the distinctions the Army itself draws between the Army as an institution serving the nation and senior Army people serving in roles of national advisers or statesmen. The formulation or advocacy of strategy implies a choice of means and ends. But such choices are not obvious to the Army in its institutional roles and missions. It must fight where and when it is told to fight; all too often, the means have been provided from the citizenry after the fact of war.

Understandably, the Army is more concerned about how well it can assimilate assigned resources and employ them than it is about the assigned objectives and resources, which it so often takes as givens. How well the Army adapts and uses its assigned resources to achieve its assigned objectives, attainable or not, is everything.[1]

The Army uses strategy, when available or articulated, usually by others, to declare what it needs. If those resources are not forthcoming, the Army will define the shortfalls and state the risks.[2] It generally will not offer strategy (and, hence, resource) alternatives. The Army is accustomed (as a citizen army in peacetime) to not having what it needs to execute declared wartime strategies; it assumes that either the resources will be made available or the strategy will have to be changed upon the event. In either case, the Army intends to fight well (i.e., demonstrate its competence, dedication, and courage) regardless of the position in which it may find itself, whether it can win or must lose.

The Air Force and Navy may advocate strategies in peacetime to their advantage, but they are not irrevocably committed to their execution in war. If their strategies do not appear to be propitious in the event of war, they are, to a large degree, free to change them accordingly by the way they commit their forces to combat.[3] The Army may be unique among the services in its acceptance in peacetime of national strategies it is both utterly committed to execute and unlikely to be able successfully to prosecute in wartime.

Generally speaking, the Army has not promoted an independent service strategy—that is, a ground-power strategy or a continental strategy—as a candidate for the national military strategy. Huntington notes that the Army may have a unique perspective here among the services:

> The Army participated in a diversity of tasks—Southern reconstruction, Indian fighting, labor disorders, the Spanish War, Cuban occupation, Philippine pacification, construction and operation of the [Panama] Canal, the Mexican punitive expedition. Accordingly, the Army developed an image of itself as the government's obedient handyman performing without question or hesitation the jobs assigned to it. . . . By following all orders literally the Army attempted to divest itself of political responsibility and political controversy despite the political nature of the tasks it was frequently called upon to perform.[4]

A few in the Army, having observed the Navy's apparent success in budget slicing, might see this passivity as an oversight that the Army needs to correct; but most would probably find an independent Army strategy inconsistent with the role of the Army or with the nature of modern warfare. It is here, on this point, that the Army can most clearly be heard saying that "the Army doesn't make strategy," and "there is no such thing as Army strategy."[5]

The nagging question is: Has the Army, by eschewing an independent service strategy, also forgone the internal institutional benefits of self-image and pride such strategies can offer? Every person, every institution must have a strategy—some concept for relating means and ends—in order to make decisions. The Army must have some kind of strategy; otherwise it would have no basis for the decisions it must make every day. To paraphrase Lacy: An Army still requires a theory of an Army. Whether stated explicitly or implicitly, there must exist something in addition to its soldiers and tanks and guns—a concept, a strategy, a notion of who it is and what it wants to be, of what it is about and what it wants to be about—a concept which is a source of inspiration and a means for explaining its actions, if only to itself.[6]

The Army strategy may not be about independent service means and national security ends because it may view such efforts by the services as predatory, counterproductive, or properly beyond its province. The Army strategy may have more to do with institutional interests and concerns, such as the prospects for its people, equipment, or funding, and as such, might be better called an institutional strategy.

If the Air Force has an air strategy, and the Navy has a maritime strategy, why does not the Army have a land or a ground-power strategy? Or a continental strategy? The question must have been asked many times since World War II—since the emergence of an independent and powerful Air Force riding upon the air strategy. The more recent expansion of the Navy, seemingly floated on the maritime strategy, can only have reinforced the significance of the question.

In fact, the Army does not have a theory that is the equivalent of the air or maritime strategy. It does have a theory of how it would prefer to fight—the AirLand Battle doctrine—but not a concept for the selection of the means and ends of war, as do the Air Force and Navy. Why this difference?

Admiral J. C. Wylie has provided a lucid analysis that explains much of this difference, which he relates to three factors.[7] It is useful to quote him at length here:

> First, the connotation of the word "strategy" is not the same to the soldier as to the sailor or airman. The reason for this is elusive but very real. It has to do with the environment in which the conception is set.
>
> Where the sailor or airman thinks in terms of an entire world, the soldier at work thinks in terms of theaters, in terms of campaigns, or in terms of battles. And the [latter] three concepts are not too markedly different from each other. This state of mind in which the soldier derives his conception of the strategic scene is brought about primarily by the matter of geography. Prominent and direct in its effect is the fundamental fact of terrain. "Terrain" as a word does not have deep meaning to the nonsoldier, but to the soldier it is everything. It is the fixed field within which he operates. It is the opponent that he must always face no matter who may be his enemy. It is the fact of terrain that establishes the field within which the soldier's professional intellect must generate its plans. (pp. 48, 49)
>
> A second factor of primary influence in the soldier's strategic pattern of thought, related closely to the status of terrain, is the nature of the soldier's combat—and thus the nature of his conception of strategy.

The sailor and the airman encounter war as a separated series of encounters. After each encounter the two sides separate. They haul off, they regroup, they jockey again for position, and to a considerable extent each combatant retains to himself the decision as to whether and where and when to fight again. In most situations, the sailor and airman fight with their opponents only when, for one reason or another, it is mutually agreeable. Mahan and perhaps others before him have found it convenient to differentiate tactical and strategic matters by the simple fact of contact. When opposing forces are in contact, the plans and operations are "tactical." Everything outside contact is "strategic."

Not so the soldier. His conception of the separation of strategy and tactics, and thus his concept of the scope of strategy, is on an entirely different footing. The "contact" thumb rule has no validity for him. The soldier makes contact when the war starts, and he makes every effort to maintain contact until the war is over. The soldier who has lost contact with his enemy is in a bad way. To the soldier the shading between a tactic and a strategy is a fuzzy and not too important one . . . what he does is tactical and what his next senior does is strategic. (pp. 50, 51)

Wylie then identifies the third factor as the soldier's limited view of the objective, which he claims is the soldier's acceptance of the Clausewitzian principle that "the ultimate objective of all military operations is the destruction of the enemy's armed forces and his will to fight." But from the discussion that follows, it is apparent that Wylie's third factor is better described as the absence of the soldier's control over his essential support:

This [soldier's focus on the destruction of the enemy] is not a theory of strategy in quite the same sense that the sailor has his maritime theory or the airman has his air theory. It is much less complex than that. It is, however, a basic concept of warfare, and appreciation of these underlying factors could do much toward helping the nonsoldier understand why the soldier thinks as he does.

It may explain for instance, the soldier's tacit (and sometimes not too tacit) opinion that air and naval forces exist primarily to transport the soldier to the scene of action and support him after he gets there. The soldier views the enemy army as the prime focal point of war, and all else should properly be subordinate. The soldier is impatient with the navy when the navy finds tasks that might interfere with taking the soldier where he wants to go, where the enemy army is, and keeping his supplies coming steadily. He is impatient with the airman who wants to put a machine tool factory out of business; he wants the airman to work on the enemy tank right across the valley from him. And the soldier, few men realize, is the only one of the military men who cannot do his part of the war alone. The airman can have his duels in the air and can bomb factories or enemy missile launchers or whatever he chooses all by himself. He does not need the soldier or the sailor to help him. The sailor can sail away and sink the enemy ships and control the seas and even extend his influence ashore, all with his own ships and his built-in air strength and his own specialized troops in the naval service.

But the soldier cannot function alone. His flanks are bare, his rear is vulnerable, and he looks aloft with a cautious eye. He needs the airman and the sailor for his own security in doing his own job. (pp. 53, 54)

In sum, the Army does not have a strategic theory as do the Air Force and Navy because its circumstances—its lack of control over terrain, engagement, and supporting resources—deny it the freedom to define war on its own terms.

If that be so, then the Air Force and Navy participate in the military planning process, through their service strategies, in an important way that the Army presently does not. The analyses presented in the previous two chapters strongly suggest that the air and maritime strategies, whatever their intellectual merits, are used by the Air Force and Navy not just to make their internal planning coherent but principally as devices for justifying the independence of their institutions, missions, forces, and, therefore, their budgets within the national security forum. If the Army is denied such independence by its inherent dependency upon others—its sister services for support and the nation's enemies and allies to define the wars it must help fight—the question still remains: What can, what should, the Army then do in the military planning process in recognition of its unique and (some might say) disadvantageous position relative to the other services?

For the Army to make itself more independent, on the model of its sister services, by claiming the independence (or dominance) of land warfare missions, flies in the face of two realities:

1. Though land warfare may, in fact, dominate some conflicts, the interdependence of air, sea, land, and even space operations is nowhere more apparent than in the conduct of land warfare. Wars isolated to space, the sea, or even the air, are at least conceivable. The isolation of warfare to the land is now credible only at the most primitive levels in situations in which both sides have no other resources. Even low-intensity conflicts, such as those now waged against smuggling, terrorism, and insurrection, are likely to involve sea, air, and, without speculating too far, even space operations.

2. The Army has never seen itself as having an independent sense of mission or purpose apart from the country's. To repeat, the Army is the nation's most loyal and obedient servant. The Army, unlike the Air Force and Navy, has no vision of a war on its own terms.[8] For the Army, war will always be on terms chosen by others—partly by the nation's enemies, partly by the nation's leadership—terms that are never satisfactory or welcome, but always to be met with a sense of duty, honor, and courage.

One obvious way out of its dilemma would be for the Army to reacquire control over its essential support, such as sea or air lift and air (or sea) fire support. It was the Key West agreements, barely forty years ago, that stripped the Army of that control. It can be argued that it is time to reevaluate those arrangements, that the Air Force will never warmly embrace close air support as a mission, that the Navy will always put sea lift and its protection at the bottom of its priorities.

The Army would be in a much better position to define an independent strategy if it had either independent missions (ends) or independent forces (means). And there is good reason to speculate that the overall defense posture of the United States might be enhanced by a reassignment of service roles and missions (e.g., separating out the nuclear forces). But whatever the logic or merit of revisiting the Key West agreements, it is a simplistic answer to an enormous problem now rooted in the nation's institutions, history, and responsibilities. Though realigning the service roles and missions may be the "right" approach, it almost certainly is not the workable approach to the Army's dilemma for at least two reasons:

1. Any steps by the Army toward controlling its own air and sea support would run head-on into opposition with the longstanding interests and actions of the Navy and Air Force to separate and keep isolated their missions and forces from their sister services. In short, it would precipitate the most virulent, highest-stakes interservice warfare.
2. It would do nothing to remove the dependency of the Army upon the nation's enemies for the choice of terrain and time of engagement in their aggressions or upon the nation's friends and allies for their support in conflicts. Removing joint dependencies would not eliminate coalition dependencies; and the Army is much more dependent upon coalitions than either of its sister services.

Thus, even if the Army did control its own lift and air support, it would still be dependent upon others in defining where and how and why it would fight.  The same is not true, to a large degree, for the Air Force and Navy, both of whom—correctly or not—see some prospect for choosing the timing, locale, and objectives in the commitment of their forces to combat.

Is the Army, therefore, without any prospect for strategy initiatives in the military planning process?  If it cannot control its essential support or the terms of its engagement in combat, it is clearly denied an independent service strategy—an independent vision of its forces (means) and the purposes (ends) to which they will or ought to be applied.

But the Army may have an advantage that its sister services do not: Though the Air Force and Navy can offer up visions of how they would prefer to fight, their visions are only preferences, not commitments.  The Army has been handed something much more concrete around which it can define both means and ends.  In the national commitments to the use of force, the Army has been given specific assignments as to where it must fight—in West Germany, South Korea, and Berlin—three overseas assignments so clear and important that the nation has already made the extraordinary decision to fight even if its forces are not attacked.  The Army, uniquely among the services, is tied to these national commitments—by alliances and the physical presence of troops—to use military force to uphold the sovereignty and territorial integrity of these nations.  I will discuss the implications of these commitments, for the Army and military planning, in chapter 13.

# Part III
# Analysis

# 9

## WHAT IS ANALYSIS?

In its broadest terms, analysis is an examination of something by its parts and the relationships of those parts to one another. Military analysis is as old as organized combat; but the science of military analysis is much more recent, and its widespread institutionalization in and around the military bureaucracies dates from World War II.[1] Today, analysis is as much a part of the military services as electronics or paperwork, but it is much more revealing about how the services see themselves and their environments: it becomes a window into their institutional minds. The window is an important one because analysis is the most logical and rigorous form of communication available for converting military concepts (i.e., strategies) into forces (i.e., hardware and personnel). Analysis has become the language of institutional advocacy for ideas and things in the military bureaucracies.

Institutionalized military analysis currently appears in many distinctive forms, and the services practice all of them to some extent. But three forms of analysis deserve special attention here because the services' attitudes toward them are substantially different. Those three—operations, systems, and requirements analysis— probably best illustrate the service differences. Other kinds of analysis include cost effectiveness, programming, budgeting, and contingency analysis, to name a few.

The three kinds of analysis can be illustrated by three successful cases in which the analyses made a real difference in the face of opposition. That is, the analyses were more than routine calculations needed to supply an answer to a question; they resolved a problem in dispute. All three examples are taken from the Air Force to illustrate first the different kinds of analysis rather than the service differences.[2] The differences among the services in their overall approaches to analysis can then be more easily appreciated.

## Operations Analysis

The first modern application of scientific methods and mathematics to military problems addressed the analysis of military operations; the techniques applied have since become generally known as Operations Research. During World War II, scientists, first in Britain and later in the United States, were employed to help military staffs solve some of their most vexing problems.[3] Through statistical and mathematical methods available at the time, basic but complex military operations such as convoying, searching, intercepting, and penetrating were analyzed and made more effective. The data required to support such analyses or their inferences were often taken from contemporary, ongoing military operations. The results from modified operations served as a test of the validity of recommendations based upon the analyses.

The achievements of operations analysts during World War II were sufficient to earn the respect of their military mentors and an enduring role in all major military institutions. The reasons for their acceptance were many: Their contributions to the improvement or effectiveness of operations were often substantial and demonstrable rather than marginal or assumed. In some cases, their answers were counterintuitive or revolutionary and, therefore, surprising: They discovered for their beneficiaries something that would not have been found by experience or trial and error. And, perhaps more important, they helped their mentors to explain why operations were being conducted as they were and with what effect.

A classic example of successful operations analysis during World War II is provided by the analysts who supported General Curtis LeMay in the conduct of his bombing campaign against Japan.[4] The initial results with the new B-29 bombers operating from the Marianas Islands were disappointing. Compared to the size of the effort being mounted, the number of targets destroyed was embarrassingly small. The operational problems included long over-water flights, modest bombloads, aircraft and engine unreliabilities, high winds, and a new and cranky airplane flown by uneasy crews.

But LeMay also faced an institutional problem: The AAF had fought hard and won its case for the B-29 bomber program in its battles with the Navy and the rest of the Army over the allocation of the available war resources. But the B-29 program had turned out to be much more difficult and costly than expected; its costs even exceeded those of the secret Manhattan Project for the development of the first atomic bombs. With such a large and contended investment riding on the AAF claims for the decisiveness of strategic bombing and the B-29, LeMay had to deliver what his institution had so publicly promised.

The AAF, true to its strategic bombardment theories of the time, sought by means of the B-29 program the heavy bomber it had always wanted: a long-range airplane specifically designed for high-altitude, daylight precision bombardment with high-explosive bombs dropped from self-defended formations. And that, of course, is precisely how it initially used the airplane over Japan. The bombers formed up over the Marianas and then flew in formation to Japan where they bombed from high altitude in daylight. The Japanese defenses against such attacks were much less effective than the German defenses over Europe, partly because of the state of Japanese defensive resources at that point in the war, and partly because of the high altitude from which the attacks were made. However, the results of the bombing were disappointing too, partly because of winds (on navigation and bombing accuracy), but mostly because the bombloads in the airplane were being sacrificed to the weight of the fuel required to fly in formation and at high altitudes, and to the weight of the bomber's defensive armament (automated gun turrets)—the very things designed to ensure its penetration of the Japanese defenses.

The AAF had finally succeeded in acquiring the airplane that could penetrate Japanese air defenses in daylight with acceptable losses only to find that it was not very effective at accomplishing its purpose: destroying Japan's capacity and will to fight. LeMay posed the problem to his small staff of operations analysts; their answers turned the B-29 bombing campaign over Japan inside out. They recommended area or carpet bombing of Japanese cities with incendiaries instead of precision bombing of the Japanese aircraft industry with high-explosive bombs.[5] They recommended flying the bombers independently at medium altitudes and stripping the planes of their guns instead of sacrificing bomb-carrying capacity to high-altitude and formation flying or to defensive armaments. They recommended flying at night to deal with the Japanese defenses.[6]

The flight crews considered the analysts' proposal that they simply "straggle" in over the target at night to be suicidal: The crews envisaged many of their airplanes colliding in the dark with hundreds of airplanes going to and from a single target. The analysts calmly demonstrated, with irrefutable mathematics, that the crews' chances of a collision were significantly less than their odds of landing in the "drink" because of the mechanical failures of all four of their airplanes' engines on a single flight. This was a statistic the crews could appreciate, since engine failures on the long over-water flights were one of their major concerns with the new B-29 and something they had to deal with every day.

LeMay adopted all the analysts' recommendations. Careful definition and analysis of the operational problem had overturned almost every design precept of the B-29 program and the AAF theory of strategic bombardment. The analysts' recommendations were counter to the intuition and doctrine of those they served, and it is unlikely that the AAF would have slowly come around to such a drastic approach to their operations. It is certainly to LeMay's credit that he had confidence in his analysts and the courage to fly in the face of AAF doctrine. But the stakes were high, and institutional doctrine had to be sacrificed to save institutional credibility.[7]

The B-29 bombing campaign then proceeded to become so highly effective in accomplishing its realigned purposes, that LeMay, upon being asked when the war would be over, simply counted up the remaining unburned cities and estimated the time for his airplanes to carpet them with incendiaries. Whatever the military or legal merits of that bombing campaign, in retrospect, it was important to the Air Force institutional aspirations nascent within the AAF. LeMay's operations analysts may have prevented a failure of such cost and expectations that it could have undone the Air Force's postwar bid for institutional independence.

## Systems Analysis

Operations analysis spawned several distinctive cousins.[8] One is known as systems analysis, and it came to full flower in the 1960s with the administration of the Department of Defense under Secretary Robert S. McNamara. If scientific methods and mathematics could be used to improve the effectiveness or efficiency of complex operations, why could not they also be extended to the problem of correctly choosing among complex alternatives? The differences between the two analytical forms is much larger, however, than a change in the question.

*Operations analysis* typically deals with existing operations about which much is known or knowable. Its recommendations are most often adjustments to existing operations intended to improve their effectiveness or efficiency; and the intended improvements can usually be measured and the analysis validated. "Real-world" data abound, and uncertainty, if present, often takes the form of well-understood stochastic processes.

*Systems analysis,* on the other hand, seeks to find and compare complex alternatives about which too little is known or knowable.[9] Assumptions or theories or models may have to substitute for facts or real-world data. If the choices depend upon weapons that have never been made, those weapons will have to be conceived on paper or captured in models. If the choices depend upon wars that have never been fought, then those wars are idealized and "fought" inside computers.

McNamara's newly arrived DoD civilian analysts saw the initial imposition of the systems analysis approach to military planning as a way to discipline the services' open-ended demands for resources.[10] No longer could the services present and argue their claims for money, people, or hardware simply, as they had, on the ground of their military experience. For a short time, the services were stymied, but they soon learned how to adapt. If systems analysis was to be the new language for military planning and debate, it could also be used as a language for advocacy. The music had not changed, only the words. Within a few years, the claims were just as strident, but the words were being written by hundreds, even thousands, of analysts in the services and their agencies, think tanks, and contractors. For the advocates, analysts had become, in effect, hired guns: Who had the best analysts to make their case? One heard the quip, "My analyst can lick your analyst!"

When the competing alternatives pose high stakes for the institutions involved, then there is an incentive—and much more maneuvering room in systems analysis than in operations analysis—to bias the assumptions, suppress unpalatable alternatives, or choose the models that give the desired answers. Such chicanery need not be deliberate or even conscious in analyses in which uncertainties, judgments, and alternatives abound. The application of the art form begged the answer. Objectivity in systems analysis is certainly desirable and possible, but it can too easily be lost in military planning when the future of a large institution is perceived to be on the line: "Military operations research has become almost completely inverted in both content and purpose in the space of forty years: What began as science unmasking the myths and choices in war has become, instead, mostly the art of cloaking predilections in the language of science and color of war."[11]

A "successful" systems analysis of the late 1960s illustrates the art form and the latitude it provides for the analyst and advocate. Some in the Air Force were looking for analytical arguments to support the major investments needed for its next bomber.[12] With the "missile age" in full flood, even the secretary of the Air Force was skeptical of the case for a new bomber as compared to additional ballistic missiles. The Navy was arguing that the strategic funds should be spent on its submarine-based Poseidon missile.

The analyst compared alternative incremental investments in sea- and land-based ballistic missiles and in bombers to see how much added survivable and deliverable destructive power could be purchased with each kind of weapon system. As expected, the sea-based ballistic missiles gave more "bang for the buck" because of their superior survivability—not a welcome answer for the mainstream of the institutional Air Force. The analyst then calculated how much the Soviets would have to spend to limit the damage inflicted on them by these same augmented forces, assuming, of course, that the Soviets attacked first and then had to face a retaliatory attack by the United States. If the Soviets were willing to accept high levels of damage (corresponding to what was then considered "assured destruction"), the U.S. forces augmented with the Navy's Poseidon would cost the Soviets more to defend against than those augmented with the new bomber or more land-based ballistic missiles—still not a welcome answer to the Air Force.

But if the Soviets attempted to limit their damage to much lower levels—to levels they might find tolerable if the stakes were high—then the bomber-augmented force stood out dramatically as costing the Soviets much more than either of the ballistic missile augmentations. The reason, of course, was that significant reductions in the damage suffered by the Soviets could only be achieved by their investing in defenses as well as offensive forces to deal with the U.S. retaliatory capabilities. With the bombers and missiles facing them, the Soviets had to buy two kinds of defense for each protected target; without the bombers, they had to buy only one type of defense.[13]

This analytical result led to the following advocacy argument for investment in the new bomber:

> While there may not be any advantage in the new bomber over ballistic missiles under the current conditions of mutual assured destruction, if the Soviets attempt to limit their damage to tolerably low levels by means of clandestine investments in defenses, the new bomber will enforce very much larger Soviet investments in defenses than would ballistic missiles; and those investments should be significantly more observable and make timely countermoves more certain.

Whatever the merits of the argument, analysis had found one though none was obvious.[14] The analyst had persisted until conditions that favored the bomber had been found. If the conditions were (or could be made) plausible, they had to be taken into account in debating the alternatives. Even if the conditions found were less likely than others, the large margin of advantage for the bomber helped its case. Presumably, the Navy was doing its own analyses of the alternatives, looking for conditions that favored its Poseidon missile among the alternatives.

## Requirements Analysis

Systems analysis provided a framework within which apples and oranges could be compared and their advocates could argue the case. But when the choice between them was made, the question changed again: How many oranges and of what size? While a systems analysis might have to consider general quantities and qualities when arriving at the choice among alternatives, the actual design and acquisition of the chosen alternative calls for a finer resolution of the kind, size, and number of oranges to be purchased. To set up a program for the acquisition of oranges requires real numbers to put into the budgets and purchase orders and contracts. And the need for such numbers leads to a form of analysis that is known as "requirements analysis."[15]

Requirements analyses typically posit conditions that allow one to answer program questions about the qualities and quantities of systems to be acquired. If the systems are weapons, the posited conditions are about possible wars, and much of requirements analyses may be devoted to the simulation or description of wars or battles. Given this war and outcome, here are the optimum characteristics for this kind of weapon, and here are the number of them that will be required.

An example of requirements analysis was setting the distances between silos for the Minuteman ballistic missile after it was chosen to succeed the Atlas and Titan I missiles. A tug of war over the silo spacing arose between those who were to operate the Minuteman, the Strategic Air Command (SAC), and those who were developing the new missile, the Air Force Systems Command (AFSC).[16] SAC had spaced the earlier missile silos at least eighteen miles apart to ensure that a single nuclear weapon could not destroy two missiles. But the Minuteman concept centered on the proliferation of thousands[17] of unmanned missile silos as opposed to the dozens for the Atlas and Titan missiles; AFSC was concerned about the cost implications of the silo spacings: the larger the spacing, the greater the travel time for the missile maintenance crews. Both sides brought their analysts into the debate as it escalated to the secretary of the Air Force, with SAC trying to maintain the existing eighteen-mile spacing and AFSC seeking something less.

Though the missile spacing was based on vulnerability considerations, SAC had set its criteria on the assumption of a salvo (or simultaneous) launch of the missiles. Since the missiles were most vulnerable as they emerged from their hardened silos during launch, the salvo launch exposed all the missiles at the same time. A lateral spacing of eighteen miles was sufficient to prevent a single large nuclear weapon from destroying two missiles if it were deliberately aimed at a point between the two missile silos.

But the AFSC analysts considered the possibilities for vertical as well as lateral spacing of the missiles by "ripple" rather than salvo launching. They argued that the missiles could be fired in a sequence over time that would distribute them in three-dimensional space when they were exposed, as compared to a two-dimensional area when they were "buttoned up" inside their hardened silos. This argument allowed AFSC to propose that the silo spacing be made as small as five miles, by balancing the vulnerabilities of the missile when in its hardened silo and when exposed during launch. The difference in missile deployment areas was more than tenfold.

The issue between SAC and AFSC was really one of focus. SAC was focused on the delivery of its nuclear weapons on their targets and on time, as its (lion's) share of the Single Integrated Operational Plan (SIOP). For that reason, SAC wanted weapons it could launch without time restrictions; it was more concerned with time restrictions on the other end of the missile's trajectory—when the missile landed on its target. On the other hand, AFSC was focused on the development of a new missile whose deployment patterns could significantly affect its cost, hence its proliferation, and ultimately the Minuteman concept itself. Ripple firing of the missiles seemed to be a small price to pay for more than a tenfold reduction in the required deployment area.

The analysts for AFSC won their case before the secretary of the Air Force. Once having accepted the ripple launch concept, SAC went on to accept silo spacings even less than five miles, depending upon silo hardness among other things. Few requirements analyses are so contended, but this one posed what were perceived as high stakes for the two Air Force institutions; it was resolved at high levels with the analysts as the advocates.

That particular requirements analysis focused on the quantitative design aspects of a proposed weapon system. Other requirements analyses focus on the quantities of the weapon system needed to perform its mission: How many interceptor aircraft would be required to defend the United States from a cruise missile attack? How many artillery shells need to be stockpiled for a war in Europe? Since these kinds of analyses typically rest upon a perception of crisis or war, they often involve complex simulations of wars, campaigns, battles, and other military operations, such as resupply and reinforcement.

All three kinds of analysis described here—operations, systems, and requirements—have become an integral, although often undifferentiated, part of defense analysis as practiced in and for the military institutions. Some elements within the institutions may practice or specialize in one kind or serve other elements that use or consume only one kind of analysis. But all three kinds find their way into the Pentagon, the services' headquarters, and into the defense planning process. And as they do, one can discern some significant differences among the services in their attitudes toward analysis.

# 10

# SERVICE STYLES TOWARD ANALYSIS

All the military services are major producers and consumers of analysis. What is of interest here is how the three services differ in their regard for, approach to, and use of analysis for their own decision making as well as those analyses that may be mandated or imposed upon them.[1] The differences are particularly discernible in services' approaches to the three kinds of analysis described in the previous chapter: operations, systems, and requirements.

## The Air Force

The Air Force, consistent with its reverence for technology, has always been the most comfortable of the three services with analysis. The Air Force has relied upon analysts from its inception to support operational, developmental, and acquisition decision making at high levels. The airplane, the focal instrument of the theory of air power and independent air forces, was itself conceived and born by means of requirements analyses. The father of the Air Force, Hap Arnold, took bold steps to ensure that the new institution could retain in peacetime some of the benefits afforded by its wartime scientists and operations analysts.

What sets the Air Force most apart from its sister services is how it regards analysis. Air Force officers, as members of an institution whose faith rests on theory and technology, are accustomed to dealing with analysis on every aspect of flight and the application of air power; supporting decisions with analysis is quite natural. Most senior Air Force officers are consumers of, even participants in, the analyses that support internal decision making. Thus, analysis in the Air Force is not restricted to the formalized planning, programming, and budgeting process; it is often regarded as the most effective medium for debate within the Air Force itself.

The Air Force is more likely to use analysis to illuminate or clarify its decision problems and options rather than to predict conflict outcomes or quantitative force requirements. Consequently, Air Force analyses tend to be relatively sophisticated and elegant in their design, execution, and presentation. Air Force analysts prize the simple equation, the single graph, or the clever model that captures and illuminates the essence of a problem. Analytic models are often fashioned ad hoc, with a life no longer than the problem at hand. Large-scale simulations and models are less prevalent in the Air Force than in the Army, but more than in the Navy. More than either of its sister services, the Air Force looks to simple (or at least clear) parametric analyses that illustrate the options or their sensitivity to the principal uncertainties.

None of the other services embraced systems analysis with the ease of the Air Force. The Air Force was willing to practice McNamara's brand of systems analysis on itself: If the institutional Air Force has to make difficult choices between dissimilar things, the internal debate can be conducted (if not always decided) with systems analytic arguments.

## The Army

The Army's approach to analysis is, in many respects, opposite to that of the Air Force. This may be partly due to the unique circumstances under which the Army must plan and fight. Unlike its sister services, the peacetime Army retains little control over the time and place where it must engage the enemy; the resources it will need (mainly people) are not forces in being, but must be conscripted from the citizenry. But its approach may also derive from the Army's vision of itself as the nation's loyal and obedient servant. If the national leadership wants planning numbers from the services, the Army will dutifully calculate them.[2]

Army analyses are oriented toward feeding numbers to the planning, programming, and budgeting process. Large-scale simulation models with long, evolutionary lives are routine. Detail and scope are prized, even at the expense of clarity or understanding. The Army appears to have an implicit faith in analysis and analysts. The stature of an analysis seems to rest upon the number of factors taken into account, the amount of detail included, and the number and credentials of the analysts who did the work. Less clear is whether that faith rests with the validity of such requirements analyses or with their effectiveness in feeding credible (i.e., acceptable) numbers into the bureaucratic programming process. In other words, does the Army believe the results or believe in the technique as a device to keep the Department of Defense satisfied?

Much Army analysis appears to be aimed at getting a single answer (often a number) rather than illuminating the alternatives in the face of recognized uncertainties. Hence, deterministic rather than stochastic methods predominate. Whereas the Air Force is more likely to use requirements analyses to define the *characteristics* of the forces it needs (e.g., the optimum payload for a new bomber), the Army is more likely to use them to define the *amount* of forces it needs (e.g., the number of 155 mm shells required).

The sophistication of Army analysis is likely to be found in computer programming and data handling or management, as opposed to problem structuring or analytic design. Army analysts are more likely to associate themselves with models (or particular analytic techniques) than with the problems to which their models are applied. In contrast, Air Force analysts tend to associate themselves with problems, which they may address with a variety of models or analytic techniques. At the risk of overstating the point, the Army uses professional analysts to get the numbers they need, whereas in the Air Force anyone confronted with the need to understand a problem or advocate a solution is likely to become an analyst.

## The Navy

The Navy's attitude toward analysis is quite different again. The Navy has been at the forefront of operations analysis—to improve the tactical or operational use of its existing platforms or forces. Some of the pioneering work in operations research was applied to naval operations, and the Navy has maintained first-rate cadres of operations analysts throughout its fleets. But it has little tolerance of analysis for planning or evaluating the Navy, by either requirements or systems analyses. Analysis of naval force requirements or effectiveness is a direct threat to the Navy's traditional institutional prerogatives. The Navy does not need analysis to define its requirements; it has always known what its requirements were.

And it knows that naval forces are effective when the Navy is left alone to use them as it sees fit. The Navy does not need systems analysis to decide whether to buy aircraft carriers or mine-sweepers—it will demand both, but buy the carriers.

The Air Force and Army may differ in their approaches to, and uses of, analysis, but both show great respect for its utility in defining requirements—qualitative or quantitative, respectively. The Navy, on the other hand, has never relied on analysis for requirements—qualitative or quantitative. Navy requirements come from its experience and traditions, and from the quality thinking of its people, well steeped in both.

When the Navy had to take up systems analysis in order to survive in the planning, programming, and budgeting process, it did so with a clear eye. If analysis was the coin of the McNamara realm, then the Navy would mint as much of it as might be necessary. Navy decisions about the needed platforms or forces, still based on its experience and traditions, could, after all, be wrapped in the language of systems analysis. It would be unfair to say that the Navy was deliberately cynical in its regard for, or conduct of, analyses because its actions were rooted in a much more fundamental perception and faith: Navy institutional judgments (like those of the true church) were infallible. If an analysis gave results that were contrary to those judgments, then, very simply, the analysis must be wrong, either in the way it was formulated or in the way it was executed.

In sum, if descriptive words had to be affixed to each of the three services to describe their approaches to analysis, they might be *sophisticated* and *elegant* for the Air Force, *ingenuous* and *credulous* for the Army, and *suspicious* and *pragmatic* for the Navy.

## An Analytical Parable

The distinctions among the service styles toward analysis are succinctly captured in a satirical "parable" I have used both to illustrate and to entertain.[3] The story goes something like this:

In 1992, the four-year election cycle coincided for the first time since 1964 with the seven-year cycle for shortages of toilet paper in Washington. The coincidence of the two cycles brought a crisis of memorable proportions. Even Congress took note: When a defense procurement bill came before the House, it attached a rider mandating that each of the services make an analysis of its wartime toilet paper needs to be sure that they were adequately stocked.

The Air Force immediately saw the advantages of being responsive to Congress with a high-quality analysis of its needs. Besides, it thought it could prove that its requirments for toilet paper were inversely proportional to the top speed of its proposed advanced tactical fighter, so it put its very best people on the problem. Its senior analyst, a three star, led a team of the Air Force's best and brightest into the statistical morass of uncertainty. The Air Force team, with elegant use of Poisson and Gaussian distributions, rigorously proved that wartime toilet paper requirements could be estimated with a precision no greater than plus or minus 10 percent with a confidence of 80 percent. Accordingly, it provided Congress with both the mean and standard deviation of its needs—normally distributed, of course. The Air Force understood the significance of its analysis, even if Congress did not.

The Army took the mandated analysis seriously. After all, 1992 was the "Year of Army Hygiene" (you remember the slogan: "Be as clean as you can be—in the Army!"). Taking toilet paper requirements seriously would demonstrate the commitment of the Army leadership to its programs. Since wartime toilet paper requirements were mainly a theater problem, the analysis was assigned to the Army's analytical agency for theater warfare. It had just the right theater-level model, called FORCEM, which it had been developing for more than a dozen years.[4] The FORCEM task force even developed a brand new "TP Module" for the model that took into account the loss of toilet paper as units were overrun and increased usage of paper by the headquarters units during enemy breakthroughs. With this, the Army analysts calculated its wartime toilet paper requirements to ten significant digits—down to the very last roll. Some Army analysts argued for an accounting by sheets since some paper was in the form of field packets, not rolls. The FORCEM modelers were pleased; the Army was pleased; and Congress was very pleased with the Army's precise and timely response to what had become a burning question.

The Navy frothed with indignation at the mandated analysis. One crusty admiral (have you noticed that admirals are always crusty?) is reported to have said that Congress could go to Hell, the Navy knew its requirements for toilet paper, had always known its requirements for toilet paper since it was first introduced into the fleet (in 1847, on September 7, at three bells into the dog watch, on the quarterdeck of the frigate *Assateague*); and the Navy did not need any analytical tomfoolery to tell it how much it needed.

When an aide respectfully noted that the analysis was mandated in the same bill that authorized the keel-laying for the next carrier, the admiral relented, but only a little. He instructed his staff to get the GS-14 Ph.D. they kept locked up in the basement for just such contingencies and to assign him the job of dressing up the current Navy estimates for toilet paper in some suitable mathematical garb. But under no circumstance was this analysis to contradict the current numbers. And that is what Congress got, begrudgingly, from the Navy. Which pleased no one.

## Implications

The point of that satirical story, of course, is that each of the services has its own unique style toward analysis. The styles of the services derive in large measure from who they are and how they see themselves.

The questions that the three services seem to be pursuing through analyses are quite different:

- Air Force: How can we better understand the problem—its dimensions and range of solutions?
- Army: What do we need to plan more precisely—to get better requirements numbers?
- Navy: How can we better use what we have?

All three questions are meritorious, but they require quite different styles of analysis, analytic tools, and perhaps even analysts.

Though their styles may fit (or reflect) their personalities, each of the services could learn something from the others' approaches to analysis:

- The Air Force's service-wide appreciation and use of analysis as an illuminative aid for its own decision making is to be admired even if its motives are not always completely altruistic.
- The Army's lavish support for analysis and analysts has built up a potential for quantitative analysis that is unrivaled by the other services, even though its application of analysis falls far short of its potential for illuminating and understanding Army problems.

- The Navy's skepticism about requirements analysis may be overdone; but it is not completely unwarranted. The Navy knows, correctly I think, that results or outcomes in war are largely incalculable. But this recognition may have caused it to throw the baby out with the bath water—to reject the benefits of analysis in illuminating important relationships between things and events in war. Walking the balance between the analysis of war outcomes and the analysis of relationships in war is tricky. The Navy has given up on both; but the Army may not yet be differentiating between the two.

Ultimately the Navy may be hurting itself as an institution by its deep internal distrust of analysis for decisions bearing upon naval force requirements and effectiveness. The Navy is correct in its discrimination between operations analysis and systems analysis; they are quite different in their purposes and methods—probably even in their analysts. One is rooted in the data of real-world operations, the other in speculative concepts and behavioral models that can rarely be validated. But if they are different in their roots, why can they not also be used differently? The value of systems analysis, even when applied to naval force requirements or effectiveness, is not in answers or numbers, but in the illumination of hidden relationships, in the hints to possible causes and effects, in suggesting where deeper examination of a problem, by whatever method, may be fruitful. The Navy need not use analysis to *determine* its force requirements or effectiveness; but it could benefit from the use of analysis to *understand* what may end up driving its force requirements and effectiveness, even within the vast uncertainties of war.

The Navy, its force requirements and effectiveness, will be the subjects of analyses, if only from the outside, if only by its critics, whether the Navy trusts such analyses or not. The Navy can, as it has, declare them to be invalid on principle. Or, as the most capable proponent and user of such analyses, it can demonstrate their limitations for its own enlightened decision making. The past and the tradition are clear enough, but the future is not.

The programming and budgeting system[5] may create a demand for point-estimate planning numbers; but that should not prevent or impede the Army from extending its analyses, perhaps with other tools, to illuminating and understanding problems rather than just calculating the answers. The real planning environment for the Army is more than the bureaucratic planning system; analysis can help the Army to understand and cope better with that uncertain environment—one that has no school solution in the back of the book of truth.

The Army's admirable commitment to the development and use of professional analysts may be fostering an association of its analysts with tools and models rather than with problems. There is a dilemma here: The specialization of Army analysts provides them with the most sophisticated tools and models. But those models have not proven themselves for anything beyond calculating the answers needed to feed the programming and budgeting system. To illuminate, to understand its problems, the Army also needs general analysts who associate themselves with problems more than tools. And if such analysts emerge within the Army, will they discover that those very sophisticated models created by the specialists are inappropriate or even unnecessary?

In short, the Army needs to confront the question of why it does analysis. Is it principally to feed numbers to the bureaucratic planning processes? Or is it, first and foremost, the means by which the Army tries to understand a murky and dangerous future in which the only certainty is that the Army will be called upon again to serve the nation it so clearly loves?

The Air Force has used analysis with more discrimination, skill, and effect than either of its sister services. However, not all is well in its analytical temples: Its analytical prowess is used *selectively* on issues of institutional interest, such as the qualitative characteristics of its next airplane. But many pertinent questions that might be amenable to its analytical capabilities are likely to receive a blind eye if the answers might threaten the Air Force or air power. In short, the Air Force has not been as admirable in its application of analysis as it has in its competency.

## What Is It All About?

At a deeper level, one needs to stand back and ask, "What is this enormous military analysis business really all about?" Much of it, of course, is the ordinary bookkeeping calculations military quartermasters and storeskeepers have done for centuries. Whether for planning or for accountablity records, these are the ledger and journal entries required for orderly logistical support of armies and navies (and for air forces or rocket forces). They are the calculations that tell the military how many "beans and bullets" they should buy or keep on hand and how to move them about most efficiently to meet their needs. Such calculations have become more sophisticated today with the size and complexity of the systems that have to be supported; the analytical techniques for projecting future demands have kept pace with their own elaboration and refinement. These are the normal calculations of orderly and prudent minds.

Another major segment of the military analysis business today is devoted to operational issues—the kinds of analysis that took hold in World War II—intended to make ongoing military operations more efficient and effective. These are the analyses that define the most effective ways to use what the military services have (or expect to have) on hand: the most efficient search patterns for finding submarines, the best matching of the available bombers and tankers, and the optimum schedule for servicing tracked vehicles. They are the analyses of tinkers and designers who would improve upon the mousetraps; they change how things get done.

These are the kinds of calculations and analysis that occupy most of the military analysts today. They make an important, continuing contribution to the functioning of the military services, in peace and in war. Like the greasing of axles and the aiming of guns, they are things that need to be done, and done well, in order to maintain and employ effective military forces. And, with other such routine and necessary activities, they are seldom visible or controversial.

But another segment of today's military analysis is not at all like those kinds just described, except that it involves analysts and analytical methods. This other segment is, by contrast, highly visible and almost always controversial. It is a peacetime rather than a wartime enterprise. It is the domain of the defense analysts; their analyses purport to be about war—how wars will be fought (or deterred), the forces required to fight (or deter) them, and the effects of weapon systems upon their conduct or outcomes. This is the new art of analysis that has emerged from seed to full flower since World War II; it was conceived by civilian scientists and academics in the think tanks during the 1950s, carried into the Pentagon by the "whiz kids" in the 1960s, and utimately adopted (or adulterated) by the military services in the 1970s. Though some of these analyses may, in academic hands, still be attempts to understand war, the military services use them for the most part not to understand war but to argue for their institutional interests—usually for the toys of war. These analyses have become a part of the language of advocacy for service interests; they have the greatest leverage and, therefore, are the ones most discussed and debated.

As a defense analyst involved in this last category of analyses, I had long suspected that our analyses were not so much about war as they were about the toys of war. But the suspicion was brought to a sharp focus for me by the events of 1982. I had spent that year in London, studying and lecturing on the possibilities for nonnuclear strategic warfare. By coincidence, it was also the year of the Falklands War. In England, it was apparent, very early, that a real war was coming. Fully six weeks before the event, it was clear where, and with what, the war would be fought. New weapon types that had never seen combat were about to be used: Nuclear submarines would be used in war for the first time, as would vertical-takeoff-and-landing fighters or "jump jets" as the British call them.

With a sense of slow motion that one often has when involved in the unprecedented, I found myself watching in fascination as the Falklands War began to unfold before my eyes, offering an opportunity I had never before had and that I could not expect to have again in my lifetime as a defense analyst: a war that could be analyzed *before* it happened! Here was a defense analyst's opportunity of the century—a chance to analyze a war and then to find out how good the analysis was through the real test of battle. Nothing was missing. There was time to do the analysis, and all the necessary information about the forces on both sides was available, weeks before they were to clash in combat.

But when I called my colleagues in America to enlist them in seizing this unique opportunity, I was met with apathy. They were too busy doing other things. They had a report to write, or they had other work piled up on their desks. Despite my enthusiastic descriptions of this once-in-a-lifetime chance to analyze a real war, I got nowhere. I suggested they "game" the war, something that would not take much time. Still, no takers. Then I thought my failure to gain their interest might be due to my not having offered them a motivation in the form of a client who could use their analysis. So I repeated my pleas with the assurance that I would deliver any useful results to the British Ministry of Defence—at a sufficiently high level to have an impact. Nothing.

That experience caused me considerable soul-searching about my chosen profession, about my being a defense analyst. Were we only willing to analyze hypothetical wars because our results could never be checked? Were we too cowardly to have our papers graded? No report cards, please; they might show that our analyses are worthless. It took me a long time to sort out what I thought was going on: Most of our analyses about war were not really about war; they were about war toys. For the most part, our clients were interested in toys, not war. But the toys of war have to be predicated on arguments about war. We were experts on the analysis of war, so our clients looked to us in the hopes that our analyses might yield good arguments, couched in the terms of war, for their favored toys. If not, our analyses could always be put aside, dismissed, or forgotten.

Thus, I came to understand that most analyses of war are not undertaken to predict or to understand how wars will go, but to predict how favored toys will do in war. And those predictions are used to argue for (or against) acquiring the toys. As I looked back upon my own experiences as a defense analyst, I realized that most of the analyses I had seen were motivated by advocacy arguments for toys. Childhood's end comes when we see, for the first time, toys for what they are: just toys.

# 11

## IMAGES OF CONFLICT

In the late 1970s, I became acutely interested in the images people have of hypothetical conflicts. Descriptions by military analysts and planners of future battles or wars tend to be in mechanistic terms—units, their dispositions, movements, firepower, survival, and so on—as if conflicts were the manipulation of things. Though such clinical detachment presumably serves to make the analyst or planner objective, it can be a treacherous or deceptive mode of description, even for military analysis and planning.

By images of conflict, I mean, literally, the picture (movie or still) that jumps into one's mind when talking about a future conflict, or some critical moment in that conflict. Such images may be fuzzy or sharp; they may be focused on critical or representative details; or they may show war from on high, in the sweep of forces as arrows on a map. But they have the common characteristic of capturing for the observer the essence of a conflict in a picture, a picture that is rich in its implication and can be mined for details and emotions. Those images, much more than analysis, may be the basis for judgments about the prospects and conduct of future conflicts. Though those images may be usefully analyzed, their source seems not to be found in analysis. I found my own inquiry into the images of conflict to be doubly revealing—about American military styles in analysis and, once again, about the American military service personalities.

### When Images Lurk Unnoticed

In the summer of 1978, the Air Force asked for an independent evaluation of the utility of a new missile to be carried on tactical aircraft for attacks against tanks and vehicles at night. The Air Force believed that the new missile was ready for production; but they were encountering resistance in Congress, which was skeptical of the missile's utility and was withholding the necessary funds. The Air Force believed that an independent evaluation of the missile's utility by outsiders would both vindicate their assessment and help convince Congress to approve the production funding.

The Air Force posed this specific question: Will the new missile represent a significant military capability in a future conflict in Central Europe? Since Congress was slated to act on the funding request in the fall of 1978, the evaluation was needed quickly. At the time, I was leading a group of several dozen analysts specializing in tactical warfare and theater conflicts. After assuring ourselves that the Air Force was willing to "let the chips fall where they may," we accepted the challenge and were given full access to all the necessary data and personnel of the Air Force and the missile contractor. Because time was so short, we treated it as a crash project and put the entire group of analysts to work on it.

The analysts quickly organized themselves into teams to pursue what they saw as the pertinent information for their evaluation. They visited the contractors to review the technical performance of the missile and plans for its improvement. They interviewed the pilots who had flown the tests of the missile on American and European test ranges. They watched video tapes of every flight test. They analyzed the weather in Europe and compared it to the weather conditions experienced on the European test range. They plotted the trajectories of the missiles and the exposure of the launching aircraft to opposing defenses. They examined the projected deployments of Soviet armored columns and compared them with the target arrays that had been set up on the test range. And they made statistical analyses of the missile reliability, accuracy, survivability, and suitability in the European weather and battle environments. This study was done quickly and competently by people who knew the subjects and who were acknowledged experts in their fields.

Then it came time to pull our findings together and make our evaluation for the Air Force. In a long day of briefings, the analysts shared with each other the fruits of all their hard work. When the briefings were finally over, they were astonished and justifiably pleased with how much technical and analytic ground they had covered in the space of a few weeks. But I spoiled the moment of pleasure by observing that I could not find anywhere in their considerable work the answer to the question posed by the Air Force. When I reminded the analysts of the Air Force's question about the missile's utility for a future European conflict, it became apparent that the members of the study group disagreed. Some thought that the new missile would be effective; others thought not; still others argued in between. The arguments quickly escalated in volume and emotion, reaching such an obvious impasse that some analysts quietly suggested that we simply turn over our technical and analytical results to the Air Force to let them judge for themselves as to the utility of the missile. I rejected that suggestion and insisted that we hammer out a consensus, even if that required the remaining few weeks available to us.

We finally did arrive at a consensus after much debate. The answer, as might be expected, was a highly qualified one. The missile could be an important contribution to a future European conflict under ideal circumstances, but (1) those favorable circumstances could not be unilaterally ensured by the Air Force, (2) the Air Force had, in a future European conflict, some larger problems that deserved more attention than the missile itself, and (3) the new missile would create some new problems as well as solve some old ones. That answer, obviously, was not entirely pleasing to the Air Force.

I was shaken by the experience of the study. What had gone wrong? Why were the analysts so confident of the work to be done and yet so divided when it came time to answer the question? What could I have done as the leader of the group to have prevented or anticipated the difficulties we encountered after the analyses had been completed? I asked myself if I might have posed the question in a different way and obtained different results. By chance, I then speculated about the Air Force's question taking a slightly different form: Would the new missile have represented a significant military capability in the World War II conflict in Central Europe? I suddenly realized that to answer this question the analysts would not have needed to do all their technical and analytical work. They could have made their judgments on the spot. They did not need to analyze World War II, they knew what it was like as a matter of history, and they knew enough about the new missile to judge its impact on that conflict in the light of history.

The difference between the two questions seemed to be in the quality and consistency of the images of conflict they evoked. The images of World War II were vivid, concrete, and widely shared. And it was not just that World War II was historical fact. A hypothetical war or battle can be so vividly portrayed in a movie that its essence (however imaginary) is captured and conveyed to a wide audience.[1] The images of a future war in Central Europe were diverse, subjective, and implicit in the analytic terms—force sizes, deployments, and so on—we used to describe them. I became convinced that the difficulty of the group in arriving at a consensus in its evaluation was not its knowledge of the missile but its differing images of a future conflict.

Though all the analysts had a fairly sharp and shared image of World War II, they did not share the same image of a future war in Central Europe. Nor were the images of future conflict as sharp or complete as those for recent, historical conflicts. Some analysts saw a future conflict as a repeat of World War II. The equipment and its capabilities had changed, but not the tactics or the kinds of battles that would be fought. They now saw, instead of propeller-driven airplanes strafing and bombing columns of trucks and tanks on the ground, jet airplanes flying over the same columns, firing missiles and dispensing cannisters of bomblets. Others had the image—perhaps from the Six-Day War—of most of the airplanes being destroyed on the ground before they, or the missiles they carried, could be effectively brought to bear. Still others saw the sky so filled with hostile projectiles or electronic noise that aircraft could not operate effectively regardless of the kind of missiles they might carry.

The important lesson was not the enormous differences of these images, but their ability to coexist without collision when future conflicts are described only in analytic terms—in the numbers of units, their deployments, speeds, and so on. Analysis may be a useful way to examine an image of conflict; but analytic terms are not much help in describing or conveying an image of conflict. And it is the image of conflict that overrides in evaluating the worth of a new machine. Thus, the focus of analysis should be on the image of conflict even more than on the machine.

My remedy for this problem—if the evaluation could have been repeated—would have been to start out with the analysts sharing their diverse images of a future conflict in Central Europe. My purpose would not have been a consensus on a single image—for who knows in advance of the event whose image is correct?—but on the exposure, comparison, and sensitivity to alternative images. I would have looked for ways to make those images as vivid as possible, perhaps through scenarios or storytelling. With those images fully developed and argued out beforehand, the analysts might have been more concerned about using their analytic efforts to explore and resolve differences in their images of the conflict rather than charging off into technical analyses in their separate areas of expertise. Some might have warmed to the images of others, and some might have cooled toward images they had too long held without critical examination.

## In Search of Images

After that experience, I actively searched for images of conflict in the minds of American military warriors and analysts, and went so far as to contemplate how such images might be more effectively generated and conveyed. On a tour of military installations in Central Europe the following year, I made it a point to ask many of the warriors I met about their images of conflict. Since they were on the front lines, if war came to them, what was the most vivid image that captured their expectations or concerns?

At an American fighter base in West Germany, I asked several pilots of shiny new F-15 Eagles about their images of conflict, if it came. The question seemed to cause a glazing of the eyes, shuffling of the feet, and mumbling. It may have been signs of embarrassment, but I am not sure whether its source was my idiotic question or their incomprehension of what I was talking about. The answer, if there was one, was quickly terminated by a change of subject: Would you like to sit in the cockpit of one our F-15s? Or do you realize how difficult it is to fly one of these marvelous airplanes to its full capacity under the restrictions imposed by civilian air traffic rules here in Europe? Clearly, these warriors were proud of their machines and preoccupied with flying them to the limits of their operating envelope, none of which should have been surprising.

At another air base, I talked with fighter pilots who flew F-4 Phantoms fitted out with sophisticated reconnaissance equipment. Though their airplanes were no longer at the cutting edge of technology, the electronic equipment they carried certainly was. I thought my questions might fare somewhat better there. Even though they were fighter pilots, their mission was to see and map the enemy, not to engage the enemy in the air. Alas, the elicited image of conflict was of these airplanes streaking along the front, sending millions of bits of electronic data to antennas on the ground. If these airplanes were not the fastest or the highest flying or the biggest, at least they spat out more electronic bits than anything else that flew.

I finally started to get somewhere when I visited an air base for what is, without any doubt, the ugliest airplane the Air Force has ever owned—the A-10 Thunderbolt II, more commonly known as the "Warthog." No prettier than its namesake, the A-10 is an aerial tank. It is heavily armored and carries a big, rapid-fire anti-tank gun. The wings, tail pieces, and engines appear to have been stuck on as appendage slabs where they would not interfere with one another or the airplane's mission. Even the nose wheel is moved to one side so as not to interfere with business—its big gun. It reportedly flies as it looks—like a tank.

Up close, the tanklike similarities of the A-10 persist: It is painted like a tank. No sky blue or gray, even on the bottom; this one is solid olive drab all over. Not even slick paint, it is gritty to the touch as if it had been sprayed with a mixture of sand and paint, just like a tank. No Air Force white star and bars on a blue field for its insignia; here it is a black star and bars, just what a tank should wear if the Air Force owned one. Everything about this airplane says that it does not really belong to the Air Force or is an airplane that the Air Force doesn't like—it is an Army tank with wings.

The A-10 pilot I talked with was the first flier to give me an image of conflict as he expected to see it: It was going to be tough to find the enemy tanks; they would be staying close to the tree lines in order to be in the shadows. To make things worse, the intelligence on where the enemy tanks might be at the moment was fuzzy because the battle was so confused. He would have to stay very low and fast not to be seen and hit by all the stuff that might be thrown up in the air. If he did spot the tanks in the shadows, they had better be right in front of him and easily identifiable as those of the enemy, because if he was forced to make a second pass, the enemy gunners would be ready to nail him. If all that came together, then he was convinced that the big gun he carried would start tearing things up—he expected to see pieces flying off those tanks. But if his plane got hit—which seemed quite likely—it was going to be tough to survive. He had to stay low and fast to avoid the enemy gunners; but the A-10 did not fly well or fast on one engine.

The A-10 pilot's image was one of dangerous, fast-breaking events in a confused environment in which he might not even get a chance to see or strike the enemy and, even if he got that chance, he could be mistaken in identifying the enemy or find himself wrestling with a crippled airplane. Though the image was of limited perspective, it certainly was vivid, and it captured his concerns and hopes if he had to fight. Perhaps it was not coincidental that he, unlike the fighter pilots I had talked with, took more obvious pride in the mission of the A-10, busting tanks, than in the airplane itself or in flying it.

Later on, at an Army headquarters in Frankfurt, a weary colonel responsible for intelligence offered up some vivid images of a future conflict in Central Europe. At the end of a long day of briefings and discussions with his visitors, I asked him my standard question on images of conflict: "If you were making a movie of the conflict confronting you here, what would be the most dramatic scene?"

He did not hesitate for even a moment: "One scene? I'll give you four from my movie."

He then proceeded to lay out four scenes, just as easily as if he were describing a movie he had seen the night before. The first scene took place in a NATO command center as the political crisis in Europe deepened. Fragmented intelligence information was beginning to suggest unusual military activities in the Warsaw Pact, but there was no clear or unambiguous pattern. Should the NATO forces be alerted and deployed forward to their defensive positions? Some were arguing for early deployments, whereas others argued that the evidence was too thin and the deployments would only make tensions worse, perhaps even precipitate the attack they hoped to deter. As the arguments continued, the NATO chiefs tried to balance the risks and come to a decision.

The second scene followed the first. The evidence of Warsaw Pact preparations to attack had become compelling, and NATO made the decision to deploy its forces. Those forces were now assembling and moving out on the roads eastward to take up their forward defensive positions. As the trucks and tanks move down the roads in the middle of the night, the soldiers realize just how vulnerable they are at this moment to a preemptive air attack. If they can just get to their defensive positions and disperse and dig in, they will gain relative safety and be better prepared to fight on their own terms. But now, and for the next several hours, they are going to be terribly exposed. Many of those on the road cast their eyes upward at the clear night sky and silently pray for the grace of a few more hours.

The third scene followed the successful forward deployment of the NATO forces, without their having been attacked on the roads.

Now an American GI sits alone in his forward observation point as the first light reveals the morning mists heavy in the defile below. He is cold from sitting and frightened by what he has heard. He was given his orders at midnight from his sergeant who told him that this time it really looked like the Cossacks were coming. And for the last hour he has heard the rumbling of vehicles to the east. Then, he can scarcely believe he is awake when the first Soviet tank appears less than a hundred meters away in the defile, followed by another, and another. This is no drill: If they see him, they will surely try to kill him; and they clearly have the capability to do just that. Should he hide? Should he melt into the woods behind him? Or should he pick up the laser designator at his feet?

The final scene was back at the NATO command post. The outlines of the war have finally taken shape on the huge battle maps covering the wall. The room hums with activity as the staff receives incoming reports, confers on phones, and updates summary boards and maps. Evidence of a Soviet breakthrough in the North is now the focus of attention. The commander turns to the staff and asks about the status of reserves that can be brought northward to block. One of the senior officers stiffens and draws the attention of all in the room as he informs the commander that all the reserves have now been committed; the last reserve brigade went into battle four hours ago.

I was very much taken aback by the colonel's four scenes. Up to that time, I had been struggling to the point of despair in my efforts to extract images of conflict from the warriors I was meeting in Europe. Then, in the space of a few minutes, I was given four, any one of which would have qualified perfectly as the kind of image I sought. Each of the colonel's scenes was vivid, human drama and presented a clear concern about unfolding events. I do not know whether or not those four images of conflict were valid, or whether or not they captured the most important concerns of the day; but my ability to recall them almost ten years later says something about their ability to hold and to convey information about the nature of a conflict.

Such images of conflict, I would argue, can tell us much more about a future war than most analytic descriptions of force counts, deployments, or movements. The analytics are useful for evaluating an image of conflict but not for describing it. If the image of conflict is truly shared, then analytical terms can help us to scrutinize, dissect, and adjust the concepts contained in that image. But I suspect that the images of future conflicts are typically not fully or widely shared. If we have thought about such conflicts, then we are likely to have formed some strong images about their essence—about what it will be like to be there, what it will really be all about. Those images (unlike the colonel's four scenes) may not surface explicitly and they may not collide with any of the analytic descriptions (as the colonel's appear not to); yet they may dominate what we think is important and what needs to be done. Little wonder, then, that analyses about conflict (outcomes or effects) are seldom convincing to anyone other than those who are already convinced. If someone's image of a future conflict leads to an implicit focus on concerns not addressed by the analysis, the analysis is, after all, irrelevant to those concerns, even if it does not explicitly contradict them anywhere.

It is tantalizing to speculate on the relative abilities of the American military services to communicate about war in terms of images of conflict. One could theorize that there might be an inverse correlation between an affection for toys or analysis and vivid images of conflict: The greater the attraction to—and identification with—machines, the more remote and abstract war may become. As analysis becomes more and more the surrogate for war, images of conflict may become the bends in graphs and the balance of numbers in tables. My evidence to support such a theory is completely inadequate, but I am no longer so perplexed by the spectrum of responses I got from warriors in Europe when I asked them for their images of conflict.

Though the battles for military toys and budgets are often waged with numbers and graphs from analyses of conflicts, the analytics may not shed much light on the real collisions of interests: On one side are the interests of institutions (or factions within them) for their well-being (in terms of independence, self-esteem, contribution, even survival); and on the other side are the interests of the warriors (cold and hot) who anticipate the war they may really have to fight. Individuals may find themselves on both sides of those interests as they shift between assignments—as between the Pentagon and a forward deployed combat unit; they may even find ways to reconcile them internally. But the analyses of war are more likely to serve the interests of the institution than they are those of the warriors. Perhaps both interests could be better perceived and addressed if the institutions could be induced to drop their masks of war and the warriors could share their images of conflict.

# Part IV
# Implications

# 12

# THE SERVICE CONCEPTS OF WAR

The distinctive service approaches to strategy and analysis are, for the most part, harmless. They are mannerisms that are more reflections than determinants of their personalities. But having sketched the personalities of the three services, and finding confirmation of those personalities in their behavior and in their styles of strategy and analysis, I will explore some implications of those institutional personalities and interests for national security.

Here is the first question to pose about the implications of the American military styles for national security. In the peacetime pursuit of their institutional interests, are the American military services preparing for the wrong war? The question is neither profound nor surprising. The immediate responses might be: So what's new? Does anyone prepare for the right war? Or so what? Does it really matter? History suggests that it does matter; and some nations or their military services have prepared better than others for their next war. The main arguments are these:

- The dominant concepts of war held by military institutions have a significant effect upon the kinds of forces they acquire and train and, therefore, upon the kinds of wars they are prepared to fight.
- The services' dominant concepts of war probably serve their peacetime institutional interests better than they serve their preparedness for the next major war.
- If the services' concepts of war are off their mark, their forces are likely, at the least, to be less effective or efficient at their tasks than they might have been. At worst, they might even lead the nation into the wrong kind of war and the loss of Western civilization as we know it.

- In any war less than cataclysmic, the Army is likely to suffer more than the Navy or Air Force because it will enjoy less latitude of choice about how, where, and when it will engage with the enemy.

Two overarching questions must be dealt with immediately lest they undermine all further consideration of these arguments. One is whether or not the military services have any latitude in their choice of concepts of war for the purposes of planning; the other is whether or not the services, even if given the latitude, are able to choose the "right" concept as a basis for planning.

Within the frameworks of the Joint Chiefs of Staff (JCS) and Department of Defense (DoD) planning processes, identifying the right war for military planning could be viewed as the proper job of the DoD, not the services.[1] From that perspective, if the services are preparing for the wrong war, they are only following the Defense Planning Guidance; and it is up to the DoD to correct that guidance accordingly. But the defense guidance does not limit the planning perspective of the military services; it serves only as the frame for DoD's brokering of the program and budget biddings of the military services. Whereas that process may largely determine the quantitative aspects of the service forces and acquisitions, the qualitative aspects are largely determined by the services themselves—by how they see themselves, who they are, and what they aspire to be. Moreover, how the services perceive the next major war they must fight is an important determinant of the types of forces they try to acquire, the doctrine they develop, and the training they follow for the use of those forces in combat.

Admittedly, there is something of a chicken-and-egg problem here: Is it the service perception of the next major war that defines the service? Or is it the service perception of itself, as an institution, that defines the service and, therefore, a compatible image of the next major war? Is the service image of the next major war a disease or symptom? I am firmly inclined toward the theory that the service's perception of itself defines the service and, hence, its concept of war; but that inclination has no significant effect on the problem as it is described here, only in the depth of change required for a cure.

The second question concerns the feasibility of institutional planning: Can institutions plan objectively for contingencies that may only diminish or challenge the institutional self-image? Institutions (or people) are seldom inclined to confront directly their most likely or serious problems. Institutional planning is too often about aspirations rather than preparations. However true those observations may be in general, they represent the risks or difficulties in planning, not its intent or its inevitable consequences. There are examples of sound planning and, though they may be rare, it is they, and not the propensity toward wishful thinking, that provide the motivation and models upon which all serious planning must proceed.

Are the services necessarily limited to a single, dominant concept of war? Might they entertain several concepts, reflecting the uncertainty of where and how and why war might come? At an intellectual level, there is little difficulty in considering several concepts of war. But when alternative concepts of war (or how to fight those wars) begin to affect the institution—its organization and aspirations—then its intellectual energies quickly become focused upon a competition for stature and survival. Competing concepts tend to resolve themselves into dominant and subordinate concepts, or the organization splits into dominant and subordinate elements, each devoted to its own dominant concept.

The Navy and Air Force illustrate both resolutions of competing concepts. The Navy has a dominant concept of war (a fight at sea for naval supremacy), with clearly subordinate concepts (e.g., a fight to protect the sea lanes). The Air Force has resolved itself into two sub-institutions, the bomber pilots (SAC) and the fighter pilots (TAC), each with its own dominant concepts of war, each contending for control of the Air Force.

Thus, through natural internal processes, institutions (and people) tend to be captured and held prisoner by a single, dominant concept or vision of themselves and the world in which they exist. Whether they should be so victimized is a question akin to asking if Darwinism, as a process, is to be admired or condemned.

## The Recent American Experience with War

If a service seriously misperceives in peacetime the kind of war it ends up having to fight, then its actual capacity for, or effectiveness in, fighting that war will depend upon its adaptability and its freedom to adapt (i.e., the degree to which the war taxes its resources). The United States has fought two major wars since World War II (i.e., within the experience of serving military officers). The U.S. military services and the Department of Defense perceived neither war before the event as the next major war. None of the services was well prepared to wage either of those wars when they came; all the services had to adapt and develop new capabilities.[2] Fortunately for the Air Force and Navy, what they could contribute to each of those wars was limited by the mismatch between their media orientation (i.e., the sea and air) and the very nature of the wars;[3] therefore, neither service was severely taxed in the application of its resources. If they were ill prepared for the kind of war they ended up having to fight, their inadequacies did not show too much. Neither the Korean War nor the Vietnam War was really a naval or air war, except to the extent that the Navy and Air Force tried to make them that.

The American conduct of both wars left impressions that the Air Force and Navy were looking for ways to contribute, to make their forces as relevant as possible to the conflicts, even when the case for relevancy was sometimes hard to make. By contrast, the Army in both wars appeared to be struggling just to manage the situation in which it found itself deeply committed. Like the Air Force and Navy, the Army was not prepared for either war. But unlike them, the Army did not enjoy much latitude in deciding when or how it wanted to contribute or participate in either war. Those wars were fought primarily in the Army's medium; they were ground wars. Unfortunately, the Army was not prepared to cope with the style and nature of those wars because of the way it had conceived of ground warfare and, therefore, because of the way it had equipped and trained its forces. Thus, when the Army found itself up to its nose in both the Korean and Vietnam wars, it had little margin for error or adaptation, and it ended up looking ineffective to many and incompetent to a few.

If the American military experience since World War II has any lesson for the future, the next major war will probably not be any of the ones that now conceptually dominate each of our services. And that war probably will not be a naval or air war and, therefore, will tax neither the Navy nor the Air Force capabilities to an extent that their planning and effectiveness are seriously exposed or challenged. But that war will probably stress the Army capabilities to the point that its preparations and competency are once again brought into question. It is not hard to conceive of such wars:

- wars that could directly challenge the security of the United States in its own hemisphere, on its own continent, or within its traditional (pre–World War II) spheres of influence;
- wars in which air and naval operations are ancillary to ground operations, providing the Air Force and Navy oppor-

tunities to exercise some of their muscles, but still without great concern about their real contributions; and

- wars that are now characterized by the services as "third world" or "low intensity" conflicts (with the connotation that they can be treated in planning as lesser included cases) but that could, nevertheless, leave the Army gasping and sweating just to keep from falling on its face.

Thus, it matters much more to the Army than it does to the Air Force or Navy to be prepared for the next major war. The Army, much more than its sister services, can ill afford to be preparing for the wrong war; it simply does not enjoy their freedom of choice in time, venue, and instruments for coming to grips with the enemy. The Navy and Air Force can suffer another Korean or Vietnam experience; the Army cannot, if only for its institutional self-esteem.

## Sources of Concepts of War

Each of the services has its own dominant image of the next major war for which it must (or wants to) be prepared to fight. That image is the one that defines (or reflects) the essence of the service—who it is and what it is about. There may be other images of war, other contingencies or missions, for which the service must be prepared, but they do not occupy that central position of importance, urgency, or priority that goes to the heart of the institution. These secondary (as opposed to dominant) images of war are the stepchildren in service planning: always finding some support from fringe elements in the institution, always clamoring for more attention and funds, but always treated as less attractive obligations by the institutional mainstream.

For example, mine warfare is a stepchild in the Navy, despite those who warn that it could, and has occasionally, become the central aspect of naval warfare. Playing around with mines—sowing them or sweeping them—is simply not the kind of business with which the Navy likes to be associated.[4] Special forces in the Army have always been stepchildren to the mainstream Army, even though they are occasionally praised or supported by those outside the Army. It has been suggested that the Army, with its roots in the citizenry, has always disliked elitism that sets any soldier as better than another. And close air support has been the most consistently neglected mission of the Air Force. Flying down in the mud instead of up in the blue and taking directions from someone on the ground are encroachments upon the freedom of flight that is so cherished by airmen.

To find the services' dominant concepts of war, one need look no further than their finest hours: When and where was it that the Army, Navy, or Air Force last displayed its institutional competence and power at its very best? Of what experience in war is it most proud? For the American military services, those moments all came in the last year of World War II, and not in the several wars they have fought since then.[5]   In the images of those moments, one can find their current concepts of war.

For the Army, its best memories of itself came in its march across Central Europe, from Normandy to the collapse of Germany. In those last ten months of the European war, the Army became a confident, effective, and robust war machine, capable of taking and holding the initiative, demonstrating courage, resilience, and innovation. The breakout at Saint Lô, the Battle of the Bulge, and the crossings of the Rhine showed ingenuity, toughness, agility, and, above all, power. By contrast, its efforts in the Pacific were frequently overshadowed by those of the Navy, the Marines, and even the Air Force. The North African campaign showed it to be plucky, but green. And it got bogged down in a stalemate in Italy. In self-imagery, nothing the Army has done since, in Korea or Vietnam, can compare with who it was and what it was doing from June 1944 to May 1945.

For the Air Force, its finest hours came with the gaining of air superiority over Germany in early 1944, finally permitting it to conduct large-scale daylight strategic bombing raids deep into Germany with tolerable losses. Up to that point, the theory upon which the Army Air Force hoped to gain its institutional independence was in jeopardy: Unescorted, daylight bombing had, so far, proven to be neither decisive nor sustainable. The AAF had dropped more weight in junked airplanes than bombs on Germany.[6]  But, by the spring of 1944, the new long-range escort fighters and the growing flood of airplanes carried the battle; the systematic destruction of Germany from the air could begin. That victory in 1944 was even sweeter, as an institutional memory, than the aerial bombardment of Japan a year later; the victory had been harder fought; and it had been fought with an able adversary in the skies.

For the Navy, rising from the debacle at Pearl Harbor, its finest imagery is of the last year of World War II in the Pacific: a triumphant Navy—100 carriers strong—sweeping across the Pacific, with fast carrier task forces ranging at will, sinking the pride of the Japanese fleet, providing the sole source for air and artillery support for massive landings, carrying the war under, on, and over the sea—right to the Japanese home islands. Midway may have been its most decisive victory, but during the last year of the war the Navy had the power it wanted, did the things it wanted to do, in the way it wanted to do them. By contrast, its operations in the cold Atlantic—convoying, antisubmarine warfare, and shore bombardment—were drudge work, done with courage and pride, but not much pleasure.

One can find more than a glimmer of these memories in the services' current concepts of war: Their concepts are as close as they could possibly be to those same images, given the inescapable realities of technology and politics more than forty years later. Indeed, one can even see where their concepts deny or denigrate some new realities that are contrary to those memories.

However costly or irrelevant these historically rooted concepts of war may be in the nuclear era, the Navy and Air Force dreams of war may not greatly undermine national security. If the recent experience in the Persian Gulf demonstrates once again that the Navy has neglected minesweepers for its carriers, it also shows that delays or stopgap measures may suffice until minesweepers can be supplied by friends or brought up from the reserves. If the Air Force's supersonic jets are once again found unsuitable to help those on the ground in irregular warfare, the application of air power can often be deferred without great consequence until other planes can be borrowed and adapted to the job.

The Army's dream of war, though, if irrelevant to the actual wars it may be asked to fight, is likely to be more costly to the nation's vital interests. Because it must generally fight on terms imposed by others, as to time and place and means, the Army cannot elect to delay engaging, borrow equipment from others, or—as the Navy and Air Force have historically been able to do—pick a time and place of their own choosing to engage. What the Army contributes most to any conflict are people trained in those arts of war relevant to the conflict at hand. From our experiences so far in the nuclear era, particularly in the Korean and Vietnam conflicts, if the Army has prepared for the wrong kind of war, its failures, much more than those of the Navy or Air Force, are likely to be apparent and to have much more serious consequences to the nation's security and to the Army's self-image as an institution.

## The Navy's Concept of War

The Navy's dominant image of the next major war is a conventional war fought with the Soviet Union over control of the seas. Though that war might have its origins in Central Europe or the Middle East, the really important war for the Navy—the one for which it wants to be prepared—would be about the defeat of the Soviet Navy at sea. The idea that the naval forces should meet each other at sea in a decisive sea battle is probably older than the American Navy, but it clearly dominated Navy thinking in its war planning between the two world wars. Though naval forces might be used for blockading, raiding, shore bombardment, and so on, the real test of forces was and is the engagement at sea.

As much as the Navy may talk in its maritime strategy about the deterrent effects of naval presence or forward deployments, or about preventing the Soviets from concentrating their efforts by attacking their flanks, or about the coercive effects of attrition of their missile-carrying submarines, those things are not what the Navy is all about. The important war, the one that really defines the Navy and the forces it wants, is the global battle to defeat the Soviet Navy at sea. All else is ancillary, for if naval power can be used unopposed, it can be used decisively.

This is basically the same theory that underlies the air power theory: If supremacy in the medium can be achieved, then the instrument of power can be used decisively through that medium. The American experiences in Korea and Vietnam are either ignored or explained away in such theorizing. In neither case did supremacy both in the air and on the sea permit either air or sea power to be used decisively. The explanation, if forthcoming at all, is that the Korean and Vietnam wars were the wrong kinds of war or were fought under the wrong kinds of rules. The implication, curiously, is that World War II was the right kind of war, fought under the right rules. When individuals exhibit such selective focusing and rationalization, they are clinically described as being fixated.

Most people believe that a nuclear war would make irrelevant those naval forces which the Navy cares most about—its carriers and surface ships. That assessment may or may not be correct in the event; but it is widely enough accepted that the Navy no longer makes any strong attempts to refute it. Instead, the Navy creatively argues that nuclear war is much less likely than the conventional war it is prepared to fight. That the Navy's ballistic missile carrying submarines (the SSBNs, in Navy notation) might be the most effective instruments for a protracted nuclear conflict gives the Navy only slight comfort; they are not its most cherished forces; to promote them could be to the detriment of its carriers and surface ships.

Likewise, the job of simply protecting the sea lanes to reinforce U.S. allies does not call for the kind of naval forces the Navy wants. Though the Navy can find ways to use its carriers for sea lane defense, they cannot be justified by or for that mission. The carriers can also be used for strikes against naval bases and shore facilities; but the range of modern aircraft with in-flight refueling makes that application of naval power less and less attractive: It brings the carriers into the range of counterattacks by land-based aircraft; and it makes land-based aircraft more competitive as alternative means for carrying out strikes against naval bases and shore facilities.

There is one situation in which the carriers and surface ships would be unquestionably better than any other means: in a conventional war in which an adversary intends to use his surface naval forces to control the use of the sea—that is, in which an opponent tries to do precisely what the Navy itself wants to do. It is little wonder, therefore, that the Navy watches with great expectancy for the emergence of Soviet carriers. They would confirm the Navy's wisdom in building its forces around carriers; they would be a signal that the Navy, at last, had an opponent who might be willing to fight the Navy's kind of war: a conventional war at sea, for control of the sea, so as to make naval power relevant to a war elsewhere.

It is not the Soviet threat that drives this concept of war and, hence, the required naval forces. It is the other way around. It is the desired forces that drive the concept of war and, hence, the interpretation of the threat. If that sounds perverse, try the following gedankenexperiment: Imagine that the Soviets have scuttled their entire fleet in its harbors overnight. Everything, all of the warships and submarines, lies sunk or wrecked. Would the U.S. Navy then say, "Well, they did our job for us, now we can safely get rid of most of our own"? Or would the Navy, as it did after

World War II, quickly find a new justification for the same forces it wants now and wanted then?

Thus, the Navy's dominant concept of the next major war is one that calls for the kind of naval forces and the kind of navy to which it aspires. It is that concept—much more than the defense guidance—which defines the qualitative character of the Navy's programs and its priorities for budget allocations.

## The Air Force's Concept of War

The Air Force, still divided as it has been from its beginnings between the bomber pilots and pursuit (now fighter) pilots, has institutionally divided itself and has two dominant concepts of the next major war for which it must (or wants to) be prepared.

The Strategic Air Command's (SAC's) concept of war is an extension of the Air Force's experience in World War II with the bomber offensives and the "maximum effort" raids, only this time in the form of an all-out nuclear exchange with the Soviet Union, one that invokes the Single Integrated Operational Plan (SIOP). This is the war that justifies the forces, plans, and procedures SAC has worked so long and hard to perfect.

The key word in understanding this concept of war is "single," the first word in SIOP. There is only one plan—the "maximum effort" plan by which the Air Force, in control of all of its resources, mounts the decisive attack, as in the last year of World War II. Time has brought subdivisions or options within the plan; it has also brought in Navy resources; but not with any pleasure. Efforts by those outside the Air Force, such as the president and secretary of defense, to have limited nuclear options designed apart from the SIOP have been treated for what they are: assaults upon the citadels of institutional independence and concepts of war. The third axiom of the air strategy is independent, central control of air power: Air power must not be divided into penny-packets.

The SIOP, with its enormous complexity of targets, resources, timing, and coordination serves to freeze in the concepts of central control and maximum effort (i.e., decisive use), while freezing out those who would meddle with either. That complexity, though real enough, is not essential to the problem, it is sought—albeit unconsciously—as a means for retaining control. If the entire SAC force had to be launched in maximum effort raids every day, the planning and coordination would somehow get done—every day instead of the year or so the SIOP requires for revision.

The Tactical Air Command's (TAC's) concept is a conventional war with competent adversary over control of the air, wherever it may be seriously challenged, but most evidently over Central Europe by Soviet aviation. The ideal model of TAC's war is probably that last year over Europe in World War II when American tactical aviation—fighters and fighter-bombers—ran "guns free" over France and Germany, shooting up everything that moved—in the air, on rails or on the roads—or that opposed them, such as the flak towers. Then, the independence of air power went right down to the pilot and his freedom of flight: With a full load of ordnance and a general area of operations, he was on his own.

That happy prospect is now tarnished by the experiences of Vietnam, SAMs, and wicked ground fire; but it was also buoyed by the Israeli slaughter of Syrian airplanes over the Beka'a Valley of Lebanon. Clearly the favorite form of combat is with an opponent in the air with another airplane. The next best thing is to go after the other's airplanes on the ground, if necessary. If ground-based defenses, such as SAMs, radars, and anti-aircraft guns interfere with the freedom or decisive use of air power, then they will come next.

After that, the use of tactical aviation against other ground targets divides sharply: If, through independently controlled air power, TAC can attack the targets, such as bridges for deep interdiction of enemy movements, then there is some interest, but not with the same affection as for airplane-to-airplane combat. If the targets require close coordination with friendly ground forces, such as supporting front-line troops, the interest declines greatly. Coordinating with other airmen in a complex strike, centrally controlled by airmen, is one thing. But losing the freedom to apply air power independently to decisive ends is to lose that which pilots have striven so hard to achieve for much of the history of the airplane.

Thus, close air support will always be an unwanted stepchild of the Air Force. The job will not be given back to the Army lest it create a rival air arm; and it will not be embraced because it relinquishes the central control of air power. The Air Force has the dilemma of a rival in air power or a sharing of its control, neither of which is acceptable. So the Army tries to make do with helicopters.

TAC's abilities to deliver nuclear weapons and SAC's abilities to deliver conventional weapons, though considerable, are clearly ancillary to their principal interests and concerns. Both the SAC and TAC concepts of war easily motivate the kinds of forces the Air Force seeks, but more important, they argue for independent control of air power. The relative priorities between their two concepts depend upon the division of power between the bomber and fighter pilots in controlling the Air Force as an institution. The bomber pilots "owned" the Air Force from the 1930s to the 1960s; but by the 1970s, the "pursuit" pilots had taken over.[7]

## The Army's Concept of War

The Army's dominant concept of the next major war is a conventional war fought with the Warsaw Pact over the territorial integrity of the Federal Republic of Germany (FRG), which for the Army, has become equated to the NATO war. Curiously, and in contrast to the other services and their concepts of war, this is not a war that the Army expects to win. At best, the Army hopes to participate in a coalition defense that could quickly stalemate (and thereby deter) a Warsaw Pact invasion of the FRG. At worst, it looks for the failure of that defense, resulting in an escalation to the use of nuclear weapons. In neither case would it expect to prevail against the tide of a determined and sustained assault by the Warsaw Pact. In effect, it is a war in which the Army expects to get rescued from disaster by the fright of others—either the Soviets by their fright of a stalemate or the U.S. leadership by its fright of losing—under the shadow of theater and strategic nuclear weapons.

To be sure, the Army is deployed and trained to fight in several other places, but the design of the Army, in its equipment and doctrine, is most clearly oriented toward a Central European conventional war.[8] This is curious if one considers how unpromising the prospective outcomes for such a war are for the Army and how the NATO coalition defense makes it impossible for the Army to control its own environment or destiny in any real fight. One might logically theorize that the Army, like its sister services, would prefer to focus on concepts of wars that would allow for the freedom of independent operations and some prospect for success, neither of which is provided in a coalition defense of the FRG.

Why would the Army want to design itself around such a concept of war? The concepts of the other two services much more clearly serve their institutional interests. But if one questions the Army on its focus on Europe, the response is usually a flurry of reasons couched in national security (rather than institutional) arguments. These are worthy of some scrutiny, if only to clear away the early debris such questioning seems to produce. Since the

Army is likely to suffer more than its sister services if its concept of war is wrong, the Army's focus on Europe deserves careful examination.

One of the first and most altruistic reasons for a European focus is the value of the region to U.S. interests: Except for the defense of its own territorial integrity, the United States has no more vital cultural and economic interests than the defense of Western Europe.

There can be no question that the security of the NATO nations represents one of the most vital interests of the United States.[9] But if the vitality of interests is the criterion, then there can be no doubt that the defense of the United States itself is more vital even than Western Europe. And the Army has significant responsibilities for ground, air, and space defense of the homeland. In terms of vital interests, the Army could make a better case for protection of Alaska from invasion, for SAM defenses against bomber attacks, and for the ground-based components of a space defense against ballistic missile attacks. Yet a war in defense of the homeland is not the dominant concept that sets the design of the Army and its priorities. So, the vitality of U.S. interests in Western Europe is not, by itself, the reason the Army is preoccupied by a war over those interests.

If it is not the vitality of the interests that governs the Army's dominant concept of war, then is it the probability of war? Nowhere else are such large and capable forces poised, toe to toe, nose to nose. The means for a major war are more readily apparent on the inter-German border than anywhere else (at least for Americans but, understandably, perhaps not for the Chinese or South Koreans). Certainly, a war in Central Europe seems more probable than an invasion of the U.S. homeland.

But is a war in Central Europe really more probable than an attack upon the United States? An attack upon the U.S. homeland could arise not only as a consequence of a war in Europe; it could evolve also from other contingencies around the world—possibly from conflicts in the Middle East, Asia, Latin America, even at sea or in space. To say that a war in Central Europe is more probable than an attack upon the U.S. homeland seems to be an arguable assertion. So the simple probability of conflict is not, or logically should not be, the reason the Army is designed around a Central European war.

By the same reasoning, even the risk (i.e., the combination or product of the consequences and probability) of a war in Central Europe does not clearly outweigh that for attacks upon the U.S. homeland. The justification for the Army focus on a Central European war, if it is based upon logic at all, must rest with factors other than, or in addition to, the probability and consequences (and the risks) of conflict.

If it is neither the vitality of our interests at stake in Western Europe nor the probability of a Warsaw Pact invasion, perhaps it is the feasibility of doing something useful that rivets the Army's attention on Central Europe. The Army can at least do something important and useful about a conventional war in Central Europe; it may have convinced itself that it can do very little about a nuclear attack upon the homeland.

That argument, however, will not withstand close scrutiny any more than the others. The Strategic Defense Initiative (SDI) is based upon the premise that defense of the homeland against nuclear attack from space or the air is not hopeless; and the Army has a historic responsibility to contribute the ground-based elements of such a defense. At the same time, it is by no means clear that the Army can, within the constraints it faces, significantly affect the outcome of a war in Central Europe if it should occur. The presence of U.S. forces in Europe may deter a conflict there, but it does not follow that the Army, by its preparations to fight there, can materially alter the outcome or consequences of such a war. It is one thing to argue for a U.S. presence to deter war (as in Korea); it is another to argue that U.S. forces will (or can) be the determinants of the outcome of a conventional war over Central Europe. Thus, the feasibility of the Army materially influencing the outcome of a conventional war in Central Europe may not be demonstrably greater than the feasibility of materially influencing the outcome of a nuclear attack on the U.S. homeland.

But the reasoning thus far has deferred two important considerations that affect the security of the NATO nations and, therefore, might justify the Army's conceptual focus on war in Central Europe: One is the importance of deterring (apart from repulsing) a Warsaw Pact invasion; the other is the importance of NATO cohesion or solidarity against Soviet coercion, short of war. It could be argued that the cohesive bonds of the NATO alliance and the deterrence of a war in Central Europe depend upon the Army's strong and continued commitment to the defense of the FRG. If that argument is valid, why does it not apply to Korea or Japan as well?

The Army presence in South Korea (ROK) is distinctly different from that in the FRG. In Korea, the size and positioning of the U.S. forces is more suggestive of a tripwire than a major partner in waging defensive war. The burden of the defense is clearly upon the ROK forces, with the U.S. forces interposed on the invasion path to the most important objective, Seoul. A serious invasion of the South would almost certainly require engaging U.S. forces. The size of those U.S. forces is not sufficient for them to hold their positions on their own; but that is not their purpose. Their purpose is to ensure U.S. involvement in the defense of the South, thereby reassuring the South and deterring the North. The same is true of the U.S. Army presence in Berlin.

Thus, if reassuring the NATO allies and deterring a Warsaw Pact invasion are the fundamental objectives of the Army posture in the FRG, then why not a U.S. Army presence on the model of South Korea or Berlin? Three or four divisions' worth, interposed forward in brigade strength on the likely invasion paths, should be sufficient for a comparable tripwire to ensure engagement of U.S. forces, reassuring allies of U.S. involvement in any conflict and, thereby, deterring a Warsaw Pact invasion. Such a suggestion, of course, ignores a host of concerns, not the least of which include:

- the legacy of history and the political symbolism behind the present U.S. force posture in the FRG,
- the role of U.S. forces as hostages to the current arms control interest in mutual and balanced force reductions in Central Europe, and
- the need for flexible responses to aggression in Europe beyond those provided by a brittle tripwire and the threat of escalation to the use of nuclear weapons.[10]

The bothersome aspect of all these concerns is that they are the logical province of the Department of State rather than the Army. They might explain external pressures upon the Army to maintain its present posture and focus on Central Europe; but the interest seems to come from within the Army much more than from the outside. The arguments do not explain the Army's own interests there. For example, a larger or constant force in Europe may be in the Army's own interests; but a reduction of forces—mutual, balanced, or not—is not.

Thus, the national security rationales for the Army's focus on Central Europe have surface plausibility more than persuasive logic. The altruistic reasons either fail upon close scrutiny or lie far outside, even contrary to, the Army's legitimate sphere of interest. What is left is not so much logic as it is explanation: The Army's focus on a Central European conventional war serves the Army's institutional image of itself. That concept of war is most harmonious with the Army's aspirations for the future, its perceptions of today's realities, and its remembrance of yesterday's glories:

- A war in Central Europe with the Warsaw Pact would be the largest land war in which the United States might conceivably participate. Thus, the war in Central Europe provides a clear rationale for a larger army than any other conceivable war.
- A war in Central Europe calls for the kinds or mix of forces that the Army prefers. Though a desert war would be dominated by armor and a jungle war by infantry, a war in Europe would call for a balance of infantry, armor, artillery, aviation, and air defense (the combat arms branches) that would best match the balance of internal institutional interests of the Army. Any other locale would disturb that delicate balance of internal power.
- A war in Central Europe can be seen as a reprise of the war that the Army remembers most positively about itself and its performance.

Though these are thoroughly plausible and legitimate reasons for the Army's focus on Central Europe for a dominant concept of war, they are just as thoroughly unsuitable as public explanations. Whatever their justification or validity, such institutionally centered reasons are uncomfortable for the Army to confront, contemplate, or articulate in the national security forums. However, their propriety and reality are two different things. They need not be publicly displayed to be weighed; they need not be advocated to be understood. If these are closer to the real reasons for the Army's focus on Central Europe, then these are the institutional benefits for which the Army may have to pay a price if it has misperceived the next major war it will have to fight.

# 13

---

# MILITARY COMMITMENTS TO COMBAT

## The Nature of Our Commitments

The wars the services claim they must be prepared to fight are not the same as the wars that the nation has clearly committed itself to fight. Although the Navy may assert that it must be prepared to defeat the Soviet Navy in a fight over control of the seas, that is a war the Navy wants to be able to fight, not one the country has made any commitment to fight, beyond providing the Navy with some of the forces it says are necessary to do so.

Here is the second question to pose about the implications of the American military styles for national security: In the peacetime pursuit of their institutional interests, including their concepts of war, are the American military services prepared to fulfill the commitments the nation has already made to go to war? Of the service concepts of war, only the Army and the tactical Air Force concepts are reasonably aligned with the wars that the nation has unambiguously committed itself to fight.

Though American military forces are deployed around the globe and on the territories of more than a dozen nations, for the most part, they are not committed to combat unless directly attacked or ordered by their commanders. The presence of U.S. naval forces in the Mediterranean, for example, is not a national commitment to fight there unless the forces themselves are attacked. A Soviet intervention in Greece or Turkey might very well be sufficient to invoke use of U.S. naval forces in the Mediterranean, but the decision to do so remains a matter of choice, which the U.S. president and the NATO leadership can consider. Though U.S. forces are stationed at bases in the Philippines and Japan, they would not be automatically involved in the territorial defense of those countries. Treaties might oblige the United States to take some action in their defense; but the form, place, and timing of the U.S. response remains to be decided by the American leadership.

However, the United States has unambiguously precommitted itself to fight in three places outside of the United States and its territories, even if its own forces are not directly attacked. These three unequivocal commitments to the use of American forces in combat are for the defense of the sovereignty and territorial integrity of Berlin,[1] the Federal Republic of Germany (FRG), and the Republic of South Korea (ROK). They are underwritten by the presence of U.S. military forces—most unambiguously, by Army forces—so positioned that they must be encountered by any serious threat to sovereignty or territorial integrity. Two of them, for the defense of the FRG and ROK, involve major commitments of U.S. forces—in division strengths—for coalition warfare alongside allied armed forces.

Indeed, it is the presence of Army combat troops that is the hallmark of these three national commitments to the use of military force. There may be little or no doubt about the determination of the United States to act in the defense of its other allies (e.g., Norway, Japan, Turkey) and friends (e.g., Philippines, Honduras), but there remains, nevertheless, some ambiguity about how that determination will be manifested. The American response in places other than those three might take a variety of military or political forms. By contrast, there can be no doubt about the circumstances, place, or time when the United States will spill blood in the defense of Berlin, the FRG, or the ROK once their sovereignty or territorial integrity is challenged.

The decision whether to fight at places other than the three now favored by these national commitments will depend upon what forces are actually available at the time, the world (including the domestic political and economic) situation, contingent threats, and other options available to the national leadership. The military leadership may, after reviewing such considerations, advise against the commitment of certain kinds of forces. For example, the Navy might argue against inserting carrier-based tactical aviation into the restricted areas of the Persian Gulf if confronted with a threat of Soviet counterstrikes. The Air Force might advise against tanker support for a long-range airlift when its strategic bomber forces are confronted with an imminent threat of attack. The Army might very well advise against a limited investment in the defense of

Thailand. Such reservations question whether a commitment would involve the right forces at the right time and right place to do the right job. But such questions do not apply to the three places where the country has already committed itself to fight if an enemy uses force to challenge the sovereignty or territorial integrity of the nations or peoples involved; they have already been answered by the positioning of Army[2] forces with the clear determination to fight.

What makes these three commitments special is that the choice about using American forces in combat has been given away—to potential enemies. In all other places and circumstances of U.S. interests, the choices of using military force—where, what kind, when, to do what—remain. These three commitments, so long as they remain in place, are the anchors to significant requirements for forces, particularly for the Army. They are anchors because they offer little scope for latitude as the nation varies in its security interests and its commitments of resources to its armed forces.

Of the many forward-deployed combat forces maintained by the United States, the Army forces appear to be the most clearly devoted to territorial defense and to defensive operations by their posture (Huntington's proposals aside).[3] By contrast, the forward-deployed air and naval forces are much more ambiguous as to their intended use: They have the potential for significantly greater effectiveness if used offensively rather than defensively against the enemy, and they may be redeployed quickly. The forward deployment of naval and air forces, as in the Philippines, Greece, Japan, or Spain, is seen by their host nations as being more in the interests of the United States for its global interests than for their defense. Indeed, that is why the forward basing for naval and air forces outside the three special commitments involves negotiating (and paying for) base rights, whereas the forward basing for air and ground forces within the three commitments involves negotiating host nation (or state) support.

As a consequence, forward-deployed troops have a political significance unlike that of naval and most air forces. The withdrawal or redeployment of U.S. naval or air forces from many of their forward deployments would be viewed by their hosts as a mixed bag: a loss of income, a reduction of the risks of becoming involved in someone else's war, and so on. But the withdrawal or redeployment of U.S. troops from their forward deployments would be cause for great concern for their host nations (or states) about the American commitment to their territorial defense.

## Pricing the Commitments

If the services or the Department of Defense treat these three national commitments to use force like other generators of requirements for forces, then there is great risk of failure to differentiate between resources that are fungible and those that are not in assessing the nation's security. Though the national leadership of the United States may be able to decide its priorities in the event of multiple conflicts (e.g., whether to reinforce NATO or South Korea or both in the event of simultaneous hostilities), the commanders (all Army officers) of the forces that now guarantee the three special commitments will have to fight, with or without reinforcements. To count these committed forces like others is to see them as part of a total pool of military force that can be summed in assessing the nation's military options. But they are not part of the military options; they are and remain commitments until withdrawn from their forward positions.

But there is more than just an accounting problem here. These national commitments to the use of force involve price tags,[4] not just coin of a different kind to be counted. The value of these commitments to the United States is largely political; their military value (if any) can be reckoned only in the context of a battle or campaign that goes beyond a simple willingness to fight. The political value of the commitments is realized through the reassurance of allies and the deterrence of enemies. The price tags are the costs, as measured in military resources and risks, associated with the peacetime maintenance of these national commitments. Those costs can be found in the answers to three questions, all in military terms:

1. What specific military purposes (e.g., destroy, delay, disrupt) are to be achieved by the commitment to use military force to defend this place at a time of choice given to the enemy?[5]
2. What military forces are required to achieve that purpose?
3. What are the military risks (possible consequences and their likelihood) associated with achieving that purpose with those forces?

Obviously, these three questions are interrelated: For every stated purpose, there are alternative combinations of required forces and associated risks. The purposes or the risks can be traded off against the size of the forces; some purposes or kinds of forces can affect risks regardless of the size of the forces. Moreover, there are tradeoffs among various kinds of forces, even with constant purposes and risks. These tradeoffs include combat forces and their support and, for the defense of allies (the FRG and ROK), between allied and U.S. combat forces and their respective supporting forces. They also include tradeoffs between air and ground forces and between lift for early reinforcement and forces in place.

Whether or not all these tradeoffs are completely understood or worked out, the important points are these:

- There is a price tag that attaches to each of the three national commitments to use force.
- Each commitment is an open contract with potential enemies (and allies in several cases) to pay that price.
- The price tag can be expressed as one or more alternative combinations of the military resources and risks associated with the achievement of a military purpose or objective.
- There are important tradeoffs among all the terms on the price tags.
- The price tags on the three extant national commitments to use force have not been explicitly assessed.

These assertions suggest that important criteria, assessments, and tradeoffs have not been provided for the least ambiguous (and perhaps the most important) of our national security commitments. And all of those are not implicit in the current force commitments or deployments. For example, the current U.S. forces committed for the defense of the FRG are the result of historical, political, budgetary, and institutional pressures, not of a deliberate consideration of objectives, force tradeoffs, or risk assessments. Indeed, the balancing of political and budgetary, as opposed to military, pressures appears to be the principal determinant of their immediate future. Should future forces be planned on that same basis? More to the point, should the American military services, particularly the Army, "go along" with their being planned that way?

The main thrust of the argument advanced here is that price tags on the national commitments to use force have nothing to do with the balancing of budgetary and political pressures. The amount of money in one's purse or the heartiness of one's appetite has nothing to do with the prices to be found on the restaurant menu. Political leaderships control the purse and have the appetite for commitments, but the professional military planner has a duty to price those commitments thoroughly and fairly.

In the national commitments to use force, the price tags attach to the commitment, not to the ability or willingness to pay the costs. The budgetary and political pressures are the realities that should bear upon making the commitments, not upon their fair pricing.[6] The price tags are the basis for planning (designing) future forces against the commitments, whereas the political and budgetary realities should determine whether or not the commitments should be sustained, expanded, or withdrawn. The military planner should not, because of budgetary and political pressures, be diverted or subverted from responsible military planning of future forces; that requires full and fair assessment of the required military forces to achieve specific military objectives, including the risks and tradeoffs in the choices among both forces and objectives.

To assess these price tags is to raise fundamental questions that the military services have every right (but may have been afraid) to ask of their political leadership (who may be afraid to answer them) and that clearly demand confronting the tradeoffs between joint and coalition forces. For example, it may be uncomfortable to state (or to hear), explicitly, the purposes and risks of the Berlin garrison force or the tradeoffs between land and air forces for the defense of the FRG. But it is folly to think that the price tag on the U.S. commitment to defend the FRG is somehow divorced from, say, Belgian force plans, Air Force tanker aircraft planning, Navy plans for protection of the sea lanes, or the risks introduced by uncertainties in all of them.

Of the three current national commitments to the use of force, the defense of the FRG is the big ticket item in the size of forces required, in the importance of the political commitment to U.S. interests, and in setting the force structure[7] of the tactical air forces and the Army. If that commitment could be fairly priced, the remaining two should be simple by comparison; and the requirements for much, perhaps the most important part, of the Army and its essential support could be clearly defined.

What might the price tag for the defense of the FRG look like? First, it would include a military objective, or a set of alternative objectives. At one extreme, an example objective might be in conjunction and coordination with allied force commitments and plans, to repulse any invasion of the FRG by the Warsaw Pact within two weeks and without resort to escalation in the scope of conflict or type of weaponry instigated by the enemy.[8]

At the other extreme, an example objective might be to ensure that any successful invasion of the FRG by the Warsaw Pact requires the destruction of sufficient U.S. forces to make escalation by the United States to the use of nuclear weapons credible, the criterion for sufficiency being at least ten thousand U.S. military combat casualties.[9]

Although both examples imply a larger, political objective of deterrence, they have been deliberately expressed here in military terms. Note that both examples address the defense of the FRG, not the defense of a sector or corps area. How does the United States see its commitment to the defense of the FRG? That question raises another: Has the U.S. Army reduced its view of the problem to the sectors assigned to it? If so, it would suggest that the bureaucratic force planning process is driving the perspective of the military problem rather than the other way around. Thus, a necessary, but not sufficient, step toward better military planning would be to shift the planning orientation from corps to national objectives.

Meeting such objectives would necessarily involve consideration of the options available to the Warsaw Pact in terms of mobilization, concentration of forces, and the employment of chemical or nuclear weapons. The forces required to achieve those objectives would need to consider allied capabilities, air and ground force contributions, air and sea lift support for mobilization and resupply, sea and air lanes protection, and so on. Force alternatives, by trading off allied for U.S. forces, air for ground forces, lift support in exchange for forces in place, and so on, would become apparent. And the alternative objectives and forces would pose different military risks. The alternative objectives, each accompanied by combinations of forces and risks associated with its achievement, constitute a set of military price tags that could be tied to a political commitment. It seems likely that a fairly negotiated price tag for the defense of the FRG would be sufficient, all by itself, to justify the current forces of both the Army and TAC.

Unfortunately, the size of the NATO security problem and the U.S. obligations to NATO have tended to blur or confuse the specific commitment the United States has made to defend the FRG. That commitment is by far the largest of many U.S. obligations to NATO, to the effect that the two are now often treated as synonymous, with detrimental consequences. The defense of the FRG is mostly a military problem; the security of NATO is mostly a political problem. Forging military means for the defense of the

FRG (or any other cooperative ally) is probably tractable; defense of all of NATO is a political pretension and probably not solvable by military means.[10]

If, however, the principal military problem is defined as successful defense of the FRG, there is some hope for the design of attainable forces. Indeed, it could be argued that it is the FRG commitment, not the NATO-wide obligations, that dominates the design of the present Army. The pessimism about NATO creeps in when the demands for the defense of the FRG are compounded by demands for the defense of the flanks (mostly of interest or concern to the Navy), which is an obligation and not a commitment. NATO is a good example of where and how clarification of military objectives could lead to better military planning.

For other possible uses of military force—beyond the three places where the nation is now committed—specific price tags of the sort discussed here (i.e., the combinations of military purposes, forces, and risks) are much more difficult because of the uncertainties attending even the decision to use military force. As for places the nation has not yet committed itself to the use of force, the setting of military objectives becomes highly speculative or hypothetical. In such cases, the association of specific forces with broad political objectives—in the style of the current Defense Planning Guidance—may be sufficient. But in the three places where the nation has already made its decision, its commitment to fight, there need be no speculation about the forces that might be committed—forces have already been committed. What remains undone is to:

- clarify the current military purposes and risks associated with those forces;
- define the tradeoffs among alternative purposes, forces, and risks; and
- rationalize the choice of a particular combination of purposes, forces, and risks to be sought in the future.

## Who Should Price the Commitments?

Who should take the initiative in seeing that price tags are put on the three national commitments overseas to use force? the Office of the Secretary of Defense? the Joint Chiefs of Staff? the Commanders in Chief for the theaters in which these three commitments exist? the military services? The prospects are not good anywhere, even though the Army and the Tactical Air Force might have the most to gain.

The Office of the Secretary of Defense is preoccupied with brokering the basic match between national security interests (including its commitments) and resources, not with writing military price tags on the commitments. Moreover, assessing force requirements and risks against military objectives has traditionally been considered as judgments properly made by the military, and not the civilian, leadership.

The JCS is, by organizational intent, the proper office to price the national commitments to use force—to define the military objectives, size the forces, assess the risks, and weigh the tradeoffs among the three. And it has the military expertise and the joint and global perspectives required to do so. But despite these propitious circumstances, the reality of the JCS is that it has, instead, become almost entirely concerned with brokering compromises among the services in their continuing competition for responsibilities and resources. Indeed, because of that concern, the JCS has become known more for avoiding or denying than for confronting the basic tradeoffs among the forces or capabilities of the services. If the price tags on the national commitments to use force are to include a full and fair accounting of the tradeoffs among joint and coalition forces, objectives, and risks, the JCS is, regrettably, not the place to get them.

The proposals to reorganize the JCS[11] might change this gloomy prospect, but one would have to be extremely optimistic to find much hope there. Current efforts at JCS reform tend toward steps to release the JCS from the blandness of its advice and the paralysis of its planning because of the pursuit of the parochial interests by the separate services. Even if successful, these reforms would only create a more conducive environment for confronting the tradeoff and price tags for the national commitments; they would not, by themselves, instigate the extraordinary process of belling the cat. Developing fair price tags for the national commitments would call for more than a permissive environment; it would require courageous activism within the Joint Staff. Because of the enormously powerful interests involved—in the White House, Congress, Department of Defense, and the military services—the need for compromise in reorganizing the JCS will be great; and the final, adopted reforms are likely to be modest and implemented with caution.[12]

The theater or regional Commanders in Chief are also plausible candidates to write the price tags on those national commitments to use force that lie within their own commands. The problem with their candidacy is their understandable preoccupation with the shortfalls between their current resources and obligations (or ambitions) for a war that they may have to fight tomorrow. They have understandable difficulties in addressing future forces, contemplating reduced objectives, or any tradeoff that might compromise the aspirations or power of the command. In short, the allegiance of the CINCs is to their command, perhaps even to their own service, more than it is to the fair and balanced pricing of the national commitments within their command. "Recent changes involving the CINCs more in the resource allocation process may alleviate some of these problems. But the fact remains that the CINCs have no program authority and cannot directly shape the forces they will have to lead into war."[13] Though the legislative attempts to reform the military may be well intentioned, they are inherently limited because they attack the perceived problem only through changes in procedures and organization—precisely the kinds of constraints within which the military institutions have always worked, more or less successfully, within and around. They will do nothing to alter the incentives and the visions that motivate those institutions. And they can never fully account for the ingenuity and adaptiveness of the institutions in the pursuit of their own interests within whatever procedural and organizational constraints may be imposed by legislation or executive order.

Of the military services, the Army would seem to have the greatest interest or incentive in seeing the commitments priced:

- The Air Force and Navy are dedicated to the independence and uniqueness of their forces; they are disinclined to consider the tradeoffs of their forces in favor of any others.
- The Army is, and will remain, dependent upon the forces and capabilities of its sister services and allies and, therefore, is very much concerned with the obvious tradeoffs among them.
- The Army would probably be the service that would most gain if the commitments were matched with adequate resources since the presence of Army troops and Army commanders is a common denominator of all three national commitments to the use of force.

In sum, although the JCS and CINCs are the logical ones to price the national commitments to the use of force, they are unlikely to do so. The tradeoffs among the services' vital institutional interests are simply too hot to touch. And, although the Army would probably benefit if those tradeoffs were made explicit, it will not touch them either because it has no desire to be the instigator of the worst kind of interservice warfare: That is not how the Army sees itself as an institution.

So the commitments remain without price tags. Fortunately, the odds are strongly against our having to pay them off in blood or treasure. But, if the commitments were called in, it is the Army that would have to pay:

> In foreign confrontations the United States is not committed until its land forces—its Army—is committed. And in the event of hostilities, the Army historically has borne the brunt of the war, the human cost, taking the great bulk of the casualties. The Army as an institution knows this and has been traditionally reluctant to go to war, its leaders seeking to ensure that war is truly necessary and that our civilian leadership exploit all other avenues before taking that final step.[14]

In its desire to keep the interservice peace, the Army may be running higher risks as to what it will have to pay if real war comes.

# 14

# IMPLICATIONS FOR MILITARY PLANNING

Here is the third question to pose about the implications of the American military styles for national security: Are the services, in pursuit of their institutional interests, failing to come to grips with some of the important military planning issues they need to face for their own future institutional well-being?

Many of the currently exaggerated images of interservice rivalry are probably rooted in the boisterous years immediately following World War II, with the birth of the Air Force as a separate service, the "unification" of the services in a single Department of Defense, and the uncharted ground of budget slicing among the services in the "atomic" era. Now, however, a long history of budgets, roles, and missions has brought considerable stability, harmony, and cooperation in their relations with one another. They take some pains to work together, particularly when their cooperation is mutually advantageous, or at least not disadvantageous, and when their cooperation can be publicly displayed.

But if the issues get too close to their vital institutional interests—their budgets, independence, or control—then barriers are likely to come up, and the threatened service typically withdraws within itself rather than striking out at the other. Even though this has made for a less tumultuous era of interservice relationships, it has not led to better military planning. Indeed, concerns for avoiding interservice strife may now override service concerns about the quality of military planning.

Examples abound of military planning suffering because of the collision of the services' institutional interests, but they tend to be "inside" stories kept within the military family, ostensibly because they hinge on details that make them classified. But examples of the inadequacies (or strengths) of American military planning are not the focus here—understanding the American military services as institutional personalities is.

A more useful example, here, is one that reveals how the particular personality and interests of one of the services may prevent it from taking the initiative for better military planning, perhaps even from increasing its own share of the defense budget. The example deals with the Army and military planning for the national commitments to the use of force. The Army's personality is the key to understanding the position it has taken. One could reasonably speculate that neither the Air Force nor the Navy, if faced with similar circumstances, would have adopted the same position as the Army has.

## The Army and Pricing the National Commitments

The Army would certainly have the most to gain through sound military planning around the nation's commitments to fight, particularly those for the defense of the FRG and ROK. So far, however, the Army has backed away from taking that initiative, for a variety of proffered reasons:

- It is not in the national interest to be too specific about military objectives, the relative capabilities of allied forces, or the risks that have been accepted. Political leaderships can seldom afford to be explicit about the military objectives associated with national commitments to the use of force.
- The true costs of the national commitments to fight are domestic and international political grenades and are, therefore, to be viewed more as a danger to the Army institutionally than as an asset to better planning.
- The tradeoffs among joint forces inherent in the national commitments to fight will affect the vital interests of the services in their independent roles, missions, and contributions and will, therefore, engender intense interservice disputes, which cannot be resolved.
- The Army does not want to be the instigator of the internecine warfare that is almost certain to accompany tradeoffs among air, land, and sea forces or their fire and lift support.[1]
- Given the historical aggressiveness of the Navy and Air Force, they might skew the tradeoffs to argue for Army

reductions in favor of their own forces.[2] The "nation's loyal and obedient servant" might be "hoist with its own petard."

- It is not the Army's job; it is a joint/coalition problem and one properly taken up by the JCS or CINCs. The reorganization of the JCS is supposed to take care of this problem.

- The Army cannot speak for the Air Force or the Navy or other countries on the supporting uses of their forces; therefore, it cannot make the tradeoffs or risk assessments required.

- The full and fair pricing of the national commitments to fight, with its demand for tradeoffs and risk assessments, is beyond the capacity of current analytical techniques or beyond the Army's analytical support resources because of their scale or complexity.

To be sure, these arguments reflect legitimate analytic, bureaucratic, and political concerns. What is remarkable about them is their number and diversity. They overwhelm and perhaps even obscure the original question as to whether or not the nation, military planning, and the Army might all be better served if the national commitments to fight were fully and fairly priced. They suggest smoke obscuring a fire. To get at the original question, it may be useful to resolve all those arguments (and possibly more) into two tough, direct questions: (1) Could the Army price the commitments, even if it wanted to? (2) Would the Army want to price them, even if it could? One is a question about means, the other of ends. Though the two questions are obviously conditionally interdependent, they can be taken up separately here.

## Could the Army Price Commitments If It Wanted To?

At first, this appears to be a question about analytical feasibility; a little reflection, however, suggests that defining the many tradeoffs among joint and allied forces is much more a bureaucratic than an analytical problem. The interactions of air, sea, and land warfare are not inherently intractable: All three services work across those interfaces with their own systems, assessing their capabilities and effects. Ships shooting down airplanes is no less tractable analytically than ships sinking ships; killing a tank from the air rather than the ground does not shift the analysis from the plausible to the incredible. The modeling or simulation of warfare of any kind is complex and can be analytically demanding, but problems of even greater complexity have been and are being subjected to analysis of varying rigor.[3] There is nothing inherent in combined, joint, or coalition warfare that poses an analytic boundary that cannot be crossed. And there is no new ground to cover in a top-down analysis of military requirements, from objectives to forces, including the risks. What is difficult, even awesome, is crossing from one service's turf onto another's. That is an institutional, not an analytical, barrier.

The Army's inability to speak for the other services or other allied nations in the use of their forces in joint or coalition warfare does not prevent the Army from portraying and analyzing those forces and their operations in accordance with their owners' statements, doctrines, and strategies. It is one thing for the Army to tell the Navy or Air Force how to fight or allocate their forces. It is quite another for the Army to repeat what its sister services themselves have declared. To claim that the Army does not know enough to portray how naval or air forces would be employed is an affront: If true, the Army is ignorant of vital information about how to fight and allocate its own forces, which are intimately dependent upon naval and air forces.

The Army can certainly portray the allocation and application of tactical air power, air lift, or air tankers according to, or consistent with, the Air Force's own doctrine, analyses, and models. Whether the Army agrees with such allocations and applications is a different problem which need not confuse the fair pricing of the national commitments. If, in the Army's view, the Air Force has not properly allocated or applied its air power, that is the Air Force's problem and can only point toward the need for more ground (or sea) forces to compensate for the misallocation of air power. If the Army misunderstands or misinterprets such sources for the application of air power, it can always welcome corrections. If there are disagreements about the effectiveness of air power, then those disagreements become part of the risk assessments that go with the price tags.

But bureaucratic barriers to analysis are real enough, even within a service, let alone among services. Analytical models and assumptions of dubious validity or relevance may be perfectly acceptable for calculating an uncontended "requirement" for spare parts or ammunition; but let them be applied to tradeoffs among the cherished symbols of a service faction—as between tanks and artillery or between carriers and submarines or bombers and fighters—and the models will quickly be found inadequate and unacceptable. The tradeoffs there, because of their vital importance to institutions, are resolved politically or bureaucratically, not analytically. Little wonder, then, that tradeoffs involving the vital interests of entire institutions have found no home in current analytical models owned, operated, or blessed by those institutions. Such vital interests are too important to be trusted either to models or analysts. The joint force tradeoffs—or more correctly, compromises—by the JCS are resolved politically or bureaucratically, not analytically.

If the Army cannot fairly define the tradeoffs among its own branches, is there any hope that it could be an honest broker in making the tradeoffs between joint or coalition forces? The Army's record on analytically examining the tradeoffs among the forces of greatest interest to its own branches is probably no worse or better than that of its sister services—that is to say, not very good. But to be credible in trading off air, land, and naval forces to fulfill the national commitments to fight, the Army would first have to have a demonstrably superior record in the tradeoffs among its own branches—as among infantry, armor, and artillery. Thus, pricing the national commitments to fight risks intraservice as well as interservice and international infighting.

This reasoning suggests that the Army is not yet institutionally prepared to price the commitments, even if it wanted to. It would first have to take the extraordinary step of subjecting itself to the same analytical disciplines required for fair pricing of the national commitments to the use of force. That step would represent a departure from the Army's current position on both branch protectionism and the way it does analysis. Not only would the Army have to tolerate, even encourage, open and explicit trading off among tanks, artillery, helicopters, and so on, it would have to realign its analytic efforts more toward tradeoffs than requirements.

Because it is still the least toy oriented of the three services, the Army is perhaps the best able to contemplate open tradeoffs among the various kinds of weapons it fields. Whether that ability to consider open tradeoffs would extend down to the resultant allocations of personnel among the Army branches is much less clear. The Army may not be so toy oriented as the other services, but the entrenchment of its branches is as deep as any. The survival of the branches may not be measured in equipment or weapons, but it is in personnel.

Then there is the matter of analytical style or preferences: The Army's analytical orientation is toward large, detailed simulations to produce and justify the specific requirements numbers needed in formal JCS and PPBS planning systems. However, the tradeoffs needed for fair pricing of the national commitments involve consideration of many cases because of the large number of alternatives, the diversity of forces, and the substantial uncertainties at almost every turn. Such tradeoffs beg for the use of simple parametric models more characteristic of the Air Force than the Army in their analytical styles. Since these differences in analytical orientations are, as much as anything else, reflections of the differences in service personalities, realignment of the Army's analytic efforts away from large simulations and toward simple parametric models would be neither natural nor easy.

In sum, there is no obvious reason why the Army could not price the national commitments if it really wanted to. The analytical means are available or known. But developing the capability to do so would require a significant reorientation of the Army's philosophical approach to the uses of analysis. And exercising such a capability would have to start with tradeoffs inside the Army itself, among the interests of its separate branches, at considerable risk to the Army's own bureaucratic tranquillity. Ultimately, even the capacity to price the national commitments could cost the Army dearly in both its peace and personality.

## Would the Army Want to Price Commitments If It Could?

The dominant concern has to be the potential for interservice strife and its consequences. The other arguments—about diplomatic and coalition sensitivities—have more the flavor of additional, buttressing arguments than they do genuine concerns. The Army has worked hard at building good relationships with its sister services, particularly with the Air Force now under the leadership of tactical pilots. All those good works could "go down the tubes" if full-scale interservice warfare broke out. The Army could find itself once again embattled over its purposes and future, as it has been several times since World War II—with its sister services amplifying, if not instigating, public questions about the need for an Army, the need for troops overseas, the dangers of becoming inextricably entangled through our ground forces in somebody else's war, and so forth.

Isolationist sentiments, ever present within American society, find expression or sympathetic vibrations in the Navy's maritime strategy and in calls for bringing American troops home or avoiding "another Vietnam." By firing the first shot in an all-out interservice battle, the Army could be the first victim.

But one needs to examine closely the particular act that would produce such dire consequences. Is it putting a price on the national commitments to use force? It is not *a price* that causes problems; it is the *menu of prices* that threatens the protocols of interservice truce. The real nub of the matter is the trading off of forces owned by different services; that is the forbidden ground. Trading off forces implies their substitutability and, hence, in any mix of forces, their interdependency, something that the Army alone among the services has accepted (or has long been forced to accept). For the Navy and Air Force, historically devoted to the independence of their requirements for forces, tradeoffs among their forces and those of the sister services are more than a tugging over budget slices; they are an assault upon their institutional integrity and independence.[4]

Given those high stakes for the Navy and Air Force, and the potentially adverse consequences for Army relationships with its sister services, does the Army have to instigate the tradeoffs in order to price the national commitments to the use of force? If the tradeoffs are the problem, why not fix the price without them?

To avoid tradeoffs is to avoid a full and fair pricing of the national commitments. If there is a declared or candidate military objective, then assessing the joint and coalition forces required to meet that objective, and the risks involved with that particular combination of ends and means, implies that the tradeoffs are understood: So much of A and so much of B, taken together, can accomplish X with some probability, P. It is the combination of A and B, whether they represent joint or coalition or combined forces, that implies an understanding of the tradeoffs. If one side of that tradeoff remains fixed, say at current force levels, then the pricing becomes advocacy for one side of the tradeoff at the expense of the other. The feasibility, credibility, and utility of pricing the national commitments to the use of force rest upon a full and fair disclosure of the tradeoffs among means and ends and risks.

If the Army does not confront the tradeoffs among those joint and allied forces upon which it is, and will remain, dependent, then the Army will find itself in a gradually worsening situation with respect to its own planning for (and its capacity to meet its obligations to) the national commitments to the use of force. The trends clearly point to increased, not reduced, reliance upon joint and coalition warfare in U.S. military commitments. If the Army avoids the tradeoffs among its own forces and those upon which it is inherently dependent, then it will continue to be a victim of the independent force theories espoused by its sister services. Although the nation may fight only with joint forces, it will continue to plan and buy them as independent forces as long as the Navy and Air Force portray them as such without challenge, while the Army, perhaps in the name of interservice harmony, remains silent about the true measures of their interdependency.

The choice is a tough one for the Army: Should it risk interservice strife for better military planning? On one side of that choice is the prospect for a continuation of the Army's recent past: improved interservice relations, accompanied by some uneasiness about the quality and extent of Army participation in the military planning process. On the other is the prospect of an uncertain tradeoff between better military planning and poorer interservice relationships. The potential gains in the quality of Army planning are probably easier to describe than the potential risks and costs of interservice strife that might follow any Army initatives toward a full and fair pricing of the national commitments.

In sum, the national commitments to the use of force, especially the commitments to defend the FRG and ROK, could provide the Army with a powerful wedge into the military planning process; but its exploitation will require defining the tradeoffs among joint and allied forces. If those tradeoffs are defined, they may or may not threaten force structure and budget slices; but they are certain to threaten the institutional independence of the Air Force and the Navy and to strain interservice relationships. If those tradeoffs are not defined, the Army will continue to lack significant control over the consistency of its obligations, resources, and risks associated with the national commitments to fight.

Taking the initiative on military planning for the national commitments, which affect the Army more than the other services, would call for the Army to take an activist's role in strategic planning, to put its force structure and budget slice on the line in the name of better or more honest planning. Such actions seem, at first glance, quite uncharacteristic of the Army in its self-image as the nation's loyal and obedient servant. Army behavior during the past two decades provides little reason to believe it would want to take such risks:

Under the several influences of the McNamara period in which there was a gradual and near-total waning of meaningful strategic dialogue in DoD and in the NSC system, the Vietnam War and the rapid retrenchment . . . organized and deliberate strategic thought directed beyond the immediate future all but disappeared from the Army. . . . Generally speaking, from 1968 forward the Army had expended its bank of strategic thought and the Army's main stream was introspective, managerial, and preservation oriented.[5]

At present, the Army's manner of fulfilling its self-image as the nation's loyal and obedient servant seems more passive than active; therefore, it seems quite likely that it will not, at this time, take great institutional risks in the cause of better military planning.

## Will the Army Be Ready to Serve?

Even if the Army is not willing to risk interservice strife for better (more honest) military planning at the national level, is it willing to risk intraservice strife for better planning and readiness for the next war it is likely to fight? The answer, again, appears to be, not yet. The Army's focus on Central Europe as the place where it will have to be prepared to fight serves its internal institutional interests in the same way that the Navy's maritime strategy serves its internal interests—because all of its components or elements get to play. Just as a battle at sea with the Soviet Navy gives all the Navy an opportunity to contribute, so a battle with the Soviet Army along the inter-German border brings all the Army's branches fully into the fray.

Note that probability or even plausibility of the scenario is not the test of these scenarios: The services will defend the scenarios on the claim that they are the most severe they will face and, therefore, should be used to set the size and qualities of their forces. But they really are not the most severe that they would face. If one asks them about a major nuclear attack on their forces, they dismiss it as being implausible or impossible to consider with seriousness. That response is a clue that their chosen scenarios are the ones they prefer to point to for their own interests.

Other than being expensive to accommodate, the Navy's choice of its planning scenario probably will not do either the nation or itself much harm in terms of military planning. The Navy may be embarrassed by such things as its lack of preparation for mine warfare, as it already has been several times before and, most recently, in the Persian Gulf; but the Navy's pertinence and capacity to participate in likely future wars are such that it does not risk being seriously taxed. The Navy, fortunately, is not sailing in harm's way. But the Army's choice could end up doing serious damage to the Army as an institution in the next war, if that war is not a Soviet invasion of Western Europe.

What effect has the Army's focus on Central Europe had upon its capabilities and preparedness to fight elsewhere? If elsewhere is taken to be Korea or Southwest Asia, the effect is probably less than it would be if elsewhere is Latin America or Southeast Asia. However, if conflicts in these other areas are considered to be smaller and less demanding than a Central European war and, therefore, to be treated as lesser included cases, then the Army's present Central European focus gains additional justification.

There is a danger of compounding two false premises in treating other potential conflicts as lesser included cases. One premise is that the dominant case is satisfied; the second is that the other cases are lesser and can be included. Neither premise is clearly safe:

- Army forces are not, in fact, adequate for a war in Central Europe. To assume that forces sufficient for one conflict are more than sufficient for lesser conflicts may have some logical merit. But to assume that insufficient forces for one conflict are also more than sufficient for lesser conflicts is not logic that will stand on its own.
- It is not clear that the other conflicts are indeed lesser on all critical dimensions, particularly in manpower, training, and logistical support. They could be lesser mainly in the rate of destruction of vehicles, but much greater in their demand for mobility, logistics infrastructure, or trained people. The Army can fail just as easily on these aspects as on not having enough tanks or armored personnel carriers.

There are two crucial questions here: The first is whether or not the present Army forces would be adequate to meet its own or public expectations if the United States became involved in a major conflict in one of these other areas. Recent history suggests that it would not; and the Army's inadequacies would be more obvious than those of the Air Force and Navy. That is to say, a major conflict in any one of these other areas would probably tax the capacities of the Army much more than its sister services, with a much greater risk of Army failure in the public perceptions.

The second question is whether or not Army forces could be made adequate for a major conflict in one of these other areas if the Army had to stay within currently available resources (i.e, within current budget and personnel ceilings). If shifting the focus for the dominant concept of the next major war would not provide for adequate capabilities, then the problem is not one of focus but of sufficient resources. But if a shift of focus away from Central Europe would allow for adequate capabilities elsewhere, the problem may be one of focus.

The second question is probably amenable to better military planning for both the nation and the Army: Stressful conflicts in areas other than Central Europe can be postulated. They need not be more intense or destructive than a European war to be stressful; they could be enormously more difficult in terms of access, terrain, weather, duration, care for noncombatants, local popular support, and so on. And they need not involve Soviet forces or support. Scenarios for stressful conflicts in any of these areas are at least plausible. The nation's painful memory of the war in Vietnam and current public attitudes toward U.S. military involvement in Central America are not absolute bars to future U.S. participation in major conflicts in the Philippines, Cuba, Mexico, or any of a half-dozen other "third world" nations. The scenarios leading to such conflicts and U.S. involvement may be less obvious or explored, but no less plausible, than a major war in Central Europe.

Scenarios leading to stressful conflicts in areas other than Central Europe would necessarily imply national objectives and public expectations for U.S. involvement. The Army forces required to meet those objectives or expectations could be estimated for various degrees of risk. Whether those required forces could be made available under current budget and personnel ceilings should not be predicated on the present deployments dominated by the Central European war scenario, but on a "clean sheet" with the other areas—one by one—taken as the dominant concept of war. If the required forces come close to or exceed the current ceilings, the problem is resources. If the required forces fall well within the current ceilings, but the current forces (by structure, training, and support) are the wrong kind, then the problem is focus. That they are the wrong kind is suggested by a cursory survey of those other areas:

- If the Korean Peninsula was the scene of the next major war involving U.S. forces, then the present Army would probably find itself regretting not having prepositioned more equipment there for rapid reinforcement and not having balanced itself more toward quantity rather than sophistication in its equipment and forces across the board. It would also likely find itself short on artillery and ammunition stocks.

- If the next major war for the United States was in Southwest Asia, then the capacities of the present Army would be limited by a host of factors, but especially by shortages of lift and logistics infrastructure. It would want to rebalance its forces more toward highly mobile armor, calvary, airborne, and aviation forces at the expense of infantry and perhaps even artillery.

- If the Army had to fight its next major war in Latin America or Southeast Asia, it would find itself poorly prepared on almost all aspects: Its sophisticated armor and air defense systems would be largely irrelevant. It would be drastically short of infantry and engineers; those available would probably not be well trained for the problems they would face. It is in these locales that the Army could most easily be made to look like a misplaced, clanking dinosaur.

## Implications of Shifting the Focus

What would the Army look like if it had been designed primarily around a concept of war in one of these other areas? More important, how would such alternative Army designs look to the present Army as an institution? Since they would clearly call for some rebalancing of the Army among its combat arms branches and between the combat and support branches, internal institutional turf would be at stake. The current internal Army agonizing over the "light divisions" presages on a small scale what could happen if the focus were to shift away from war in Central Europe. It is not the shift in focus that poses the problem; it is the implied shift in branch turf. But the internal institutional battles will nevertheless be argued out in terms of the national security imperatives because of the proprieties.

These arguments will ultimately raise the question of which war should the Army be most prepared to fight? To date, the answer to that question has been the war in which we face the biggest and most sophisticated threat, the one that would be the most destructive of equipment. Though that answer clearly supports the maximum requirement for equipment (and, less obviously, the current splits among branches), it is silent about the probability of the occurrence of that war or the Army's ability to be effective in waging it if it did occur.

A future ground war with the Soviet Union is conceivable in only three places: Central Europe, Southwest Asia, and Northeast Asia. None of those could be the Army's war for very long. Anywhere on the periphery of the Soviet Union, the Soviet's central position would eventually work to its logistical advantage. Therefore, such wars would have to end quickly (perhaps because of fright) or else escalate (vertically or horizontally). More important, within current (or realistic) resource constraints, how well the Army is prepared to fight such wars may be largely immaterial in determining their outcomes. The Army simply cannot win a war with the Soviets on their doorstep any more than the Soviets could on ours. Deterrence of such conflicts on the periphery of the Soviet Union does not (cannot realistically) rest on the Army's ability to prevail, but only upon its credibility for interposing, for becoming directly involved in a military confrontation.[6]

The Army must prevail in order to meet public expectations in those so-called low-intensity or Nth-country conflicts, wars in which Soviet involvement is either indirect or negligible. Such wars, with origins typically in internal economic, social, and political conditions, are not subject to deterrence through the preparedness of the U.S. Army to intervene. The Army will not be measured by its ability to deter such wars, but by its ability to intervene effectively if they occur and if vital American interests are at stake.

The places where the combination of vital U.S. interests and the fomenting conditions for war might coincide are legion: throughout Latin America, the Middle East, and the Pacific. Many of those wars would, indeed, be small and well within the capacity of the Army even though ill prepared because of its focus on Central Europe. The past U.S. interventions in Grenada and the Dominican Republic are examples.

But not all such wars would be walkovers. Mexico and the Philippines stand out as having significant potential because of their historically close associations with the United States, large and rapidly expanding populations, and severe economic, social, and political problems without obvious solutions. A major revolutionary conflict in either country is quite conceivable and, particularly if the conflict appeared to be inspired or supported by the Soviets or Soviet proxies, U.S. interests are implicit. Revolutionary wars on the scale that could be expected in Mexico or the Philippines are more than enough to tax any U.S. Army that could be raised and employed under realistic constraints.

The possibility, before the end of the twentieth century, that the U.S. Army could be ordered to intervene in a major war in Mexico or the Philippines (or to reoccupy Cuba) is hardly less likely than a Soviet invasion of Central Europe. If the Army oriented itself toward such a possibility, it could probably be quite effective in meeting both its military objectives and the public's expectations. If the Army continues with its current focus on a war in Central Europe, a major war elsewhere will probably tax its capabilities to the point at which its performance will please no one except its enemies.

The costs and benefits of that shift in focus must be reckoned both for the Army as an institution and for the nation in its security. Neither reckoning can be done until alternative designs for the Army, within resource constraints, are laid out and evaluated. Such designs and their evaluation are sound military planning—for the nation and the Army. The institutional risks to the Army in undertaking that reckoning are probably less than they would be if the reckoning is left to others whose primary motives and interests lie with neither the Army nor, if truth can ever be known in the political arena, national security.

# 15

## IMPLICATIONS FOR REGIONAL SECURITY

If the services' pursuit of peacetime institutional interests has left us unprepared to fulfill the commitments the nation has already made to fight, have they also led us to be overprepared to fight in conflicts for which the nation has neither such commitments nor the need to fight? The American military planning and force posture for the Pacific would suggest that possibility.[1]

If any American insitution has an interest in the Pacific, it is the U.S. Navy. Indeed, for American military planning, the Pacific *is* the Navy's theater, just as Central Europe is the Army's theater.[2] Since the Spanish American War, the American Navy has looked to the Pacific as its "lake"—the best place for it to exercise international influence with naval power and, if necessary, to demonstrate that power in combat. In the interlude between the two world wars, before the ascendancy of the aircraft carrier to capital ship status, the Pacific offered the American Navy almost everything it could want as a theater of operations for a military institution:

- Japan posed the perfect antagonist with a strong naval force that could be met and defeated in a battle at sea, consistent with the Navy's longstanding, dominant concept of war.
- The region was one in which naval forces were the central elements of military power by sheer geography and in which the maintenance of a naval presence offered a pleasant, even gracious style of life.

The war with Japan, when it came, justified the American Navy's prewar focus on the Pacific, even as it invalidated much of its prewar thinking about the roles of battleships and airplanes. And its own stepchildren, the aircraft carriers and submarines, ultimately proved themselves to be the decisive elements of naval power there.

When Japan faded from view or prospect as a potential enemy after World War II, the Pacific remained the Navy's theater of interest, dominance, and affection. Today, on almost any measure, the American Navy continues in its ownership of the Pacific with respect to its potential adversaries, including the Soviet Union, and with respect to its sister services. Much of American security policy and interests in the region reflect the Navy as the dominant military institution in the Pacific: To have a security policy or force posture inconsistent with the Navy's interests on its most hallowed waters would be a challenge to the Navy. This longstanding Navy ownership of the Pacific appears to have resulted in military planning and a force posture that probably serve the Navy as an institution as much or more than they do American security interests. They may have stimulated reactions by the other services, by our allies, and by our enemies that are not beneficial to American security interests there.

## The Pacific as a Military Theater

Americans do not appear to have any consensus on the role of the Pacific in a global war, nuclear or conventional. Despite the growing recognition of the economic shift to the Pacific, the most immediate and consequential military threats to U.S. interests abroad are perceived to remain first in Western Europe and then on the Persian Gulf littoral. Some have suggested that the United States might want to take the initiative against the Soviets in the Pacific if a conflict should start elsewhere on the presumption that Soviet forces could be pinned down in East Asia and prevented from being sent elsewhere, or that the Soviets are more vulnerable to being hurt in the Pacific. Another, more extreme, argument suggests that the United States could "afford" to lose Europe if it could hang on in the Pacific, using the enormous economic base of the Pacific as the springboard for a return to Europe.

The most common political view, however, sees the Pacific as neither the likely spark for a global war nor an advantageous arena for the expansion of a war started elsewhere. For U.S. military institutions, this view undercuts arguments for expanding or even justifying their Pacific forces. The services have differing attitudes toward the argument that the Pacific, as a military theater, is, and ought to be kept, benign.

- The Army probably welcomes that perspective, being oriented toward forces and tactics for a European war on the central front. Two grinding, unpopular wars in East Asia since World War II appear to have left the Army with too little glory or pride to design itself for a third.
- But the Navy would prefer even more emphasis on the Pacific theater, its arena by history and geography. Anything that would expand the military importance of the Pacific would work to the Navy's advantage, both in the absolute sense and relative to its sister services. Thus, the Navy has seized upon the increase in Soviet naval activity in the Western Pacific and the Soviet use of Camranh Bay as evidence of the Navy's need for more forces to counter the growing Soviet naval threat.
- The Air Force attitude toward the Pacific fits somewhere in between those of the Navy and Army. It would like to use the Pacific to justify its need for more and better aircraft; but the command of the theater (CINCPAC) is deeded in perpetuity to Navy hands; Navy views and interests therefore tend to dominate the region.

The words that best describe the three services' attitudes toward the Pacific as a potential theater for military operations are unambiguously devoted for the Navy, patiently opportunistic for the Air Force, and weary and wary for the Army.

Though tactical and strategic nuclear forces are deployed in the Pacific, they have not assumed the same character as those in the European theater. The U.S. tactical nuclear weapons in the Pacific serve as a deterrent to a successful conventional attack against South Korea by the North; but that eventuality is not expected in the absence of contingencies involving the Soviet Union—on the peninsula or elsewhere. By contrast, NATO expects to resort to the use of tactical nuclear weapons in the event of the expected failure of its conventional defense against a Soviet onslaught. The deployments of ballistic missile submarines in the Pacific by both the United States and the Soviet Union reflect convenience for basing and coverage of their assigned strategic targets rather than theater orientations. In the European theater, however, some of the U.S. ballistic missile submarines have been assigned a distinct and separate role in the NATO alliance plans for a theater nuclear war. These differences between the European and Pacific theater perceptions of the roles of nuclear weapons are reflected in differences in the numbers of weapons and in the political heat they generate.

## Northeast Asia Dominates

In the wake of the war in Vietnam, the focus of U.S. national security interests in the Pacific fall on the intersection of the three East Asian powers: where the shadows of China, Japan, and the Soviet Union overlap—the environs of the Korean Peninsula and the Sea of Japan. To the extent that considerations of potential military threats provide the rationale for the U.S. military force posture in the Pacific, the defense of Northeast Asia, specifically Japan and the Republic of Korea (ROK), dominates.[3] Conflicts in Southeast Asia are no less likely and would require somewhat different forces, but the forces required to meet the threats posed in Northeast Asia are quantitatively and qualitatively much more demanding and, therefore, will always better serve the U.S. military institutions in their advocacy of larger and more powerful forces. Specialized forces for Southeast Asia, such as riverine and counterinsurgency forces, have been treated as marginal add-ons to a force posture that has been rationalized for Northeast Asian contingencies—one that treats conflict in Southeast Asia as a "lesser included case."

In Northeast Asia, there are three salient threats that justify the U.S. military force posture in the Pacific:

1. The threat of invasion of South Korea by North Korea, with or without the encouragement or assistance of the Soviet Union or the People's Republic of China. That threat justifies much of the U.S. Tactical Air and Army forces allocated to the Pacific.

2. The threat against U.S. naval and air forces deployed in and around Japan posed by the growing Soviet long-range bomber forces in Northeast Asia. The Backfire bombers[4] increasingly drive the U.S. demands for air defense capabilities—for protection of its aircraft carriers, its land bases, and Japan.

3. The threat against sea lines of communication in the Pacific—both commercial and military—particularly that posed by the substantial Soviet attack (torpedo and cruise missile carrying) submarine force. Countering this perceived threat is the rationale for much of the U.S. naval forces in the Pacific—surface action groups, submarines, and maritime patrol aircraft.

To be sure, the United States perceives other threats that determine its requirements for forces in the Pacific; but these three, by
themselves, carry the burden of the U.S. force posture in the
region. As such, each deserves closer scrutiny.

## The Korean Peninsula

The invasion threat facing South Korea appears to be changing,
even though the geography of the peninsula is not, and the political
hostility that divides it seems glacial. The relative economic growth
of the two Koreas favors the South; the military postures that ride
on the backs of those economies may soon also favor the South.
The prospects for invasion between the two Koreas may actually
reverse in the next decade: "The two Koreas are no longer the weak
pawns of the past; the South, in particular, has considerable potential as a medium-sized power. By the 1990s, as the overall balance
of advantage—economic, diplomatic and military—swings in its
favor, it will be seen increasingly as a threat to the North—at least
by the North."[5] In the absence of Soviet or Chinese participation in
a North Korean invasion of the South, the ROK may soon be able
to stand on its own against the North. The American security
problem for the future may be damping the political ignition potential on the Korean Peninsula for larger Pacific conflicts, not the
maintenance of the military force balance there.

## The Backfire Bomber Threat

The Soviet long range bomber threat in Northeast Asia is really
most acute for the U.S. Naval aircraft carriers and their escorts
(collectively called carrier battle groups or CVBGs). Though the
Backfire bombers can certainly attack land bases, it is less clear that
their destructiveness against most ground targets would compensate
for their own losses. Their effectiveness, with conventional ordnance against command and control installations or air bases, is as
problematic as the effectiveness of our own bombers against comparable targets. Our long experience with bombers and bombing
suggests that such land targets tend to be difficult to destroy and, if
destroyed, are often more easily reparable or replaceable than the
bombers or crews lost in attacking them.

Against the carriers, however, the potential destructiveness of bombers with antiship missiles is worthy of almost suicidal losses.[6] But it is important to remember that, for the Soviets to bring their bombers to bear against the carriers, the CVBGs would have to be approaching within strike range of Soviet bases. Thus, the most severe threat posed by the Soviet long-range bombers is their ability to counter the strike threat posed against them by the U.S. CVBGs. The Backfire bombers are a problem only if we insist upon pushing our carriers under (or up) the Soviet nose, which is exactly what the Navy insists is its right: "The main threat to our fleet [as it moves forward] are the 'Backfires' and other missile-carrying aircraft of Soviet Naval Aviation. The United States cannot allow our adversary to assume he will be able to attack the fleet with impunity, from inviolable sanctuaries."[7] Note how the Navy asserts that it is the nation's duty not to allow the Soviets to attack the Navy's fleet—an example of the Navy's unique perception of its relationship to the U.S. government. Note also that the injunction is silent on why the fleet has to be moved forward and brought within range of the Backfires, so that it can threaten or attack the Soviets!

## The Sea Lanes Threat

Though the perceived Soviet threat to the Pacific sea lanes is most often portrayed as cutting the vital flow of resources, such as oil to Japan, closer examination suggests that the most threatened flows would be military forces and supplies moving into Northeast Asia from U.S. bases in and around the Pacific. Interruption of the flow of commerce and raw materials becomes a severe problem only if it persists for months and years.[8] But military forces and supplies must be moved within days or weeks if they are to be effectively employed; and much of these forces and supplies must be moved by ship. The prospects for a long war of attrition in the sea lanes between two nuclear-armed superpowers are arguable, to say the least. Thus, the Soviet threat to the sea lanes poses the most immediate and gravest effects, not for Pacific commerce, but for U.S. military forces and their employment in the Pacific. And the U.S. military posture is vulnerable to that threat mainly because it is based and deployed *forward* for overseas operations.

Thus, though the United States has successfully encouraged Japan to assume responsibility for protecting a portion of her own sea lanes, pointing to Japan's dependency upon the flow of oil, such burden sharing will more likely serve in crisis or conflict to protect U.S. military reinforcements and supplies and to relieve U.S. forces for offensive operations elsewhere.  Certainly, the expansion of the Japanese capabilities for sea lane protection serves the U.S. Navy's interests and plans in the Pacific.  And it must be welcomed by any nascent naval interests in Japan.  But it is less clear that it serves the Japanese well in the political perceptions of their uneasy neighbors to the south or their traditional enemies to the north and west.

## Offensive Postures Favored

Over the years, the U.S. military posture in the Pacific, led by the Navy, has been developed and deployed with a preference for offensive over defensive systems and operations.  The evidence can be seen in the following choices:

- the bulk of the American aircraft carriers, with decks devoted more to offensive strike aircraft than to defensive antisubmarine, early warning, or patrol capabilities for the protection of shipping;
- the preference for long-range fighter aircraft, which can be employed offensively, over surface-to-air missiles for the air defense of our allies in the region;
- the maintenance of significant amphibious (Marine) assault capabilities forward in the Western Pacific as opposed to the rear; and
- the stationing of ground-attack-capable F-16 aircraft (as opposed to interceptor-only models of the F-15) at Misawa in northern Honshu, where they are closer to Vladivostok and Sakhalin than they are to most of Korea.

These forces and deployments are matched, perhaps less obviously, in offensive concepts for their employment: The aircraft carriers are, first and foremost, the principal strike arm of the U.S. Navy.  It is they that would strike and sink an opposing fleet.  If the opposing fleet would not meet them at sea, then they would advance and strike it in its ports.  And having defeated the opposing naval forces at sea or in port, they would carry the attack to the enemy ashore.

The U.S. Air Force is doctrinally and tactically oriented toward using its aircraft offensively in the Pacific. It would prefer to "carry the war to the enemy" and to "seize the initiative" in offensive operations, whether against North Korea or the Soviet Union. Though the U.S. Air Force does not enjoy anywhere near the abundance of the U.S. Navy forces in the Pacific, even in numbers of airplanes, the types of Air Force aircraft, their deployments, munitions, and training, all speak to a preference for offensive rather than defensive operations against the "enemy."

It is only fair to ask if these offensive plans and posture are truly required by the regional threat, our security commitments there, or the limited forces available to us. In other words, do the offensive plans and posture in the Pacific reflect more the service's institutional interests or the nation's security interests? The answer depends upon:

- whether the services really have a choice between offensive and defensive postures;
- if they do, which one best serves American *military* capabilities; and
- whether the choice affects American regional security interests.

## Regional Implications

The U.S. preference for the offensive—in forces and in plans for their employment—probably makes the Soviets jittery about their vulnerabilities in the Pacific, which are substantial. Some might argue that making the Soviets jittery about their vulnerabilities is a good idea; others might argue that such a motive is not in the long-term interests of the United States or the other regional states. Nevertheless, the Soviet force posture speaks much more to Soviet vulnerabilities than opportunities in East Asia. The overriding security concern for the Soviets, outside the stability of their Eastern European bulwark against the West, has been (and remains) the sheer bulk of China as a border adversary. Much of the enormous buildup of Soviet military forces in East Asia reflects and is focused toward that concern. Only after attending to those larger concerns has it been possible for the Soviets to address their long-term vulnerabilities to U.S. initiatives in the Pacific.[9]

The offensive capabilities of the U.S. CVBGs, from the beginning of the Cold War, have been a reminder to the Soviets that they are subject to punishing, even humiliating, air strikes into their homeland, which they could not easily match in kind. The buildup of the naval Badger bombers was an earlier attempt to blunt that threat. Now the deployment of substantial numbers of naval Backfire bombers on the Pacific poses, perhaps for the first time, a credible counter to the freedom of the CVBGs to strike at will into Soviet East Asia.

The Soviets might reasonably perceive the deployment of F-16s at Misawa as a regeneration, in a new form, of the threat that they had hoped to counter with their Backfire deployments. The Soviet military commander in the Far East could reason that the F-16s at Misawa are a threat to their Backfire deployments which were, in turn, intended primarily as a counter to the threat of the CVBGs. The suggested spiral is more qualitative than quantitative: The CVBGs begat the Backfires, which begat the Misawa F-16s, which might logically beget Soviet conventionally armed ballistic missiles aimed at Japanese air bases. That spiral may be kept somewhat in balance as between the United States and Soviet Union, but Japan's security seems to be suffering with each escalation.

The Soviets have other vulnerabilities to be concerned about: They are not secure about the survivability of their ballistic missile-carrying submarines because of the technological prowess of American ASW (antisubmarine warfare) and the Navy's declared intention to attack their submarines,[10] even though the Soviets have developed missiles with sufficient range to keep their submarines close to home—in the Barents and Sea of Okhotsk. Much of the Soviet surface fleet, including the new carriers, seems to be aimed at preventing U.S. ASW forces from penetrating the bastions of their ballistic missile carrying submarines.[11]

And the Soviets probably remain insecure about their possession of the disputed islands in the Kurils. The Japanese persistence in their claim to the Northern Territories, even if not accompanied by any indication of their being willing or able to wrest them back by force, sustains the question of Soviet legitimacy there and feeds the historic Soviet fears about the adequacy of their security and stature. The character of recent reinforcements for the Soviet bases there suggests insecurity more than opportunity. Their territorial insecurity probably extends to Sakhalin and the Kamchatka Peninsula as well. They are aware, even more than we, just how isolated and vulnerable these areas are to invasion and occupation by the military might of the United States if it is supported by Japan.[12]

The Navy frequently cites the deployment and operation of Soviet forces out of Camranh Bay as evidence of Soviet opportunism associated with their force buildup in the Pacific. That evidence might be more alarming if Camranh Bay were serving as a base for projecting significant Soviet military power into the region, but so far it seems to be used only to keep track and limit the freedom of U.S. naval forces to project their power into the same region. The vulnerability of Camranh Bay to U.S. military forces in the region, in the event of war, does not seem to be in much doubt on either side.

China probably finds itself the most ambivalent of the regional powers about the U.S. force posture in the Pacific. As a counterbalance to their most salient threat, the Chinese want to see America as a powerful and preoccupying adversary for the Soviet Union. But they do not want the United States to be so powerful as to pursue its own hegemonic interests in Asia to China's detriment; nor do they want the Americans to be disturbing the peace of the region with military provocations or adventures. For these reasons, China would probably prefer to see a U.S. force posture that was more offensive at the global (or intercontinental) level and more defensive regionally, in the Pacific. Thus, the character of China's relationship with the Soviets may be more affected by the strength of the U.S. strategic force posture, whereas its relationship with the United States may be more influenced by the qualities of the U.S. Pacific force posture.

For Japan, the dilemma posed by the offensive nature of the U.S. force posture is more acute: It, even more than South Korea, is dependent upon the U.S. military presence for security against the portentous coercive threat of the Soviet Union. Yet, the offensive character of the U.S. force posture necessarily presents a source of concern for them in peace or war. In peacetime, Japan, along with others, such as Australia and New Zealand, sees the offensive character of the U.S. posture as inviting military adventurism or aggressive behavior that could bring the region into a conflict threatening its security. In crisis or war, particularly one involving the two superpowers, the notion of the Americans conducting offensive strikes from Japan into the Soviet Union raises terrifying prospects of a larger, more violent war and of reprisals against Japan as the host of the attacking forces. On the other hand, defense of Japan against such attacks, if initiated by the Soviet Union, carries no such burden of escalation.


## Military Implications

Even if the regional political implications did not mitigate against offensive postures, there are good military reasons for being cautious about relying upon them. Almost all the offensive operations that might be contemplated by the United States in the Pacific would have to be conducted by means of aircraft, either carrier or land based. Offensive air operations against defended targets, in the absence of surprise or overwhelming superiority, have historically been costly in losses and marginal in their effectiveness.[13] For example, the U.S. Air Force F-16 fighter-bomber aircraft in Japan, even though compromised in their performance by their dual roles, would probably be much more effective against the Soviet long range bomber threat if they were used in purely defensive (intercept) operations instead of in offensive strikes against the bomber bases.

Obviously, there are some significant advantages to offensive over defensive military postures—for deterrence as opposed to denial, for posing or truncating a threat that ties down forces, and even for efficiency in the use of military force. But these are the more traditional rationales for the traditional offensive postures preferred by the Navy and the Air Force and, therefore, are expressed more often than they are scrutinized. Since such offensive postures are two-edged swords, politically and militarily, they deserve much more careful examination before being accepted as the only or the best solutions for U.S. military objectives in the Pacific.

The U.S. preference for certain kinds of weapons rubs off on (or is urged upon) allies, of course.[14] The selection of weapon systems by U.S. allies is heavily influenced by the military-to-military institutional liaisons, along with some self-interest and aggressive support of the U.S. arms industry. Some doubt that the F-16 is the best solution for the modernization of the ROK aircraft inventory because of its cost and complex support requirements. One might also question whether the F-15 is the best solution for Japanese air defenses: Long-endurance (turboprop) aircraft fitted with air-to-air missiles and fire-controls (like the Phoenix and AWG-9) and good early-warning radars (like the one on the E-2) would appear to be a much better match to Japan's geographically focused air defense problem, much more harmonious with its established aircraft industry, and clearly, unambiguously more defensive in nature. But it is an approach to air defense the U.S. military institutions have long and consistently rejected as being culturally unattractive.[15]

## Qualitative Options

It can be argued that it is not possible to adopt a military posture, in the Pacific or elsewhere, that is clearly defensive and not offensive, given the flexibility and power of modern weaponry. Though it is true that weapons are not offensive or defensive, per se—that their use determines their character—nevertheless, some weapons are perceived to be more likely than others to be employed for offensive operations. Among those in the Pacific whose offensive strike potential is most evident are:

- the CVBGs with strike aircraft such as the A-6;
- long-range strike aircraft such as the B-52s at Guam;
- amphibious and airborne assault forces;
- short-range strike aircraft based forward, such as the F-16s at Misawa; and
- land-attack cruise missiles, whether carried by truck, aircraft, submarines, or ships.

By way of contrast, forces whose offensive strike potential is limited include:

- maritime patrol aircraft, such as the P-3;
- surface-to-air missiles, such as the Hawk;
- aircraft carriers largely devoted to antisubmarine aircraft, such as the S-3, and reconnaisance aircraft, such as the E-2; and
- air defense and antisubmarine ships, when operated as pickets or barriers independently of the attack carriers or amphibious assault forces.

Though many other forces—such as aerial tanking, mobility forces, and naval surface action groups—constitute the U.S. military posture in the Pacific, those cited above appear to be the most likely to influence the posture's perceived character as being offensive or defensive. The balancing among these choices, more than their collective quantity, may be the most important determinant of security in the Pacific.

A less offensive and more defensive U.S. military posture in the Pacific might involve the following changes:

1. A shift in the emphasis of aircraft carriers toward defense of the sea lanes and away from land attack or "force projection" missions. It would involve shifting their deck loadings to antisubmarine, reconnaisance, and maritime attack aircraft at the expense of ground attack and interceptor aircraft. Even more antithetical to the Navy, it might, as well, point to smaller and fewer carriers in the Pacific.

2. A substantial increase, perhaps as much as 50 percent, in maritime patrol aircraft, such as the P-3, for antisubmarine and sea lanes protection. But these land-based patrol aircraft, despite their effectiveness in antisubmarine warfare, have never enjoyed the stature of carrier-based aviation in the Navy.

3. A much greater reliance, probably severalfold, on surface-to-air missiles for the air defense of Japanese, Korean, and U.S. bases in the Pacific. It would permit some reduction in interceptor aircraft, which have a greater potential for supporting or conducting offensive air operations.

4. Rearward basing of offensive forces, such as amphibious assault forces and long-range strike aircraft. It is not easily demonstrated that these forces must be deployed forward in order for them to be brought to bear in a timely fashion in a conflict with the Soviet Union, with all that such a conflict would portend for global and nuclear violence. Indeed, it is not clear that U.S. forward bases, particularly in the Philippines, but also in Japan, any longer represent an overall benefit to U.S. regional interests, even as they remain vital to U.S. Navy and Air Force interests there.

Though such changes in the U.S. military force posture might actually make it more effective in the event of conflict and might make it better serve national and regional security interests in the Pacific, they would be perceived, especially by the Navy and, to a lesser degree, by the Air Force, as counter to the American military institutional interests in systems and operations. For that reason, they are not likely to suggest or promote them. In the Pacific and elsewhere, the reality is that the military institutions will be the ultimate arbiters of the force qualities, whereas the political institutions will control only the force quantities through the budget. So long as that division of responsibility persists, the quality of force postures will change very slowly in peacetime.

Though the quantity of forces is much debated and the quantitative force balances are much measured, the tone of Pacific security—for enemies and allies alike—is probably more affected by the quality of the force postures there. Given the long term offensive character of the U.S. force posture in the Pacific, it is not clear whether the Soviet force posture in the Far East is independently becoming more offensive in its character or is responsively becoming a more effective counter to the U.S. posture. Some would say it does not matter which because significant offensive capabilities are now latent in the Soviet posture.

But it may matter in the following sense: If the Soviet force posture in the Far East is primarily an effort to achieve a favorable offensive balance of forces for the Soviet Union, perhaps the better to intimidate her neighbors, then further buildups may be in lock step with U.S. offensive forces in the Pacific, unless one believes that the Soviets will exhaust themselves before the United States in that race. But if the Soviet force posture in the Far East is primarily to counter or neutralize the offensive forces opposing them, then changes in the qualitative character of the U.S. force posture toward a defensive stance might have a moderating effect on Soviet deployments. But how could anyone tell? Unfortunately, the action-reaction times for such changes are so extended and confounded by other events, on political and global dimensions, that the cause-and-effect can only be argued and not proven.

Nevertheless, quite apart from Soviet reactions, if the United States were to move its military force posture toward defensive rather than offensive systems and deployments, it could have favorable effects upon the perceptions and security of its friends and allies in the Pacific, and even upon the effectiveness of its military response if one became necessary. But, more likely, if the United States persists in its past approach to military postures in the Pacific, it will find itself with increasingly fragile options—options that are unpalatable to its own political leadership, unacceptable to its allies, and even unattractive to its highest military leaders, those who ultimately must contemplate the gains and losses in blood and destruction.

# Part V
# Prospects

# 16

# THE ARMY'S IDENTITY CRISIS

The international and American security arenas are now undergoing a number of simultaneous changes likely to confront the Army, perhaps even more than its sister services, with difficult choices in the near future. These changes include:

- the prospects of declining military budgets;
- an expanding scope of arms control agreements;
- shifting perceptions of alliance obligations, American interests, and the threats to those interests; and
- evolutions, if not revolutions, in the technical, institutional, and social environments in which the Army functions.

All the services will find themselves battered by these changes, but they are likely to prove more difficult for the Army to deal with because its sense of identity:

- was skewed by its experiences during World War II;
- has been frozen there by the interests of its powerful branch structure; and
- appears to be inappropriate, if not inadequate, for the circumstances of the nuclear era.

The compounding experiences of the two world wars have left the Army with a strong and positive image of itself in the role of defender and liberator of Europe. Late in World War I, the Army, forged from citizen soldiers and led by regulars, went to Europe as an expeditionary force and, with allies, defeated the enemy. Between the two world wars, the Army continued in its role as "the government's obedient handyman,"[1] quelling the veterans' riots, patrolling the Mexican border, running the CCC (Civilian Conservation Corps) camps during the Depression, and so on. Without the positive, reinforcing experience of World War II, the Army might have seen its exploits in World War I, like those in the Spanish American War twenty years earlier, as simply another of its military chores for the nation.

But the experience of the Army in its final and finest year of World War II, from the invasion of France to the collapse of Nazi Germany, made an impression that has persisted with remarkable tenacity and effect right down to the present. The Army's experiences in Korea and Vietnam have been relegated to unpleasant aberrations—the wrong kinds of wars because of political constraints or lack of public support. The suggestion that the Army's experience in World War II was the aberration, and that such peripheral conflicts might be the only kind of wars the Army will be asked (or permitted) to fight in the nuclear era, has probably been rejected unconsciously, not because it is clearly wrong, but because it undermines a much more satisfying self-image.

Is the Army overly fixed on a Central European war? Some dissenters point to the many aspects of the Army oriented elsewhere: the Southern Command (for Latin America) and Central Command (for Southwestern Asia) the Army forces in South Korea, the Rangers, Airborne, and Special Forces. Similar arguments can be offered up to counter the claim that the Navy is overly fixed on big aircraft carriers. But the existence of adjunct capabilities in the Navy, such as land-based patrol (VP) aircraft, says nothing about where the mainstream of the Navy flows— about its first love, its first priority, or who really runs the Navy. Despite interests elsewhere in the Army, the part of the Army configured for the main battle of Central Europe is, I think, the mainstream Army—that is its first love and priority.

Despite the Army's focus on preparations to refight the battle for Central Europe, its actual duties throughout the nuclear era have been a continuation of the "handyman" list started by Huntington: The Army has participated in a diversity of tasks—occupying Japan and Germany, fighting the Korean War (a "U.N. police action"), standing guard on the inter-German and Korean borders, defending South Vietnam, invading Grenada, and interdicting drugs in Bolivia. The list of the future—just from today's news, let alone tomorrow's—might very well include interventions in Latin America, the Western Pacific, arms treaty verification, or without too much imagination, a U.N. pacification of South Africa. None of this long list of duties—for the recent past or the likely future—

includes the war toward which the Army has devoted so much of its energies and equipment designs. Whether or not the Army likes the image or label, it has been, is, and will likely continue to be the nation's obedient and loyal military servant. Its remembrance of itself as the defender and liberator of Europe may make for nice memories; but it is not a realistic image for the present.

The Army's image of fighting its big war in Central Europe is doubly unrealistic. First, a conflict there is unlikely, for reasons that have much more to do with the vitality of the interests of four nuclear-armed nations than with the conventional forces any of them has stationed there. Second, the Army's ability to affect the outcome of any serious conflict there through its peacetime posture or actions is totally disproportionate to the resources required or available.[2]

I have argued earlier, in chapter 12, that the Army's excessive focus on a Central European conflict cannot be explained or justified by either the probability or the consequences of a conflict there, or even by the Army's ability to deter or contribute to such a conflict. The Army may claim that its posture in the Federal Republic of Germany has been the bulwark to the deterrence of war in Central Europe for the past forty years; but it would be easier to argue that the Soviets have been much more deterred by the prospect of nuclear war in any conflict over such vital interests as Europe, even if no American forces were present. Though there are historical and political reasons for the U.S. military presence in Europe—as there are for the U.S. forces on the Korean Peninsula—they are not the same as the Army's reasons for wanting to design itself to fight a major war there.

The litmus test for the Army and its presence in Europe goes something like this: Would the Army, as an institution, be happy if our NATO allies really stepped up to the challenge of defending Western Europe and said, "America, thank you very much, now you can take your troops back home again if you like"? At that moment of truth, the Army might admit, realistically and in pain, that it is concerned about a withdrawal of U.S. forces from Europe because the withdrawn forces may be lost—not reconstituted—when they come home. But the Army is unlikely to admit that the forces in and for Europe are ultimately what drive the rationale for the kind of army the Army wants to be. For the Army, Europe is the only invitation it will get to the prom of its fondest memories.

## The Frozen Image

To let go of fond memories and to confront the realities are not simple for individuals or institutions. Even if the separation between the dream and reality is recognized, it may still be terribly painful to let go of the dream in order to serve the reality. The Prom Queen may have more need for a vacuum cleaner than a ball gown; but she would prefer to identify herself with the latter. The Army may have more need for linguistic skills than main battle tanks; but that is not how the Army would like to imagine itself or its needs. To the extent that neither can let go of dreams, the realities may become increasingly punishing.

The problem for the Army in adjusting its self-image to the realities of the nuclear era is more than suffering the pain of letting go of fond memories of itself: The Army, like most large institutions, is a captive of its own internal fiefdoms. The guilds of the Army—its branches, particularly the powerful combat arms branches—freeze the Army by their understandable interests in maintaining the continuity and stability of internal power. Any change in the Army poses a potential threat to the internal balance of the branches; the branches, therefore, will instinctively move to paralyze the Army leadership against changes.

The other services have not been trapped by their internal structures in the same way that the Army has been by the stable balance of power among its three traditional combat arms branches—the infantry, artillery, and cavalry (now armor). The Navy has experienced a shift of power and control over the institution—from the battleship admirals to the aviators in World War II, with the submariners now increasingly challenging for its leadership. The independent Air Force was conceived by the bomber pilots who prevailed over the pursuit (fighter) interests in the Army Air Force; but forty years later, the tactical pilots have ascended to leadership. In the Army, however, the three traditional guilds, in a fraternal embrace of interdependencies in combat, have created a remarkably stable troika of control over the Army that shows no sign of weakening. The Army ethic, with its distaste for elites and its devotion to both fraternalism and the notion of "One Army," may have contributed to its frozen stability.

The Army's agonies over the light divisions is a case in point: Whatever the merits or faults of the concept, light divisions threaten the balance of power among infantry, armor, and artillery in favor of infantry. The maintenance of that balance by the three branches is the key to the control of the Army: Unlike the aviators in the Navy, or the bomber pilots in the emerging Air Force, no single branch is sufficiently powerful, by itself, to run the Army. But the three traditional (senior) combat arms branches, by their fraternal relationship and mutual protection of one another's turf, can collectively retain the power over the other branches and, hence, run the Army. To permit any significant shift in the balance among the three would undermine the fraternity and mutual protection enjoyed by the three; and the control would soon collapse. For the Army to shift its focus away from a conflict in Central Europe would almost surely undercut the need for heavy armor and artillery. So even if the Army leadership sees the need for changing the Army's image of itself and, therefore, its combat focus, it will almost certainly face collective, internal resistance from its strongest components.

Dealing with the internal interests that now freeze the Army into its focus on conflict in Central Europe is probably the most important institutional problem confronting Army leadership in the next decade. If the Army cannot break itself free from the current grip of its own internal power balancing, then events outside the Army will probably force the fracture. The fracture could be painful, if not tragic, for the Army because it could find itself suddenly stripped of any ability to maintain pretenses toward its preferred self-image. The loss of self-image because of externals is likely to be much more traumatic than a deliberate, internal changing of images.

Budget reductions, arms control agreements, and changing perceptions of both our alliance commitments and the Soviet threat, all point toward the future possibility of troop withdrawals from Europe. At some point, the role of U.S. forces in Europe will have to be reconciled with their size, the destructive pace of modern warfare, and the possession of ample stocks of central strategic nuclear weapons by at least four of the nations involved. These are not new realities; but up to now, the Army has been a willing accomplice in the political avoidance of their confrontation in European security arrangements. Any significant withdrawal of U.S. forces from Europe will demand a new accounting; and the future role of the U.S. Army there is almost certainly not going to be that of the principal defender of Central Europe. Its role there is likely to become similar to that which it long ago accepted in South Korea: sufficient presence, position, and capabilities to ensure that the United States will become militarily involved in the conflict and will have a political stake in its outcome.

If outside events make the Army's role in Europe the equivalent of its present role in South Korea, will the Army then be forced to confront a different, perhaps truer, image of itself? Two of the three powerful, traditional branches—armor and artillery—will resist, of course. The infantry and the other branches may not. Indeed, the elite units—the rangers, airborne, and special combat units—will probably rejoice at the prospect of greater attention being paid to those conflicts and contingencies which they, and the Army, are most likely to face.

## Shifting Images

If such re-imaging is likely to be forced upon the Army by external developments, is there any advantage to the Army in taking the initiative? The impediments to shifting the Army self-image—the internal difficulties and pain—are evident, but the advantages to the Army of instigating the shift on its own are less clear. If the alternative images are obviously more attractive than being "Europe's protector," the advantages of shifting will be easily identified. But if the historical role of the Army as the nation's obedient and loyal military servant is closer to the new image, would the Army gain anything by precipitating the shift any earlier than absolutely necessary? The role of the "good servant" or "handyman" certainly does not appear to be as inspiring as that of defender and liberator of Europe.

I would argue that there is more opportunity for initiative and pride in the role of the good servant than is at first apparent. To use the analogy, the good servant not only does his master's bidding, but also anticipates his master's bidding: He uses his initiative and expertise to anticipate what his master will likely demand of him in the future and then prepares himself so that he can ably carry out that demand.[3] He does not rely entirely upon his master to anticipate needs or demands; he may even discover that what his master thinks might be needed and what his master actually ends up demanding are two different things; he focuses his attention on the latter. The good servant is not judged on his ability to deliver what the master might ask of him; he is judged on his ability to do what is asked of him.

To illustrate the point with the circumstances of a house servant: If a master most often expresses his expectation of fifty for dinner, yet never has more than six and, in fact, does not even have the capacity to serve more than a dozen, should the good servant permit the quality of his dinner service for the few to be seriously degraded because of his efforts to accommodate his master's continued expectation of the many? The good servant will devote his greatest efforts to those duties which are most likely to be demanded of him and which his master will expect him to perform most ably. And the good servant will warn his master of which duties are likely to be beyond his capacity to perform with the resources that are available to him. Yet, if the servant takes great pride in the possession of grand arrays of silver, crystal, and china, based upon his memories of a grander time, he may be tempted to co-opt his master's expectation of fifty for dinner as justification for acquiring and maintaining the table settings. His choice will depend upon the principal source of his pride and initiative: Is it in service or possessions?

Can the Army honestly and courageously differentiate between its institutional interests and those of the nation? If one looks at the sweep of history, the answer must be an emphatic yes. The Army, more than either of its sister services, has sacrificed its blood, comfort, and popularity for the needs of the nation—actual or as perceived by the body politic. "[I]t always has been and will be the Army's role to expand and contract and otherwise change internal form as needed to serve the democracy."[4] If the Army has ever failed in that separation of interests, it would seem to be in the forty-odd years since World War II, when the Army appears to have first aspired to a new identity—not the nation's servant, but Europe's protector.

Is the Army truly willing to anticipate the nation's likely needs? to take the initiative in preparing for the demands on the Army? to warn if the available assets are insufficient for the demands? It was up to World War II; at the deepest levels of the Army consciousness, that spirit or ethos probably remains intact.

The military operations that the nation has actually asked its Army to undertake during the entirety of the nuclear era are:

- to maintain an American military presence as evidence of a commitment to the defense of allies who face immediate threats on their borders,

- to intervene militarily in areas where America has no presence but has real or declared interests that have been threatened, and
- to act as the military agent of the U.S. government in the prevention or relief of disorders and disasters.

Of the three, I would argue that the second is the most important and most likely contingency—the one for which the Army must be creatively prepared to act quickly and ably. In areas where the Army already has an established presence for the defense of allies, the probability of direct conflict with a nuclear-armed adversary is not only reduced—the Army is no longer the salient force if conflict should occur. Though the presence of Army forces may deter conflict, it is not their size or capabilities that deter so much as it is their unavoidable involvement in any conflict, which, in turn, invokes the shadow of nuclear weapons. This relationship between interposing military presence and deterrence implies that, in many contingencies in which we have no military presence, establishing an Army presence quickly may be much more important than its size or its actual fighting capabilities.

If the Army, with the resources it has been given, cannot successfully defend Berlin, West Germany, or South Korea against the full onslaught of our adversaries, few would be surprised or remonstrate the Army for its manifestly inadequate capabilities. But, if the Army, with those same resources, cannot successfully intervene against third-world forces to preserve American interests, many will be surprised and will be quick to remonstrate the Army for the inadequacies in its planning, training, doctrine, and equipment. Thus, the Army, which intends to be the nation's obedient and loyal military servant, ought to be best and most prepared to intervene militarily in areas where America has no presence but does have declared interests that might be threatened. And, that is a significantly different Army from the one we have today.

Conflicts requiring American military intervention are not likely to be winnable by the means now configured for the main battle of Central Europe. For example the greatest contribution that the Army might make in many third world conflicts would be to support indigenous forces with information in the form of surveillance, reconnaisance, intelligence, communications, and analysis through small, high-tech units. That, clearly, is a direction that would be vigorously resisted by the traditional combat arms branches. Yet, it is a direction that history, technology, and even common sense seem to commend.

In areas where the demand for an American military presence is to serve as a bulwark against the threat of a nuclear-armed opponent—as in West Germany and Berlin—defeat of the enemy is no longer a reasonable military objective. Instead, those forces have become, like the homeland cities from which they spring, hostages to the enormous power of destruction on each side. Thus, two roles the nation has previously asked its Army to fulfill are no longer relevant in the nuclear era:

- to defeat its principal (i.e., nuclear-armed) adversaries overseas, and
- to defend the territorial integrity of the United States against its principal adversaries.

The existence of nuclear weapons in large quantities has made these two roles highly improbable. To attempt the invasion or defeat of a nuclear-armed state is now a naked invitation to one's own destruction. We are therefore unlikely to attempt to defeat our principal adversaries, and they are unlikely to attempt to challenge our territorial integrity. When nuclear-armed powers collide, it is the vitality of their interests and the shadows of their nuclear weapons, much more than the force balance at the collision point, that will determine their behavior. This reality of the nuclear era may now be more widely appreciated by political leaderships than by the military. That gap in understanding needs to be reversed, especially within the Army, for the Army's own sake.

# 17

---

# IMPLICATIONS FOR THE FUTURE

If this exploration of the institutional personalities of the American military services has any utility, it is in understanding those personalities well enough to recognize them in their behavior and, therefore, to predict their behavior. If those personality characteristics are strong and persistent, and if the American military services are the most powerful institutions afoot in the national security arena, then they should be powerful guides to future events in that arena.

## The Services and Nuclear Weapons

The service personalities described here have no fundamental affection for nuclear weapons. Their affections, if for things at all, are for the more traditional vehicles or platforms for war, particularly those that must be manned for war. Nuclear weapons may make some of these vehicles or platforms more effective or more justifiable, but the services have no greater intrinsic love for nuclear weapons than they do for a Mark 82 "iron bomb" or a 155-mm projectile.

Nuclear weapons were the instruments that finally made the dreams of the air power theorists possible. Up until 1945, the theory that air power, by itself, could be decisive in war remained a theory whose proof was arguable. But with the dropping of the atomic bombs on Japan, few could doubt that air power, with this kind of bomb, could be a decisive instrument of war, all by itself.[1] It was to be expected that the air power advocates within the Army Air Force would be the first to embrace nuclear weapons, not because they liked them or even understood them, but because they finally justified the concept of aerial bombardment that, in turn, justified the big airplanes they loved. The story of the Air Force and the Strategic Air Command in their early years is one of an institution riding into its independent future, sitting on the saddle of a theory that could finally be carried by a horse called nuclear weapons. Any other horse that could have carried the burden would have done as well for the Air Force.

One of the Air Force's early worries was that atomic bombs did not require thousand-plane raids; but the planes were getting bigger and faster, and quality was always more important than quantity for American pilots. The Strategic Air Command built a powerful fiefdom based upon the air power theory taken to the extreme: Air power could be made so awesomely destructive (decisive) that it would never have to be used—just acquired, maintained, trained, and exercised—all the things pilots really wanted to do with their splendid machines.

All the time, the Air Force's love affair was with the airplanes, not the atomic bombs that served as their justification, twice removed. But when all of the necessary airplanes had been acquired, the only institutional excitement was the prospect of the next new airplane: After the B-52, there would be the double-sonic B-58 (an expensive disappointment), the triple-sonic B-70 (canceled by McNamara), a shot-gun marriage to the FB-111, and a long lustful chase after the elusive B-1. Much of the romance began to slip out of the Strategic Air Command with the advent of ballistic missiles in the late 1950s; with them, came the Navy's nose under the tent flap with its Polaris Fleet Ballistic Missile program. By the late 1960s, certainly by the early 1970s, the pilots of the Air Force saw the future excitement elsewhere—in tactical aviation, specifically in fighters. Even for those in the Air Force more interested in missiles than airplanes, the Minuteman, like the B-52, appeared to be the high water mark of the Strategic Air Command.

If the Air Force is, in the future, confronted with arms control measures or budget cuts that reduce the nation's inventory of either nuclear weapons or delivery vehicles, or both, its response will be highly sensitive to the effect upon its airplanes, not the number of bombs or ballistic missiles. If the Air Force can elect its cuts, the ballistic missiles will go first. Therefore, one would expect the so-called Midgetman missile development program to be triply vulnerable:

1. It is a missile and not an airplane program.
2. It will provide a smaller, less capable "bird" than the big MX missile the Air Force had long sought as an advancement over the old Minuteman missile (i.e, bigger is one measure of better in missilery).
3. It will generate substantial future "streams" of costs because it has not yet been acquired.

Thus, despite the Scowcroft Commission's call for a small missile and Congress's affection for its lack of the counterforce or first-strike qualities they attributed to the MX, the mainstream Air Force would probably just as soon see that baby die in its crib.[2]

The Air Force would probably not object at all to reductions in the number of missiles if it were to be accompanied by increases in the number of bombers. Indeed, the devil's bait for the Air Force would be to promise it a new bomber in exchange for reductions in missiles or nuclear weapons. The personality sketched here would suggest that it could not resist a new airplane of its choice.

And of all the services or their factions, none has embraced nuclear weapons as comfortably as the Strategic Air Command. The Tactical Air Command is certainly prepared to use them, but shows no particular affection for them.

The mainstream Navy has, for the most part, rejected nuclear warfare as irrelevant to the kind of navy and naval forces it cares most about. The Navy's ballistic missile submarines are a triumph for sea-based strategic forces, but they make for boring naval forces and missions. A world with reduced reliance upon nuclear weapons is not one that worries the institutional Navy personality. Indeed, the mainstream Navy might welcome such a world even if it resulted in cutting back its fleet of ballistic missile submarines, which has been a drain on its budget and its most skilled people.

The Army has evidenced no love for nuclear weapons even as it has obediently taken them up in a wide variety of forms, from mines to air defense, from artillery shells to ballistic missiles. The Army would not weep if it were told to rely less on nuclear weapons or upon fewer of them, for several reasons:

- The Army has fewer vehicles that are strictly nuclear in character.
- Nuclear weapons are typically adjuncts or alternate "rounds" for the Army to use in conjunction with its traditional forces.
- The Army sees itself as the military servant of the nation and will make do with or use whatever it is given to use or ordered to do.

Senior Army officers may speak to the point of the nation's security if nuclear weapons are reduced or removed; but they will show or have little institutional concerns about such a decision.

These institutional personalities suggest that nuclear weapons are not generally central to the services' self-images. They can probably be reduced or taken away from the services without much fuss if attention is paid to the effects upon their real interests in airplanes, ships, and divisions. If those vital interests are affected, one should expect the Air Force to be the most concerned because more of the things it cherishes have been justified on the basis of nuclear weapons delivery. But the degree of the Air Force's resistance will depend upon whether its airplanes, rather than its missiles, are to be cut, and, unfortunately, its arguments will be couched in terms of national security rather than its deeper (and legitimate) concerns about airplanes and flying.

Those who would reduce nuclear weapons, or the means for delivering them, might further their cause by giving greater consideration to the vital interests of the institutions that have been entrusted with them. If the reductions are to be forced down the throats of the services solely in what some perceive to be the interests of national security and without regard to the institutional interests of the services, they will be confronted with some very effective adversaries who are well prepared to argue the opposite case in terms of national security interests. But if the reductions are "sweetened" with compensating institutional benefits, such as more airplanes, ships, or divisions, the services will probably support them. To be sure, some factional interests are bound to be affected by any change, and some will complain or protest; but the mainstream interests of the services should be reckoned with and addressed if arms reductions are to be successfully pursued.

Some will find the above suggestion objectionable—that the services would put their own institutional interests above that of the nation's security, or that the nation should pander to the services' self interests. I will defend the suggestion by noting that if the services have unique institutional personalities—the central premise of this book—then they should be treated as persons and not as gods or as perfect, altruistic things. If people are treated with care as to their self interests, even if those self-interests are not admired or even shared, then so should institutions who have developed a personality. To treat the services, or any other institutions, as if they were somehow more perfect, more noble than the people who compose them is to court deception on both sides of the relationship.

The masks of war that the services hold up before their faces to explain or justify their deeper self-interests is one side of a mutual deception. The other side is treating the services as more than human, just as people often do with their medical doctors.

## Whither Star Wars?

Understanding the services as institutions that are, in peacetime at least, compelled to pursue their own interests even as they attempt to fulfill their obligations to the nation's security provides a basis for understanding and predicting their behavior in future situations. President Reagan's initiative for the development of a protective shield against ballistic missiles—the so-called Star Wars or Strategic Defense Initiative (SDI)—offers a clear and unambiguous opportunity to forecast events on the basis of the institutional interests of the services.

Whatever its merits or fallacies, promises or dangers, President Reagan's call for SDI has set in motion a significant program of research that will amost inevitably lead those most deeply involved or committed to the program to urge its conversion into system development and, if that be successful, into force deployment. Those two future situations, the conversion of Star Wars research into systems or forces, will require that one or more of the military services assume responsibility for its development and deployment. So long as Star Wars remains in the research stage, it can be a protected child of the Department of Defense. The research establishments within the services may participate in that research; they may even run the research programs through the posting of some of their officers.

But once that research is converted to development, its program ownership must change from that of the research community or the Department of Defense to the mainstreams of the services themselves. The change is due to the requirement that the development of modern weapon systems anticipate their operation or use by the services. Weapons can only be designed, developed, and deployed by those who must command, use, and support them. Star Wars, if it is developed at all, must eventually belong to one of the three services (or a fourth service must be created to be its owner). When that conversion occurs, Star Wars will have to compete as a concept, system, weapon, and force with all the other mainstream interests of the service that has assumed its ownership. It is then that Star Wars will really have to fight for its existence.

The ownership of Star Wars, if it includes heavy reliance upon space systems, is most likely to pass to the Air Force. The Army is likely to have a subordinate role, if any, in the ownership of any ground-based weaponry. How are those two services likely to react? The answer is best found by thinking about how the ownership of Star Wars is likely to affect their institutional interests. And when doing that, one must look look beyond the common characteristics attributed to institutions in general—to the unique personalities of the services. For example, most institutions are seen as seeking growth, power, and prestige, among other things. On that basis, any of the services, as institutions, should welcome the acquisition and ownership of Star Wars; it should afford them growth, power, and new prestige. And, from that, one might suppose that the services would compete for the ownership of Star Wars. But, like the generalization that "everyone wants to have a bigger house," it fails to take into account the personality of a particular institution. There may be those—when one looks closely enough to see who they are and what they are about—who do not want a bigger house or who have much higher priorities to serve than a bigger house.

The Air Force is not about growth, power, or prestige in the abstract; it is about flying and flying machines. For the Air Force, there cannot be too much of flying and anything less than the very best flying machines that technology can provide. Other things, such as institutional growth, power, or prestige are then of interest primarily as means or adjuncts to the ends of flight. If they adversely affect flying or flying machines, they are impediments to the Air Force's vision of who it is and what it wants to be. From that perspective, the ownership of Star Wars is not an unalloyed prize for the Air Force.

Though conveyance of the deed to Star Wars might be accompanied by a budget increment, initially, none of the services would expect that budget advantage to persist very long—certainly not so long as the obligations of its ownership. Eventually, the costs of Star Wars would have to be taken out of the Air Force's share of the defense budget, whatever that might be at the moment. This is precisely the situation the Navy found itself in with its Fleet Ballistic Missile (FBM) program: Initially, the ownership of a fleet of submarines carrying ballistic missiles was welcomed by the Navy as an opportunity to expand its submarine fleet and to expand its role in (perhaps eventually even dominate) the long-range strategic nuclear forces. However, after ten or so years, the Navy found itself paying for an expensive force that was not at the center of its real institutional interests: the forces to defeat the Soviet Navy at sea, the forces centered on the large carrier battle groups. Since then, the Navy would have preferred that someone else (i.e., the Department of Defense) pay for the costs of those forces, that they not be paid for out of the Navy's slice of the defense budget, or that the Navy receive an additional compensatory allotment in the budget to pay for them. The Navy has, apparently, gone so far as to argue that point, noting that these forces, after all, serve the country more than the Navy—a remarkable separation of its interests from those of the nation, but not inconsistent with the Navy's personality! "Many naval officers . . . are convinced that the FBM Program came out of the hide of the Navy, that the opportunities forgone for the Polaris were naval opportunities. . . . Complaints that the Secretary of Defense had promised the Navy that the ballistic missile programs would be funded independently of *the regular allocations* were of no avail; the Navy had to make part of the initial investment."[3]

Though Star Wars is, as conceived, high-technology weaponry, and the Air Force worships technology, Star Wars is not airplanes or flying. If Star Wars necessarily involved sending manned flying machines into space and back (as in the so-called aerospaceplane concept), the Air Force could develop some enthusiasm. But if it involves sending unmanned spacecraft into orbit, then there is little to draw the Air Force beyond the technology. Although the Air Force includes "space cadets" and "technology freaks" among its factions, they are not the mainstream or close to the heart of the institution. The ownership of Star Wars by the Air Force would produce institutional reactions that are similar to those induced by its ownership of ICBMs. Ballistic missiles are a spliced-on stepchild for the Air Force as compared to its favored-child affection for airplanes. If a budget crunch forces it to cut back, the Air Force will propose cancellation of a ballistic missile program before cancellation of a bomber or fighter program.

Eventually, programs not at the heart of an institution's interests will come into competition for that institution's limited resources. Then, those programs will suffer, regardless of the enthusiasm of their initial sponsors or of the loyal faction that gathers around them. To flourish, such programs need strong and continuous protection within the institution. That is the history lesson provided by Billy Mitchell, Hyman Rickover, and John Medaris. Outside protection, from Congress or the Department of Defense, may work for a while; but when backs are turned, even for a moment, the institution will have its day and way.

The Army, if deeded part ownership of Star Wars, would probably be no more enthusiastic than the Air Force, but for different reasons and interests, and with different effects. Within the Army, the ground-based components of Star Wars would fall outside the purview of its three dominant combat arms—infantry, armor, and artillery—which have historically defined the Army. Though the Army is organizationally prepared to participate in strategic defense of the country and in ballistic missile defenses generally, the organizational elements are the vestiges of the Army's Nike air defense— thence Safeguard ABM—programs,[4] which have never been close to the mainstream interests of the Army as an institution. The Army has generally been better than its sister services in broad support for all of its branches and factions—mainstream or not—but if faced with severe budget cuts, it would probably rather keep its division flags than build ballistic missile defenses. On the other hand, the Army, in its self-image as the nation's loyal and obedient military servant, would probably be the most compliant of the three services in shouldering the duties of strategic defense.

The introduction of the modern ballistic missile into the services in the 1950s offers some insight into institutional behavior of the services when confronted with new technological initiatives. Although all the services had some factional interests in ballistic missiles, they were vested in minorities that had more in common with one another than they did with their parent services. None of the services evidenced great enthusiasm for major investments in ballistic missiles even as their factions noisily pursued research, experiments, and proposals. The mainstreams of the services were much more concerned with pursuing their established interests in aircraft carriers or bombers or divisions.

When it became apparent that the nation would have to develop ballistic missiles because the Soviets were doing so and because such missiles would provide the Soviets with capabilities the United States did not have, the mainstream services' enthusiasm for ballistic missiles did not change—only their environment had changed. Instead of pushing away something that would only compete with their primary interests if they accepted it, the services were now confronted with an event that was going to intrude upon their primary interests whether they liked it or not. At that point, ballistic missiles became part of the competitive landscape for the services: If the nation was going to have ballistic missiles, who was going to own and operate them and, therefore, who was going to develop them? All three services then scrambled for ownership of the ballistic missile program, not because they really wanted it, but because they did not want to be left out of what had clearly become a part of the future.

If Star Wars is an elective choice, none of the services will embrace it even though factions within them may. If Star Wars is pushed upon the country because the Soviets do it (or are truly believed to be doing it), then the services will compete for its ownership even though they are not enthusiastic about it. And once they own it, it will remain an unwanted stepchild for a long, long time. If the stepchild becomes strong enough, if it proves itself beyond doubt in war, if it becomes rebellious, it may survive and eventually flourish. Examples of successful survival despite institutional neglect or hostility include the advocates of air power and the aircraft carrier. Stepchildren that have still not found the mainstream of the armed services despite their obvious potentials include mines (for both land and sea warfare), guided missiles or remotely controlled vehicles, and special forces. Those stepchildren will be accepted and modestly supported by the services; but they will never be fully embraced at the heart of the institution until something forces a change.

## Can Nothing Be Done?

If the American military services are driven by glacial engines for stability, can we only stand back and watch them "do their thing"? If their own chiefs or a secretary of defense cannot change them, can anyone?

In a benign funding environment, in the absence of involvements in major wars, the services will change very slowly, mostly in response to the changes in the society in which they are embedded and share. But none of those conditions or factors should be counted upon too highly by those who hope for, or want to bring about, change in the services.

Funding constraints may rein in the service acquisitions, but not their desires. They may have to do with lesser quantities, but they will continue to pursue the qualities they want in their institution and in the forces they are able to acquire. Congress may put them on a diet, but the services will retain their menu and their appetites. Moreover, the services will tend to see such a diet as a temporary state of affairs—one that will change when the "enemy" manifests itself or when the political winds shift again in their favor. Thus, funding constraints result in the services tightening their belts, but not losing their grips on their institutional identities or dreams.

War may force changes upon the service, but not assuredly. Wartime traumas that shake the institution to its foundations may cause change; but such traumas are uncommon. The Navy's loss of half its battleships in one morning to carrier aircraft was a trauma that forced the Navy to recognize the new capital ship of World War II; the Navy had no choice but to change. But many "lessons" of a war can be ignored or explained away to preserve the institution's adherence to its glacier movement: The decisiveness of air power in World War II is arguable; but its apparent failure to be decisive in the Korean and Vietnamese wars could be explained by the defenders of air power as wars that either were the wrong kind or were fought with the wrong rules. The Army's failure in Vietnam could be explained away in similar terms. Thus, unless war utterly wrecks an institution or its precepts, it will try to persist in its ways.

The German and Japanese armed forces were utterly wrecked in World War II; those that have emerged since then are quite different institutions from their predecessors. But those changes were the product of the complete defeat of nations, which included the death and rebirth of many institutions besides their armed forces. Short of national defeat, it is hard to imagine wartime traumas that would induce major changes in the American services. The sudden loss of half the Navy's carriers to Soviet submarines and missiles is conceivable and would force the Navy to change; but that possibility is highly unlikely in anything less than a war that would make the issue trivial by comparison to other losses. The failure of strategic bombardment to be decisive, even if completely unleashed, is also conceivable, but under such circumstances that no one would any longer care.

The Army, however, alone among the American services, could face a wartime trauma short of Armageddon, yet sufficient to force fundamental and painful institutional changes. If the Army were confronted with a major irregular war on its doorstep (e.g., in Latin America), under circumstances in which air or naval power were clearly unnecessary, and then unleashed to do its "thing," it might conceivably fail. That kind of failure could cause the Army to change.

To the extent that American society changes, there are pressures for the services to change in the same direction. But there are counterpressures as well: "Military men have always cherished a sense of separateness from the civilian sector, a sense of special calling deriving from their choice of a profession involving the risk of life. They feel this separateness confers a distinction that compensates them to some extent for the risk of the profession."[5] The American society changes slowly, too, unless the issue is brought to focus by pain or fashion. A society that is generally critical of, or hostile toward, the military is likely only to isolate the services more from the surrounding society, without significantly reducing their power or their ability to attract new members.

The military reformers, even though they may often be correct in their assessments of the failures of the American military institutions, will not succeed in forcing the changes they seek. Their prescriptions for a cure fail to treat the personality within the institution: They shout for rational or altruistic behavior; yet, like all of us, they tolerate occasional irrational or selfish behavior in themselves as simply a part of being human. They would reorganize or restructure or legislate to make the institutions behave as they should, even though that approach seldom succeeds in producing favorable changes in human behavior. The prescriptions for reform treat the institutions as if they were not human, as if they were machines that needed different linkages, gears, input feed, or control levers. Instead, these institutions are living, breathing, and, most important, adaptive, self-motivated human organisms that, like individuals, will look to their own survival, security, and esteem. They will find ways to ensure their survival, security, and esteem even if they are reorganized or restructured or legislated; and, like us, they will pretend to rationality and altruism as they do so.

Thus, calls for restructuring the military services are not likely to lead to any significant changes. They do need to change; but they will not be changed from the outside, given the current political and social environments. Political reformers of the military, if elected or appointed to positions of power, will only succeed in prodding the American military institutions into rallying their many supporters in Congress and throughout American society. Millions of citizens have served in or had some other close association with one or more of the services; millions more are currently working in or for the services. Most will rally to the concerns of the institution they have served or now serve. And over the years, the services have cultivated agreeable relationships with those in Congress and the press who can and will support them. The services will close ranks and effectively resist any radical restructuring of their institutional powers and independence. A real fight over military reform will inevitably end up in Congress, where the services know how to look after their interests and would not expect to lose. Significant restructuring will occur only if the society as a whole aligns itself in such a way that Congress must comply with its wishes; and such an alignment is not likely in the absence of a major trauma.

Possibly the best hope for change in the American military institutions—and the one that ultimately motivates this book—is through a better understanding of institutions by those within them and by those who must deal with them. People change their ways by being constrained (deterred or restricted), by trauma (accompanied by pain), by gaining an understanding themselves (through insight or education), or by association with people who do understand them (as with teachers or therapists). If institutions have identities and personalities, as they have been characterized here, then perhaps, like people, they may be changed by something other than constraints or trauma. If those who are members of an institution and those who deal with institutions understand why the institution behaves the way it does, then the ways of modifying that behavior equals or exceeds the number of people who have that understanding, for each can take actions, even if only for one's self, that will contribute eventually to change.

When we or those around us understand a certain kind of behavior, that behavior is likely to become modified. If most people are made aware that the folding of one's arms is "body language" signifying a protective or "closed" attitude, many will make a conscious effort not to fold their arms in conversation. The awareness, the understanding of behavior induces change: If many people understand the services and why they behave the way they do, then the collective institutional behavior will change if only to preserve self-esteem. Pretensions or facades, once pierced and widely discussed, are likely to be dropped. Foibles or follies, once discovered and publicly analyzed, are likely to be avoided.

Undesirable behavior is often cooperatively induced: The treatment of medical physicians as gods by their patients (or the patient's friends and relatives) requires both sides to play. The patients want to believe the doctor is a god who can make them well; and being treated as a god is flattering and enjoyable to most humans at one time or another. But, if both sides to that cooperative game become fully aware of what they are doing, and know that the other side also knows what is going on, they will generally both want to change that behavior. Likewise, much of the services' pretensions about altruism in the cause of national security are supported by cooperative behavior: Both the public and the services want to believe it, even if it mostly is not so, and behave accordingly. If we can deal with these institutions in the light of their personalities, we shall be looking past the masks they have used too long to hide their legitimate, but less noble, motivations and interests: the masks of war.

# NOTES

## Preface

1. Both reports were published under the same title and author: Carl H. Builder, *The Army in the Strategic Planning Process: Who Shall Bell the Cat?* The CAA report was published as a Technical Paper, CAA-TP-86-12, dated October 1986, and the RAND report was published as R-3513-A, dated April 1987.

2. Subsequently published as: Carl H. Builder, *On the Army Style in Analysis*, RAND Corporation, P-7267, Santa Monica, October 1986. It was then republished in *Phalanx: The Bulletin of Military Operations Research* 20, no. 2 (June 1987), under the same title.

3. Perry McCoy Smith, *The Air Force Plans for Peace, 1943–1945* (Baltimore: Johns Hopkins University Press, 1970).

4. James L. Lacy, *Within Bounds: The Navy in Postwar American Security Policy*, Center for Naval Analyses, CNA 05 83 1178, 28 July 1983.

5. J. C. Wylie, *Military Strategy: A General Theory of Power Control* (Westport, Conn.: Greenwood Press, 1967).

6. Arnold Kanter, *Defense Politics: A Budgetary Perspective* (Chicago: University of Chicago Press, 1979).

7. Arthur T. Hadley, *The Straw Giant—Triumph and Failure: America's Armed Forces* (New York: Random House, 1986).

## Chapter 1

1. An excellent summary of this rational, logical approach to military planning is provided in *Foundations of Force Planning: Concepts and Issues*, edited by the Force Planning Faculty, Naval War College (Newport, R.I.: Naval War College Press, 1986).

2.  Lawrence Freedman, *Strategic Defense in the Nuclear Age*, International Institute for Strategic Studies, Adelphi Paper 224, London, Autumn 1987, p. 3.

3.  My colleague William Jones, who shares my interest in institutional analysis, has pointed out that institutions are also, in some respects, less than the sum of their human individuals. For example, institutional change requires considerable renegotiating of the roles of the institution's human components and, since that usually requires lots of time, change can seldom occur at more than a glacial pace.

4.  Of course, the service, as an institution, may itself limit the range of views that its members may safely express in dealing with "outsiders," reinforcing the appearance of a single voice.

5.  Hadley, *The Straw Giant*, pp. 71–72.

6.  The Marine Corps falls within the Department of the Navy and the Coast Guard within the Department of Transportation.

7.  For example, the Marine Corps has enjoyed a reputation with Congress for its competency within a well-defined, if limited, role and for its relatively modest claims for resources. Thus, the Marines have generally been bystanders in the almost continuous jostling and bumping of the Army, Navy, and Air Force over military strategy and resources. They appear to be protected from harm by Congress and quite comfortable with hand-me-down equipment developed by the other services, taking more pride in who they are than in what they own.

8.  My colleague William Jones points out that a military service, as viewed by one of its own members, necessarily has a strong belief in its vital relevance to national security. Therefore, a member of that institution finds no contradiction between the interests of the institution and those of the nation. This is apparent even with most retired officers, who no longer have any career or financial interest to protect, when they speak for or about their particular service's interests.

9.  Ministry of Defence, *The Future United Kingdom Strategic Nuclear Deterrent Force*, Defence Open Government Document 80/23, 15 July 1980.

10.  Herbert G. Hoover, a RAND colleague with a distinguished career as an Air Force analyst.

# Chapter 2

1.  Some other aspects considered were the differences among the services in how they program and budget and how they relate to one another and to the JCS. These could be interesting studies all by themselves.

2.  The most useful sources for differentiating among the services varied with the aspect being considered. Some aspects are treated extensively in the literature and have been cited accordingly. For other aspects

that have not yet received attention in the literature, I have drawn upon my own experiences or conversations in suggesting the differences among the services. If my literature support is sparse, I welcome relevant citations, anecdotal support, and alternative interpretations, for this aspect of my research will never be completed.

3. This comparison was suggested by Rear Admiral James A. Winnefeld, USN (ret.), who offered, as an example, a possible answer for the Navy.

4. See, for example, Samuel P. Huntington, *The Soldier and the State* (Cambridge: Harvard University Press, Belknap Press, 1957), pp. 248–49.

5. Ibid., p. 303; with the quotations taken from Henry L. Stimson and McGeorge Bundy, *On Active Service in Peace and War* (New York: Harper Bros., 1947), p. 506.

6. Even as the Navy discusses its maritime strategy, it reiterates its need for independence in command and control: "One of the truly unique aspects of naval warfare is its awesome complexity. . . . The complexity of the tasks makes it essential that we not attempt to micro-manage the war from Washington" (James D. Watkins, "The Real Reformers," *The Maritime Strategy* [Annapolis: U.S. Naval Institute, January 1986], p. 13).

7. One evidence of a slowing in the expansion of the aeronautical technologies is the growing lifetimes of aircraft before obsolescence. The most successful (or ubiquitous) models of aircraft have always had useful lifetimes about equal to the time interval between Kittyhawk (1903) and the year of their design. That thumb rule can be applied across more than eighty years of aviation during which airplane designs have generally succumbed to technological obsolescence. It can be applied equally well to the Curtiss Jenny, the Douglas DC-3, and the Boeing 707. The best military aircraft designs have had somewhat shorter useful lives, but have followed the same trend. This continuing extension of useful lifetimes implies that technological obsolescence in aircraft is slowing. This slowing might be welcomed by those paying the bills for aircraft, but not by those devoted to designing and building new ones; they have to search harder for reasons—the threat or competition or technology—to replace the existing aircraft.

8. Evidence of the Army's roots in the citizenry is to be found in its composition—over a third of the Army's force structure (as measured in divisions) is vested in National Guard units.

9. Bruce Palmer, Jr., *The 25-Year War: America's Military Role in Vietnam* (New York: Simon & Schuster, 1984), p. 209.

10. Bernard W. Rogers, *The Army*, Field Manual FM-100-1, 29 September 1978, i.

11. *The Army*, Field Manual FM-100-1, 14 August 1981, p. 24.

12. Robert J. Murray, "JCS Reform: A Defense of the Current System," *Naval War College Review* 38, no. 5 (September/October 1985): 25.

13.  Kanter, *Defense Politics*, p. 5.

14.  See John F. Lehman, Jr., "The 600-Ship Navy," *The Maritime Strategy* (Annapolis: U.S. Naval Institute, January 1986), pp. 35–36.

15.  The persistence of these goals for Navy ships was pointed out to me in 1971 by Arthur Herrington, who served as the director, Naval Forces, in the Office of Assistant Secretary of Defense for Systems Analysis during the Johnson administration. For further evidence of this constancy, see Vincent Davis, *Post War Defense Policy and the U.S. Navy, 1943–1946* (Chapel Hill: University of North Carolina Press, 1966), p. 202. See also Samuel P. Huntington, "National Policy and the Transoceanic Navy," *U.S. Naval Institute Proceedings* 80, no. 5 (May 1954): 484.

16.  The Air Force sought seventy groups after World War II, when it was dominated by strategic bombing enthusiasts. See Paul R. Schratz, "The Admiral's Revolt," *U.S. Naval Institute Proceedings* 112, no. 2 (February 1986): 70. More recently, under leadership dominated by the Tactical Air Command, the Air Force has sought twenty-seven tactical fighter wings. See Murray, "JCS Reform."

17.  My colleague William Jones notes that the Army's focus on people is not surprising since combat success is traditionally measured in the taking and controlling of territory. With the technological age, the taking of territory may increasingly depend upon equipment and machines; but the controlling (secure occupation) of territory remains a task mostly for people—lots of them. Jones observes: "Pity the poor Soviet army planner trying to plan the conquest of China."

18.  Several colleagues have objected to my use of the term "toys" instead of equipment, platforms, or weapons. They find the term pejorative, even insulting, given the destructiveness of these machines and the seriousness with which their operators treat them. Nevertheless, I have observed an excitement and enthusiasm over these machines best captured by possessing toys. To call them toys is not to say that their operators are children or that they will be used like toys; rather, it is an attempt to capture a particular relationship between a machine and its operator. Note that the relationship between a child and its toy is quite different from that, say, between a pet and its master or between workers and their tools.

19.  Colonel Clifford R. Krieger (USAF) has pointed out to me that the association sometimes goes beyond the model designation, right down to the block: "Flying a Block 30 F-16C is more fun than just about anything else in the world" (from a letter to the author dated 19 September 1987).

20.  General Jack Ryan, when he was chief of staff of the Air Force, promoted the slogan "The job of the Air Force is to fly and fight—and don't you ever forget it!" Yet, the two were probably not equally attractive: To be told that you will fly but not fight is not the same as being told that you will fight but not fly.

21.   There were not prominent instances of American volunteers for the British Army or Navy in World War II, although Americans in the French Foreign Legion in World War I were fairly numerous.

22.   Davis, *Post War Defense Policy*, p. 120.

23.   Ibid., p. 45.

24.   Samuel P. Huntington, *The Common Defense: Strategic Programs in National Politics* (New York: Columbia University Press, 1961), p. 407.

25.   Kanter, *Defense Politics*, p. 18.

26.   The submariners are now increasingly challenging the naval aviators for the top of the hierarchy, probably because of the twenty-year ascendancy of the bright young officers who were handpicked by Admiral Hyman Rickover for the Navy nuclear power training program.

27.   Davis, *Post War Defense Policy*, p. 120.

28.   See Kanter, *Defense Politics*, p. 108.

29.   Aviation and air defense artillery are more recent additions to the combat arms; they probably do not fully share the higher status of the traditional branches.

30.   Kanter, *Defense Politics*, p. 19. This may be definitional rather than symptomatic: The name "general" was originally intended to apply to those officers capable of commanding all the branches in a combined arms force. It is fitting, therefore, that they no longer associate themselves with a single branch but with all branches under their command.

31.   This does not mean that the branches are free from rivalry. Like brothers, they frequently tease one another about their respective abilities and chores but not about their contribution to the Army or its missions.

32.   Smith, *The Air Force Plans for Peace*, p. 27.

33.   William R. Emerson, "Operation Pointblank: A Tale of Bombers and Fighters," *Harmon Memorial Lectures in Military History*, no. 4 (Colorado Springs: United States Air Force Academy, 1962), p. 40; quoted by Smith, p. 27.

34.   Walter Millis, *Arms and Men: A Study in American Military History* (New York: G.P. Putnam, 1956), p. 283; quoted by Smith, p. 35.

35.   Smith, *The Air Force Plans for Peace*, p. 28, emphasis added. My colleague William Jones suggests that old saw about the military "planning to fight the last war" is imprecise: They really plan to refight the last battle of their last victorious war. That point is discussed at greater length in chapter 12.

36.   Lacy, *Within Bounds*, pp. 2, 19, 60.

37.   However, that transfer was effected only through the trauma of World War II and the disastrous losses of battleships to aircraft by all the major naval powers.

38.   Not surprisingly, each service tends to focus on the kind of war that would make its own forces the principal player. By elevating the importance or likelihood of its particular brand of war, each service raises the stature of its own role, mission, and forces. These differences are explored in chapter 12.

# Chapter 3

1. Davis, *Post War Defense Policy and the U.S. Navy*, p. 56.
2. David C. Jones, "What's Wrong with Our Defense Establishment," *New York Times Magazine*, 7 November 1982, p. 73; quoted by Lacy, *Within Bounds*, p. 536.
3. Quoted by Huntington, *The Soldier and the State*, p. 262.
4. Jones, "What's Wrong with Our Defense Establishment," p. 70; cited by Lacy, *Within Bounds*, p. 596.
5. Smith, *The Air Force Plans for Peace*, p. 18.
6. Barbara W. Tuchman, "Human Nature Is Responsible," in *The American Military: Opposing Viewpoints*, edited by David L. Bender (St. Paul, Minn.: Greenhaven Press, 1983), p. 74.
7. There is some ambiguity about the motto for the Air Force Academy, whereas the mottos of the Military and Naval academies are to be found on everything from cuff links to glassware; there appears to be no comparable consistency for an Air Force motto. The one used here for the Air Force Academy appears on the base of the sculpture of a falcon in the cadet area opposite Mitchell Hall and has appeared on class rings. Over a portal to the cadet area, however, is "Bring me men" (to match my mountains); and a current exhortation is "Commitment to excellence," which appears on the academy stationery. Inquiries to the academy staff and graduates have provided no further resolution of this ambiguity.
8. The ordering of the three words probably has more to do with their sound than with logic. One could argue that the logical order is country, duty, honor. The country is the object of worship; the worship is demonstrated through duty; and that duty to country brings honor to those who serve.
9. The B-49 bomber was the jet-powered version of Northrop's B-35 flying wing and, at the time the Air Force Academy was designed, perhaps one of the most graceful airplanes to have flown.
10. E. B. Vandiver III, an astute observer of military institutions, suggested this comparison to me.
11. Only one of the six cases contained the instruments of space flight, striking a balance that seemed somehow appropriate to the institution's preference of air over space as its medium.
12. Peter B. Vaill, "The Purposing of High-Performing Systems," *Organizational Dynamics* (Autumn 1982): 23–39.
13. Ibid., pp. 24, 26; emphasis in the original.
14. See the discussion in chapter 2, under "Intraservice Distinctions."
15. The resignation of Navy Secretary James Webb in 1988 was triggered by a dispute, inter alia, over whether the Navy could decide how to absorb budget cuts. The Navy did not have difficulty in deciding the budget cuts it wanted to take; but it had great difficulty with that decision being taken out of its hands by political leaders. And this was not the first

such dispute that has led to a Navy resignation. Again, see Schratz, "The Admiral's Revolt."

16. E. B. Vandiver has cautioned me that two other important dislocations in the post–World War II era have influenced the Army's historical perception of itself: First, the Army enjoyed decisive victories in all its prior wars except the War of 1812, whereas the wars in Korea and Vietnam ended in stalemate and withdrawal, if not defeat. Second, since World War II, the Army has maintained the largest peacetime force—in both absolute and relative terms—in its history. Both these experiences represent important breaks with the past for the Army.

17. See Arthur T. Hadley, "The Split Military Psyche," *New York Times Magazine*, 13 July 1986, pp. 26–33.

18. A Navy wife confided to me that when she "joined" the Navy, one of the attractions was the life style of its most senior officers, particularly the large Navy-furnished quarters staffed with enlisted personnel for household services. That prospect made the sacrifices demanded of junior officers and their families seem a little more bearable. But over the space of twenty-five years, American societal attitudes changed to make that Navy tradition intolerable. When her husband attained flag rank, they got the big home but not the servants to make full use of it. Her implicit contract with the Navy was broken and she was bitterly disappointed. If the change had not been imposed from the outside, she (and probably many others) would have resisted from inside the institution any efforts for change.

19. Perhaps the best modern example of a military institution being decimated and therefore able to build a new personality is the Wehrmacht. If the Japanese self-defense forces significantly rebuild themselves, they, too, may emerge with personalities distinct from those of the Imperial Army and Navy up to 1945.

20. President Dwight D. Eisenhower's farewell address on 17 January 1961; emphasis added.

## Chapter 4

1. These definitions were taken from the following sources: *Webster's Third New International Dictionary*, unabridged ed., 1969; *Random House College Dictionary*, revised ed., 1982; *American Heritage Dictionary*, 2d college ed., 1982; and *Department of Defense Dictionary of Military and Associated Terms*, JCS Pub. 1, 1 April 1984.

2. While discussing these definitions, a retired general noted that the JCS appeared to have taken its definition from Webster's. Asked why the JCS found it necessary to interchange the words "science and art" and elaborate upon the other words, the general quickly replied, "That, of course, was the value added by the JCS."

3. Wylie, *Military Strategy*, p. 13.

4. Caspar W. Weinberger, secretary of defense, *Annual Report to the Congress, Fiscal Year 1987*, 5 February 1986, p. 33.

5. Ibid.

6. Keith A. Dunn and William O. Staudenmaier, "The Retaliatory Offensive and Operational Realities in NATO," *Survival* 27, no. 3 (May/June 1985): 109.

7. Wylie, *Military Strategy*, p. 13.

8. Carl H. Builder, *A Conceptual Framework for a National Strategy on Nuclear Arms*, RAND Corporation, R-2598-AF, Santa Monica, September 1980, p. 3; emphasis in the original.

9. A colleague, Robert L. Perry, suggests that doctrine often does not truly relate means to ends because the claimed ends are often beyond the actual means. Be that as it may, doctrine relates the institutionally preferred ends and desired means in a concept that reflects an image acceptable to the institution.

10. Russell L. Ackoff and Elsa Vergara, "Creativity in Problem Solving and Planning: A Review," *European Journal of Operational Research* 7, no. 1 (May 1981): 8.

11. Weinberger, *Annual Report*, p. 32.

12. It can be argued that deterrence is more likely to be a political end than a military strategy.

13. To make them instantly digestible, the dozen examples have all been taken from recent history, from World War II to the present.

14. See "World Wars," *Encyclopedia Britannica*, 15th ed. vol. 19, 1978, p. 992.

15. A colleague, Robert L. Perry, notes that separate wars were also being fought by branches or commands *within* each of the services. For example, the submarine war against Japan was carried out, for the most part, separately from the surface fleet operations. And the latter were, in turn, divided between a war against the Japanese fleet and support for MacArthur's war against the Japanese Army in its occupation of Pacific islands.

16. The air strategy is perhaps more appropriately attributed to Douhet or Mitchell or Trenchard. However, Major Alexander P. DeSeversky's book *Victory through Air Power* (New York: Simon & Schuster, 1942) and the Disney film derived from it did much to popularize the strategy and spread its vision beyond those directly involved with its advocacy or implementation.

17. The maritime strategy, like the air power strategy, can claim many authors, including Bing West and Admiral James Watkins. But Secretary of the Navy Lehman has used the maritime strategy as the basis for his effective advocacy of the 600-ship Navy. See Lehman, "The 600-Ship Navy," pp. 30–40.

18. See Samuel P. Huntington, "Conventional Deterrence and Conventional Retaliation in Europe," *International Security* 8, no. 3 (Winter 1983–84): 32–56.

19. See Bernard W. Rogers, "The Atlantic Alliance: Prescriptions for a Difficult Decade," *Foreign Affairs* 60, no. 5 (Summer 1982): 1145–56.

20. Kanter, *Defense Politics*, p. 83.

21. Kennan's strategy surfaced in an anonymous article in the July 1947 issue of *Foreign Affairs*. See "Containment," *Encyclopedia Britannica*, vol. 3, p. 109.

22. According to Michael Howard, "the concept of 'grand strategy' was introduced to cover those industrial, financial, demographic, and societal aspects of war that have become so salient in the twentieth century" ("The Forgotten Dimensions of Strategy," *Foreign Affairs* 57, no. 5 [Summer 1979]: 975). Paul Nitze sees grand strategy as "something broader than military strategy . . . in which all factors bearing on the evolving situation—including economic, political and psychological factors as well as military—are taken into account over long periods of time, including times both of peace and war" ("Strategy in the Decade of the 1980s," *Foreign Affairs* 59, no. 1 [Fall 1980]: 82).

23. See "United States, History of," *Encyclopedia Britannica*, vol. 18, p. 993.

24. I am indebted to a colleague, David J. Stein, for suggesting this principle by implication while he was explaining why the United States had difficulty in formulating or adopting strategies.

25. This principle is remindful of (but not strictly analogous to) the Heisenberg uncertainty principle in physics, which states that "it is impossible to know both position and momentum [of atomic particles] with sufficient accuracy at the same time" ("Mechanics, Quantum," *Encyclopedia Britannica*, vol. 11, p. 795). Strategy, too, appears to have relativistic properties.

26. James T. Westwood, "Some Notes on Strategy," *Military Review* 65, no. 10 (October 1985): 65.

27. The ambiguity in NATO's strategy of flexible response (MC 14/3) is generally seen as deliberate (Karl Kaiser and Georg Leber, "Nuclear Weapons and the Preservation of Peace: A German Response," *Foreign Affairs* 60, no. 5 [Summer 1982]: 1150), but that may be making a virtue of the necessity to compromise in a coalition strategy for sixteen nations.

28. "One . . . uniquely American phenomenon is that strategic ideas . . . have more the smell of the seminar room about them than of the trench or missile silo" (Colin S. Gray, "Defense Planning and the Duration of War," *Defense Analysis* 1, no. 1 [March 1985]: 32).

29. "As the record of the past suggests, broad policy declarations and the fashions of official military strategy have considerable limitations. Strategy proclamations are more likely to embellish than to enlighten, and while they may not therefore be misleading, they are not likely to be particularly instructive either" (Lacy, *Within Bounds*, p. 525). The same

point is made by Gray in "Defense Planning and the Duration of War," p. 31: "The ideas and assumptions on strategy that have the authority of official blessing today have . . . had their intellectual shape molded very much by trends in fashionable opinion, by considerations of public acceptability, and by the sometimes very arbitrary outcomes of the budgetary process, and by the preferences of entrenched bureaucracies."

30. "Societies in which communication is open, which safeguard pluralism with legal sanctions, and which normally tolerate a high degree of political dissent find it much more difficult to develop and maintain a consensus of commitment to the legitimacy of strategic objectives. Yet the maintenance of that consensus is one of the key objectives of national strategy" (Charles F. Kriete, "The Moral Dimension of Strategy," *Parameters* 7, no. 2 [1977]: 67; quoted by Harry G. Summers, Jr., *On Strategy: The Vietnam War in Context*, Strategic Studies Institute, U.S. Army War College, Carlisle, Pa., n.d. pp. 21-22).

31. "In the United States, policy and strategy proceed by innuendo, persuasion, compromise and almost infinite negotiation and transaction. So it is that U.S. national policies and strategies are subdued and subtle, becoming highly implicit in plans and programs" (Westwood, "Some Notes on Strategy," p. 65).

32. The continuing difficulties of the United States in formulating a strategy toward the possession and use of nuclear weapons (ever since the early 1960s when Soviets acquired a significant capability to reply in kind) can be contrasted with the so-called dual-track strategy that successfully (if not quietly) ushered in the NATO deployment of theater-range ballistic and cruise missiles.

33. Barry R. Posen and Stephen Van Evera, "Defense Policy and the Reagan Administration," *International Security* 8, no. 1 [Summer 1983]: 4; emphasis in the orginal.

34. Inadequacies may include the failure of a strategy to confront explicitly actual ends or real constraints. For example, a defense strategy that observes, but pretends to ignore, fiscal contraints or strong bureaucratic pressures or real (but embarrassing) interests is an inadequate declaration of ends, means, and the concept for relating them. What is unsaid about a strategy may be more important than what is said. Thus, political sensitivities may vitiate a declared strategy, leaving one to infer the operative strategy, if any.

## Chapter 5

1. For a discussion of structured national security ends (goals), see Builder, *A Conceptual Framework for a National Strategy on Nuclear Arms*, pp. 5, 6.

2. The war plan of CINCSAC, the Single Integrated Operational Plan (SIOP) for the employment of U.S. strategic offensive forces in strike operations, is one widely discussed example.

3. Typical documents incorporating statements of the defense strategy include the Defense Planning Guidance, the Joint Long Range Strategic Appraisal, and The Army Plan.

4. Service strategies are likely to be implicit rather than explicit because of their purposes. An explicit example of a service strategy, presented as a component of the defense strategy, is found in the Navy's Programming Objectives Memorandum (POM) submission, according to Watkins, "Reforming the Navy from Within," *Defense 85* (Washington, D.C.: U.S. Government Printing Office, November 1985), p. 20.

5. Examples are General Bernard Rogers's scheme in Europe for countering the Soviet follow-on forces and Admiral Robert Long's proposed swing strategy for the Pacific.

6. An example of the general political ends might be the proposals for "horizontal escalation," which surfaced in the early 1980s, alongside or integrally with the maritime strategy. An example of the specific military means might be the Rapid Deployment Force. One called for new political objectives in the event of war, without specifying the means to achieve them; the other specified forces that had to be acquired, without defining the military objectives for those forces.

7. This perception of the importance of the service strategies in the military planning implies that the services retain powerful influences upon the *kinds* of forces acquired and the concepts that guide their use, even though they may not have so much influence upon the *amounts* of forces acquired or total resources devoted to national defense.

8. This substitution has happened at least twice. In the 1940s, the emerging Air Force proposed that the national military strategy should be centered on air strategy; in the 1980s, some sea-power enthusiasts have argued that the nation would be better served if it shifted to a maritime strategy.

9. This orientation of efforts within the Navy is one of the claims for the maritime strategy by James D. Watkins, "Reforming the Navy from Within," p. 20. See also Watkins, "The Real Reformers," p. 15.

10. Lacy, *Within Bounds*, p. 24.

11. Huntington, *The Common Defense*, p. 399.

12. Lacy, *Within Bounds*, p. 532.

13. Kanter, *Defense Politics*, p. 100; emphasis in the original.

14. Lacy, *Within Bounds*, p. 542.

15. Kanter, *Defense Politics*, p. 101; emphasis in the original.

16. Lacy, *Within Bounds*, p. 528.

17. Summers, *On Strategy*, p. 90; with the quotation cited from Townsend Hoopes, *The Limits of Intervention* (New York: David McKay Co., 1969), p. 3.

18. Summers, *On Strategy,* p. 117.

19. Huntington, *The Common Defense,* pp. 407, 408.

20. Ibid., p. 412.

21. Kanter, *Defense Politics,* pp. 92, 93.

22. Huntington, *The Common Defense,* p. 419.

23. Horizontal in the geographic sense, as opposed to vertical in the destructive sense.

## Chapter 6

1. Both the Army and Navy have assigned specific responsibility for strategy to flag officers in their headquarters. For the Army, it is the Strategy, Plans and Policy Directorate (DAMO-SS); for the Navy, it is the Strategy, Plans and Policy Division (NOP-60). In the Air Force, the responsibility for strategy is assigned two levels further down (in AFXOXIS), as a part of planning integration, which, in turn, is a part of Air Force plans.

2. Giulio Douhet, *The Command of the Air* (New York: Coward-McCann, 1942), translated by Dino Ferrari from the 2d ed. published in 1927; originally published in 1921 under the auspices of (the Italian) Ministry of War.

3. The idea of air power as an independent instrument is usually attributed to Hugh Montague Trenchard, principal organizer of the RAF (see, for example, "Trenchard," *Encyclopedia Britannica,* vol. 10, p. 109), but Jan C. Smuts is given that credit in the semiofficial history of the British air arm in World War I, according to *The War in the Air,* edited by H. A. Jones (Oxford: Oxford University Press, 1937), Appendixes (as cited by Bernard Brodie, *Strategy in the Missile Age* [Princeton: Princeton University Press, 1959], p. 71 n.).

4. This claim was more strident in the middle of the twentieth century than it is today. Then it was claimed that air power was *the* decisive instrument of war. Today, air power theorists claim that it can be decisive if used correctly by either side to a conflict. For an updated perspective of the evolution of the air strategy, see David MacIsaac, "Voices from the Central Blue: The Air Power Theorists," in *Makers of Modern Strategy,* edited by Peter Paret (Princeton: Princeton University Press, 1986).

5. Douhet, *The Command of the Air,* p, 30; emphasis in the original.

6. "Mitchell," *Encyclopedia Britannica,* vol. 6, p. 943. For a more detailed examination of the roles of Douhet, Mitchell, and DeSeversky in the evolution of air power, see Edward Warner, "Douhet, Mitchell, Seversky: Theories of Air Warfare," in *Makers of Modern Strategy,* edited by Edward Meade Earl (New York: Atheneum, 1966).

7. DeSeversky, *Victory through Air Power.*

8.  Smith, *The Air Force Plans for Peace*, pp. 14, 15.

9.  DeSeversky, *Victory through Air Power*, p. 70.

10.  Wylie, *Military Strategy*, p. 66. Wylie goes on to say: "And nearly everybody missed the point. The strategic bombers were then, as they are now, fully able to do their job. The only hitch was that the assumptions did not coincide with reality. The Korean War was real enough; it was the assumptions that were not valid for that particular reality. Whether the reality—i.e., the Korean War—was 'right' or 'wrong' was irrelevant."

11.  Smith, *The Air Force Plans for Peace*, pp. 30, 31.

12.  DeSeversky, *Victory through Air Power*, p. 102.

13.  See Lacy, *Within Bounds*, p. 550.

14.  Smith, *The Air Force Plans for Peace*, p. 116.

15.  *Basic Aerospace Doctrine of the United States Air Force*, AFM 1-1, 16 March 1984, pp. 1–3; emphasis added. Only aerospace forces are described as having decisive potential. The discussion of the other members of the team—land and naval forces—notes that they are dependent upon aerospace power and makes no reference to their having the potential to be decisive.

# Chapter 7

1.  "Mahan's Strategy of Seapower," *Encyclopedia Britannica*, vol. 19, pp. 562, 563.

2.  See Maurer Maurer, *Aviation in the U.S. Army, 1919–1939*, Office of Air Force History (Washington, D.C.: United States Air Force, 1987), pp. 113–29, 406–8.

3.  Davis, *Post War Defense Policy and the U.S. Navy*, p. 42; emphasis in the orginal.

4.  Ibid., p. 256.

5.  Lacy, *Within Bounds*, p. 11.

6.  Ibid., p. 16.

7.  DeSeversky, *Victory through Air Power*, p. 25.

8.  Davis, *Post War Defense Policy and the U.S. Navy*, p. 149; emphasis in the original.

9.  Ibid., p. 130, quotation cited from Fletcher Pratt, *The Compact History of the United States Navy* (New York: Hawthorn Books, 1957), p. 319.

10.  Lacy, *Within Bounds*, p. 551.

11.  Ibid., p. 540; emphasis added.

12.  Huntington, *The Common Defense*, p. 423.

13.  Lacy, *Within Bounds*, p. 529.

14. Robert W. Komer, "Maritime Strategy vs. Coalition Defense," *Foreign Affairs* 60, no. 5 (Summer 1982): 1124–44.

15. Stansfield Turner and George Thibault, "Preparing for the Unexpected: The Need for a New Military Strategy," *Foreign Affairs* 61, no. 1, (Fall 1982): 123; emphasis added.

16. James D. Watkins, "The Maritime Strategy," *The Maritime Strategy* (Annapolis: U.S. Naval Institute, January 1986).

17. Ibid., p. 1.

18. See Watkins, "Reforming the Navy from Within," pp. 18–20.

19. See the Comment and Discussion department of the *U.S. Naval Institute Proceedings* in the months following the publication of *The Maritime Strategy* by the U.S. Naval Institute in January 1986.

20. That the United States is a maritime nation by geography and overseas interests is not enough, by itself, to justify the need for a maritime strategy. Other nations, such as Japan and Norway, are also maritime nations by geography. The Soviet Union is a maritime nation by interests, even if not by geography. Yet it is not apparent that these nations are driven to maritime strategies. The argument that the United States needs a maritime strategy is inferential rather than explicit in its basis.

21. Ambassador Robert Komer wondered aloud: "It is interesting that the maritime supremacy school never suggest [*sic*] that the United States pull back forces from Northeast Asia. . . . Could it be because the Pacific is a Navy-dominated theater?" (Komer, "Maritime Strategy," p. 1140, n. 10). Davis noted: "One of the dominant characteristics of U.S. naval strategic thought during the half century from 1890 to 1940 was a strong emphasis upon security problems in the Pacific and Asia and a relative neglect of the Atlantic and Europe. This enduring traditional Navy concern for the Pacific and Asia, and the corollary lack of concern for the Atlantic and Europe, was evident again from the outset of the Navy's planning for the post–World War II period" (*Post War Defense Policy and the U.S. Navy*, p. 76).

22. If deterrence fails, the only agreed-upon U.S. objectives are to terminate the war as quickly as possible, at the lowest possible level of violence, and upon favorable terms. It is not at all agreed that the United States will seek to protract or expand any war, anywhere, any time, with the Soviets. Though it might certainly be desirable, under some circumstances, to protract or expand a war with the Soviets, that is not the general or accepted case.

# Chapter 8

1. It is here, on the effective and efficient use of available resources, that the Army concentrates its conceptual energies. The AirLand Battle concept is not strategy but doctrine: It says, whatever the means and ends

that may be assigned to us, here are concepts for the most effective and efficient use of those means toward those ends. This is how we would prefer to fight if we have the opportunity.

2.   But in defining the shortfalls and stating the risks, the Army is typically not confrontational. These things are said and accepted quietly, as with a partner in a venture. There is a duty to say what must be said, but loyally, without challenging the national leadership.

3.   For example, the Navy abandoned its Rainbow war plans in the aftermath of the Japanese attack on Pearl Harbor.

4.   Huntington, *The Soldier and the State*, p. 261.

5.   Summers, *On Strategy*, p. 2.

6.   See Lacy, *Within Bounds*, p. 24.

7.   Wylie, *Military Strategy*.

8.   Unless it would be to pick up where it left off in Europe in 1945, and complete the job of European liberation as General George S. Patton is supposed to have proposed. It could be argued that the AirLand Battle doctrine provides an Army vision of war; but that vision is true to its name: It is about a battle, not a war.

# Chapter 9

1.   For a concise summary of the institutionalization of scientific military analysis, see J. A. Stockfisch, *The Intellectual Foundations of Systems Analysis*, RAND Corporation, P-7401, Santa Monica, December 1987. He suggests early signs of the institutionalization during World War I in the British military air establishment (p. 3).

2.   To be sure, the choice of examples was influenced by my familiarity with Air Force analyses and the opportunities to talk with the analysts directly involved. But it should also be noted that the Air Force has probably done more analysis and more with analyses than the other services.

3.   The first of the World War II analytical scientists were probably Churchill's "boffins." Stockfisch suggests that Churchill used them to provide a critical, independent assessment of the bureaucratic reports and requests he had to deal with as prime minister. The motivations, elsewhere, may have been, in part, simply to find something worthwhile for the technically capable volunteers to do in helping with a total war effort. The United States soon copied the idea, with many scientists and mathematicians being lured or assigned to radar and weapons development projects.

4.   This example is drawn from several conversations in the late 1950s with Professor Alex Boldyreff of the University of California at Los Angeles who served as an operations analyst for General LeMay during World War II. My memory of the details of those conversations thirty years ago may not be completely reliable, but the point of the example is almost certainly consistent with that put forward by Professor Boldyreff.

5. The rationale given at the time for this indiscriminate form of city bombardment was that the Japanese war industry had, after three years of war, become a cottage industry—almost any home could be involved in the making of aircraft engine components. The validity of that rationale seems dubious today; but at the time it seemed plausible to many; some such rationale was necessary if the bombing was not to be a violation of the Geneva Conventions, which prohibit indiscriminate attacks upon civilians.

6. The Japanese radar capabilities were correctly judged to be insufficient for accurate direction of anti-aircraft artillery or night-fighter aircraft.

7. My colleague William Jones points out that LeMay, at the time, was probably not at all concerned about the AAF as an institution. He was a bomber man and a forceful manager who was determined to make the B-29 bombers under his command work.

8. A "genetic" relationship in the development of various forms of analysis is discussed by Giandomenico Majone in "Systems Analysis: A Genetic Approach," in *Handbook of Systems Analysis*, edited by Hugh J. Miser and Edward S. Quade (New York: North-Holland, 1985), pp. 33–66.

9. If the information about the alternatives is complete or certain, the choice has probably already been made and systems analysis is unnecessary to make that choice.

10. Indeed, the concept of "assured destruction" was first advanced by McNamara and his systems analysts as an analytical device to cap the rapidly expanding demands of the services for more nuclear weapons: If the number of nuclear weapons was sufficient to absorb any surprise attack and remain assuredly able to destroy the enemy's society, why was there any need for more? Unfortunately, some seized that analytical device and turned it into a "strategy," whereas others subverted it in a continuing escalation of demands for weapons.

11. Carl H. Builder, "The Crowd Roars," *Phalanx: The Bulletin of Military Operations Research* 19, no. 3 (September 1986): 26.

12. At the time, this bomber was known as the Advanced Manned Strategic Aircraft (AMSA). Subsequently, it became the B-1 (canceled by President Carter) and, finally, the B-1B (revived by President Reagan).

13. It was assumed that a ballistic missile defense would be unable to deal with a low-altitude aircraft threat, and that without a new bomber there would be no low-altitude aircraft threat.

14. Several analysts suggested to me that this argument was instrumental in bringing the secretary of the Air Force into the bomber advocates' camp.

15. The differences between, and need for, systems analysis and requirements analysis may be analogous to the separate jury deliberations for a verdict and for sentencing. The first decides whether there is to be any sentencing; the second decides what the sentence shall be. Systems analysis decides which alternative shall be chosen; requirements analysis then defines the selected alternative. To be sure, a verdict may be deliber-

ated with some consideration of the sentencing possibilities, just as a systems analysis considers the possible qualities and quantities of the systems involved; but the final resolutions in both cases await the basic choices.

16. This example was suggested by my colleague Herbert G. Hoover who, as an analyst for AFSC, was one of the participants in the tug of war.

17. Initially, the Air Force contemplated as many as 3,000 Minuteman missiles being deployed. The number was later cut about in half by Secretary of Defense McNamara in the early 1960s, and ultimately was set at 1,000.

## Chapter 10

1. These observations on the differences among the military services in their styles toward analysis are based almost entirely upon my own experiences. They have been previously summarized in Builder, *On the Army Style in Analysis.*

2. The Army seems quite willing to calculate any requirement. Indeed, the Army may do more calculations and less analysis than either of its sister services if one assumes that analysis leads to understanding and calculations lead to numbers.

3. This parable was first publicly presented during a banquet talk I gave at the Twenty-fifth Annual U.S. Army Operations Research Symposium on 8 October 1986, at Fort Lee, Virginia.

4. The FORCEM model is real enough. It is a massive and highly detailed simulation of theater warfare developed by the U.S. Army Concepts Analysis Agency. The model represents an advance over its predecessors most notably in its treatment of theater logistics.

5. I deliberately omitted planning, as have others, since the first *P* in PPBS is regrettably missing.

## Chapter 11

1. Subsequently, we experimented with a BBC film, *The War Game,* which described a hypothetical nuclear war through both imagery and analytics. The images were of events before, during, and after the war, affecting typical people; the analytics were tables of statistics and maps that described the scope and consequences of the war. We found that in this hypothetical war audience recall of imagery was much richer and more persistent than its recall of analytic information, even with audiences of military analysts.

## Chapter 12

1. In this view, the role of the services is that of supplier and supporter of forces, not the owner or operator of those forces.

2. An example for the Navy was the development of riverine forces; an example for the Air Force was the aerial gunships.

3. The contributions from the Air Force and Navy in both wars were mainly in the form of air power. It was DeSeversky who correctly foresaw that "total war from the air against an undeveloped country or region is well-nigh futile" (DeSeversky, *Victory through Air Power*, p. 102).

4. Admiral David Farragut expressed the Navy's historic attitude toward mines more than a hundred years ago: "Damn the torpedos [which is what mines were then called], full speed ahead!"

5. The fondness of the services for their memories of World War II may not lie entirely with the sweetness of victory. It was a time, also, when the services enjoyed enormous public support at home and very little intervention by civilian control—circumstances that they long for today.

6. My colleague William Jones, who was there, explains why: The B-17 and B-24 bombers were carrying only one-sixth to one-seventh of their weight in bombs on their missions to Germany, yet as much as one-fifth of the bombers were being lost on those early missions. It was in March 1944 that the weight tallies of bombs dropped and planes lost finally crossed over.

7. The reasons for the ascendancy of the fighter pilots over the bomber pilots in control of the Air Force invites speculation. My theory goes something like this: The deployment of ballistic missiles in the 1960s encroached upon the mission of the bombers and their numbers. But since the Air Force is about flying and is run by aviators, fighters much more than missiles seemed to have a better future for those who loved flying and airplanes. By the late 1960s, one could discern the growing power of the fighter pilots; in the 1970s, the control of the Air Force began to shift.

8. AirLand Battle doctrine is supposed to apply generally to conflicts the Army might face; but its relevance is obvious only in Europe. Though its principles can certainly be stretched to apply in a few other places, such as Southwest Asia or Korea, it would be difficult to imagine it emerging from the contemplation of conflict anywhere else. Perhaps this is why the Army and the TAC-dominated Air Force have been able to cooperate as well as they have in recent years in the development of the AirLand Battle doctrine: They appear to be able to share a concept of the next major war—a conventional war with the Soviets in Central Europe. The Army still worries, however, that the Air Force will fight its war for control of the air, even as the Army loses its war for the territorial integrity of the FRG.

9.  The growing importance of the Pacific in U.S. trade relations has caused some to question the future validity of America's historic emphasis on the security of the Atlantic community. But this is not an argument for the United States to discount the importance of Europe so much as it is to increase the attention it gives to Asia.

10. If we are willing to accept a trip wire posture in South Korea but not in the FRG, the implication is that we find it easier to threaten the North Koreans with nuclear weapons when they have none with which to reply than it is to threaten the Soviet Union which could respond in kind.

## Chapter 13

1.  Including, probably, the right of overland access to the city from West Germany.

2.  In the FRG and ROK, Air Force units have also been positioned to assist in territorial defense (or to carry the war to the enemy); but the very mobility of air power makes the form and timing, if not the continuance, of their commitment somewhat less certain than that of Army forces.

3.  See Huntington, "Conventional Deterrence and Conventional Retaliation in Europe."

4.  The term "price" is used here in the sense of "the cost at which something is obtained," not in the economic sense of "the quantity of one thing that is exchanged or demanded in barter or sale for another" (*Webster's Ninth New Collegiate Dictionary*, 1986).

5.  It is not enough to say, as some do, that their purpose is deterrence of conflict. Deterrence, in the absence of criteria for its success, is not a military purpose, as the term is used here. The prospect of destruction, delay, disruption, or even uncertainty may deter; but then the criterion for deterrence—how much destruction, delay, disruption, or uncertainty is expected to deter—needs to be specified.

Secretary of Defense McNamara proposed that the threat of assured destruction should be sufficient to deter a nuclear attack on the United States by the Soviets; but he then went on to define the criterion for deterrence—the ability to destroy certain specified fractions of the Soviet population and industrial floor space following a specified Soviet attack—thereby providing an explicit, though legally dubious, military purpose to be achievable by the strategic nuclear forces. For a discussion of the legal issues raised by the concept of assured destruction, see Carl H. Builder and Morlie H. Graubard, *The International Law of Armed Conflict: Implications for the Concept of Assured Destruction*, RAND Corporation, R-2804-FF, Santa Monica, January 1982.

6.  Fair pricing here means the full and honest assessment of the required military forces and risks associated with specific military objec-

tives, without regard to political sensitivities, fiscal constraints, or service proprietaries.

7. Force structure is defined as the "numbers, size, and composition *of the units* that comprise" the forces assigned (See *Department of Defense Dictionary*, emphasis added).

8. It is almost certain that this objective would demand more forces than the United States could (or would be willing to) provide. But such an objective might be useful as a reference point in terms of minimizing risks and maximizing forces. Lesser objectives and their associated risks and forces would then provide a spectrum of price tags and a rational basis for negotiating a match between military commitments and capabilities, whatever the political aspirations might be.

9. Although this objective may appear to be frivolous or macabre, it is probably, unfortunately, not far removed from the current, but implicit, objective of U.S. forces in the FRG. The reasons for making such objectives implicit rather than explicit are more political than military; but the tradeoff between the interests of political rectitude and military planning needs to be confronted sometime, if not continuously.

10. For the Army (or Department of Defense) to define itself mostly in terms of defending NATO by military means is to drive itself crazy and leads to much of the pessimism about NATO planning. Trying to design forces for impossible tasks is not only futile, it is discouraging and demeaning as well.

11. Most notably, the so-called Packard Commission's Report—*A Quest for Excellence*, Final Report to the President by the President's Blue Ribbon Commission on Defense Management, June 1986.

12. For an early assessment of the prospects for JCS reform, see Jeffrey S. McKitrick, "The JCS: Evolutionary or Revolutionary Reform?" *Parameters* 16, no. 1 (Spring 1986): 63–75. For a later and more comprehensive assessment of the several efforts to reorganize the Department of Defense, see Don M. Snider, "DOD Reorganization: Part I, New Imperatives," *Parameters* 17, no. 3 (September 1987): 88–100, followed by "Part II, New Opportunities," no. 4 (December 1987): 49–58.

13. McKitrick, "The JCS: Evolutionary or Revolutionary Reform?" p. 68.

14. Palmer, *The 25-Year War*, p. 209.

# Chapter 14

1. This view was expressed to me by one high official in the Army.

2. Such arguments often find fertile ground in the ever-present American isolationist tendencies or play to occasional interests in a pull-back from NATO because of some tiff with the Europeans.

3.  Good examples are to be found in the current efforts to simulate the earth's atmospheric, climate, and weather phenomena.

4.  The tradeoffs between the assets of the Army and those of the Air Force will be the more obvious, immediate, and direct for the three national commitments to the use of force. But the Navy may be the most sensitive of the services to any tradeoffs involving its forces. Thus, it is not clear which of the Army's sister services would perceive itself as the most threatened by force tradeoffs.

5.  Summers, *On Strategy*, p. 111, referred to a memorandum from Major General John Elder to Lieutenant General Donald Cowles, DCSOPS, 8 March 1973, on the subject of "Army Strategic Thought."

6.  A mirror example for the Soviets would be Cuba: The Soviets could not hope to prevail over the United States in a protracted war over Cuba. But the Soviets' ability to insert their ground forces in brigade or division strength would pose a powerful deterrent to U.S. armed intervention because of the Soviet options (and incentives) for horizontal escalation and the heightened risks of vertical escalation.

# Chapter 15

1.  For a good summary of American military strategy options in the Pacific, see Francis Fukuyama, "Asia in a Global War," *Comparative Strategy* 6, no. 4 (1987): 387–413. Many of the observations made here have their source in my participation with Fukuyama in RAND research on strategy alteratives for the Pacific. The views expressed here, however, are presented as my own.

2.  Colonel Clifford Krieger of the Air Force has reminded me on more than one occasion that the Air Force also has its principal theater of concern: the Trans-Polar theater.

3.  For a summary of the military forces in that region, see Anthony H. Cordesman, "The Military Balance in Northeast Asia: The Challenge to Japan and Korea," *Armed Forces Journal International* 121, nos. 4, 5 (November/December 1983).

4.  As did the Badger bombers that preceded them and as may the Blackjack bombers now projected to succeed them.

5.  Peter Polomka, *The Two Koreas: Catalyst for Conflict in East Asia?* International Institute for Strategic Studies, Adelphi Paper 208, London, Summer 1986, p. 56.

6.  Though the "lessons" of the 1982 war in the South Atlantic are still subject to considerable debate, the value of the British ships destroyed by the few Argentine Super Entendards with Exocet missiles would have made it worth the loss of the aircraft, if that had been necessary.

7.  Watkins, "The Maritime Strategy," p. 12.

8.  Fukuyama, "Asia in a Gobal War," p. 390.

9.  For an excellent analysis of the Soviet buildup, see Harry Gelman, *The Soviet Far East Buildup and Soviet Risk-Taking against China*, RAND Corporation, R-2943-AF, Santa Monica, August 1982.

10.  John D. Perse, "The Maritime Strategy," *U.S. Naval Institute Proceedings* 113, no. 12 (December 1987): 29–30.

11.  See David R. Rivkin, Jr., "No Bastions for the Bear," *U.S. Naval Institute Proceedings* 110 no. 4 (April 1984): 36–43.

12.  Moreover, the Soviets are not yet able to pose a comparable threat to either Japan or the United States. Their prospects for conducting, supporting, and exploiting an invasion and occupation of northern Hokkaido or the Aleutians against Japanese and American opposition are not promising.

13.  See chapter 12. Recall that it was only in the last fifteen months of the war in Europe that the United States dropped more weight in bombs than junked airplanes on Germany.

14.  The American military institutions, of course, would like to see the wisdom of their preferences reflected in the "choices" of our allies. But they also have an interest in our allies having capabilities to support American equipment if it should be needed in their defense.

15.  When I have voiced these arguments with American military officers, they have countered with the observation that U.S. allies do not want anything less than the best—the same first-line systems that the United States acquires for itself. But that observation only begs the source of the views of what is the best. The views could be as much a cultural transfer of system preferences as a reasoned assessment of allied or American defense needs.

## Chapter 16

1.  Huntington, *The Soldier and the State*, p. 261.

2.  To make the available peacetime resources more nearly proportionate to the improbable task of war in Central Europe, the Army is forced to redefine the problem creatively—to make it something considerably less than it is in its full dimensions. Thus, we hear such creative objectives as defeating the first echelon of Soviet forces, stopping the Soviet advance by the first week (or month), providing a conventional pause before escalation to nuclear weapons, and so on. What happens after these diversions is left to the imagination of others.

3.  My colleague Ed Cesar notes that the Army, unfortunately, has several masters it must serve: Congress, the president, the joint chiefs, the secretary of defense, and even the citizenry. They can confront the Army with demands that are, if not directly conflicting, often in tension. I take

his point, but the good servant either finds ways to finesse the tension or to ascertain who the real master is. Admittedly, the Navy finds it somewhat easier to deal with the problem because it thinks it is, or should be, the master, not the servant. The Air Force, the aviators, do not even think in those terms; their relationships are with their media (air and space) and the machines that take them there.

4. Snider, "DOD Reorganization: Part II, New Opportunities," p. 52.

## Chapter 17

1. Only much later would some come to doubt that large, dispersed, agrarian cultures, such as China, could be decisively defeated even with lavish use of thermonuclear bombs.

2. After these words were written, the Air Force, indeed, proposed to cancel the Midgetman missile: "In recent weeks, Midgetman's congressional supporters began picking up quiet indications that Air Force officials, led by [Chief of Staff General Larry] Welch, were preparing to kill the small missile. Welch was described by sources as unwilling to fund three strategic modernization programs within the smaller fiscal 1989 budget total he has been allocated." (*Defense Week*, 14 December 1987, p. 1.) That the Air Force faces budget constraints is undeniable. What is significant here is the Air Force choice of the programs to be sacrificed. When Congress forces the services to cut—and they often do in times when they are preoccupied with other budget cutting concerns—it is the services who then decide whose baby dies in its crib.

3. Harvey M. Sapolsky, *The Polaris System Development*, (Cambridge: Harvard University Press, 1972), pp. 168–69, emphasis added. Whether those views are correct or not is in some dispute; but the perception of those within the institution is relevant in determining the institution's behavior.

4. These programs, in turn, have their roots in the Army's air defense artillery and, before that, in the coast defense artillery. This is a part of the Army that has been searching for its institutional niche ever since the airplane eliminated the sharp boundary between land and sea in warfare and obsoleted the systems specifically designed to control that interface: coast defense artillery and naval monitors (shore bombardment ships).

5. Tuchman, "Human Nature Is Responsible," p. 77.

# BIBLIOGRAPHY

Ackoff, Russell L., and Elsa Vergara. "Creativity in Problem Solving and Planning: A Review." *European Journal of Operational Research* 7, no. 1 (May 1981).

Bender, David L., ed. *The American Military: Opposing Viewpoints.* St. Paul, Minn.: Greenhaven Press, 1983.

Brodie, Bernard. *Strategy in the Missile Age.* Princeton: Princeton University Press, 1959.

Builder, Carl H. *The Army in the Strategic Planning Process: Who Shall Bell the Cat?* CAA Technical Paper, CAA-TP-86-12, Bethesda, October 1986.

————. *The Army in the Strategic Planning Process: Who Shall Bell the Cat?* RAND Corporation, R-3513-A, Santa Monica, April 1987.

————. *A Conceptual Framework for a National Strategy on Nuclear Arms.* RAND Corporation, R-2598-AF, Santa Monica, September 1980.

————. "The Crowd Roars." *Phalanx: The Bulletin of Military Operations Research* 19, no. 3 (September 1986).

————. *On the Army Style in Analysis.* RAND Corporation, P-7267, Santa Monica, October 1986.

————. *On the Army Style in Analysis.* Republished in *Phalanx: The Bulletin of Military Operations Research* 20, no. 2 (June 1987).

Builder, Carl H., and Morlie H. Graubard. *A Conceptual Approach to Strategies for the Control of Air Pollution in the South Coast Air Basin.* RAND Corporation, R-2917-SCAQMD/RC, Santa Monica, September 1982.

————. *The International Law of Armed Conflict: Implications for the Concept of Assured Destruction.* RAND Corporation, R-2804-FF, Santa Monica, January 1982.

Cordesman, Anthony H. "The Military Balance in Northeast Asia: The Challenge to Japan and Korea." *Armed Forces Journal International* 121, nos. 4, 5 (November/December 1983).

Davis, Vincent. *Post War Defense Policy and the U.S. Navy, 1943–1946.* Chapel Hill: University of North Carolina Press, 1966.

DeSeversky, Alexander P. *Victory through Air Power.* New York: Simon & Schuster, 1942.

Douhet, Giulio. *The Command of the Air.* New York: Coward-McCann, 1942.

Dunn, Keith A., and William O. Staudenmaier. "The Retaliatory Offensive and Operational Realities in NATO." *Survival* 27, no. 3 (May/June 1985).

Emerson, William R. "Operation Pointblank: The Tale of Bombers and Fighters." *Harmon Memorial Lectures in Military History,* no. 4. Colorado Springs: U.S. Air Force Academy, 1962.

*Foundations of Force Planning: Concepts and Issues,* edited by the Force Planning Faculty, Naval War College. Newport, R.I.: Naval War College Press, 1986.

Freedman, Lawrence. *Strategic Defense in the Nuclear Age.* International Institute for Strategic Studies, Adelphi Paper 224, London, Autumn 1987.

Fukuyama, Francis. "Asia in a Global War." *Comparative Strategy* 6, no. 4 (1987).

Gelman, Harry. *The Soviet Far East Buildup and Soviet Risk-Taking against China.* RAND Corporation, R-2943-AF, Santa Monica, August 1982.

Gray, Colin S. "Defense Planning and the Duration of War." *Defense Analysis* 1, no. 1 (March 1985).

Hadley, Arthur T. "The Split Military Psyche." *New York Times Magazine,* 13 July 1986.

————. *The Straw Giant—Triumph and Failure: America's Armed Forces.* New York: Random House, 1986.

Hoopes, Townsend. *The Limits of Intervention.* New York: David McKay Co., 1969.

Howard, Michael. "The Forgotten Dimensions of Strategy." *Foreign Affairs* 57, no. 5 (Summer 1979).

Huntington, Samuel P. *The Common Defense: Strategic Programs in National Politics.* New York: Columbia University Press, 1961.

————. "Conventional Deterrence and Conventional Retaliation in Europe." *International Security* 8, no. 3 (Winter 1983–84).

————. "National Policy and the Transoceanic Navy." *U.S. Naval Institute Proceedings* 80, no. 5 (May 1954).

————. *The Soldier and the State.* Cambridge: Harvard University Press, Belknap Press, 1957.

Jones, David C. "What's Wrong with Our Defense Establishment." *New York Times Magazine,* 7 November 1982.

Kaiser, Karl, and Georg Leber. "Nuclear Weapons and the Preservation of Peace: A German Response." *Foreign Affairs* 60, no. 5 (Summer 1982).

Kanter, Arnold. *Defense Politics: A Budgetary Perspective.* Chicago: University of Chicago Press, 1979.

Komer, Robert W. "Maritime Strategy vs. Coalition Defense." *Foreign Affairs* 60, no. 5 (Summer 1982).

Kriete, Charles F. "The Moral Dimension of Strategy." *Parameters* 7, no. 2 (1977).

Lacy, James L. *Within Bounds: The Navy in Postwar American Security Policy.* Center for Naval Analyses, CNA 05 83 1178, 28 July 1983.

Lehman, John F., Jr. "The 600-Ship Navy." *The Maritime Strategy.* Annapolis: U.S. Naval Institute, January 1986.

MacIsaac, David. "Voices from the Central Blue: The Air Power Theorists." In *Makers of Modern Strategy,* edited by Peter Paret. Princeton: Princeton University Press, 1986.

McKitrick, Jeffrey S. "The JCS: Evolutionary or Revolutionary Reform?" *Parameters* 16, no. 1 (Spring 1986).

Majone, Giandomenico. "Systems Analysis: A Genetic Approach." In *Handbook of Systems Analysis,* edited by Hugh J. Miser and Edward S. Quade. New York: North-Holland, 1985.

Maurer Maurer. *Aviation in the U.S. Army, 1919–1939.* Office of Air Force History. Washington, D.C.: United States Air Force, 1987.

Millis, Walter. *Arms and Men: A Study in American Military History* New York: G. P. Putnam, 1956.

Murray, Robert J. "JCS Reform: A Defense of the Current System." *Naval War College Review* 38, no. 5 (September/October 1985).

Nitze, Paul. "Strategy in the Decade of the 1980s." *Foreign Affairs* 59, no. 1 (Fall 1980).

Palmer, Bruce, Jr. *The 25-Year War: America's Military Role in Vietnam.* New York: Simon & Schuster, 1984.

Perse, John D. "Discussion: The Maritime Strategy." *U.S. Naval Institute Proceedings* 113. no. 12 (December 1987).

Polomka, Peter. *The Two Koreas: Catalyst for Conflict in East Asia?* International Institute for Strategic Studies, Adelphi Paper 208, London, Summer 1986.

Posen, Barry R., and Stephen Van Evera. "Defense Policy and the Reagan Administration." *International Security* 8, no. 1 (Summer 1983).

President's Blue Ribbon Commission on Defense Management. *A Quest for Excellence.* Final Report to the President, June 1986.

Rivkin, David R., Jr. "No Bastions for the Bear." *U.S. Naval Institute Proceedings* 110, no. 4 (April 1984).

Rogers, Bernard W. *The Army.* Field Manual FM 100-1, 29 September 1978.

————. "The Atlantic Alliance: Prescriptions for a Difficult Decade." *Foreign Affairs* 60, no. 5 (Summer 1982).

Sapolsky, Harvey M. *The Polaris System Development.* Cambridge: Harvard University Press, 1972.

Schratz, Paul R. "The Admiral's Revolt." *U.S. Naval Institute Proceedings* 112, no. 2 (February 1986).

Smith, Perry McCoy. *The Air Force Plans for Peace, 1943–1945.* Baltimore: Johns Hopkins University Press, 1970.

Snider, Don M. "DOD Reorganization: New Imperatives." *Parameters* 17, no. 3 (September 1987).

———. "DOD Reorganization: New Opportunities." *Parameters* 17, no. 4 (December 1987).

Stimson, Henry L., and McGeorge Bundy. *On Active Service in Peace and War.* New York: Harper Bros., 1947.

Stockfisch, J. A. *The Intellectual Foundations of Systems Analysis.* RAND Corporation, P-7401, Santa Monica, December 1987.

Summers, Harry G., Jr. *On Strategy: The Vietnam War in Context.* Strategic Studies Institute, U.S. Army War College, Carlisle, Pa., undated.

Tuchman, Barbara. "Human Nature Is Responsible." In chapter 2, "Is the U.S. a Militaristic Society?" of *The American Military: Opposing Viewpoints*, edited by David L. Bender. St. Paul, Minn.: Greenhaven Press, 1986.

Turner, Stansfield, and George Thibault. "Preparing for the Unexpected: The Need for a New Military Strategy." *Foreign Affairs* 61, no. 1 (Fall 1982).

U.S. Air Force. *Basic Aerospace Doctrine of the United States Air Force.* AFM 1-1, 16 March 1984.

U.S. Army. *The Army.* Field Manual FM 100-1, 14 August 1981.

Vaill, Peter B. "The Purposing of High-Performing Systems." *Organizational Dynamics* (Autumn 1982).

Warner, Edward. "Douhet, Mitchell, Seversky: Theories of Air Warfare." In *Makers of Modern Strategy*, edited by Edward Meade Earl. New York: Atheneum, 1966.

Watkins, James D. "The Maritime Strategy." *The Maritime Strategy.* Annapolis: U.S. Naval Institute, January 1986.

———. "The Real Reformers." *The Maritime Strategy.* Annapolis: U.S. Naval Institute, January 1986.

———. "Reforming the Navy from Within." *Defense 85.* Washington, D.C.: U.S. Government Printing Office, November 1985.

Weinberger, Caspar W. *Annual Report to the Congress, Fiscal Year 1987.* 5 February 1986.

Westwood, James T. "Some Notes on Strategy." *Military Review* 65, no. 10 (October 1985).

Wylie, J. C. *Military Strategy: A General Theory of Power Control.* Westport, Conn.: Greenwood Press, 1967.

# INDEX

A-6, 179
A-10 Thunderbolt II ("Warthog"),
    120–21
Abrams tank, 24
Advanced manned strategic aircraft
    (AMSA), 15, 100, 222 n.12
Aircraft. *See specific type*
Aircraft carriers, 76–77, 172–73, 174,
    176
  importance of, 78, 79, 135
Air Force
  balance of power in, 61–62
  concept of war of, 129, 136–38
  institutional legitimacy and relevance
    of, 27–29
  intraservice distinctions in, 26
  love of, for machines and flight, 23,
    32–33
  measuring size and composition of,
    21–22, 210 n.16
  Pacific, posture of, in, 170–75
  Pentagon corridor of, 35–36
  responsibility of, for strategy, 218 n.1
  reverence of, for technology, 19, 23,
    32–33, 72, 209 n.7
  self-image of, 199
  sense of identity and interests of, 37
  Star Wars and, 199–201
  struggle by, for autonomy, 72, 73
  style of, in analysis, 104–5, 109, 111
  World War II and, 132, 224 n.6
Air Force Academy Chapel, 34
Air Force strategy
  autonomy as postwar concern in,
    69–70, 71
  pioneers in, 67–69
  strategic bombardment as, 70–72

Air Force Systems Command (AFSC),
    102–3
AirLand Battle doctrine, 88, 220 n.1,
    221 n.8, 224 n.8
Air power
  concepts of, 136–38, 224 n.7
  as decisive instrument of war, 68,
    218 n.4
  evolution of, 218 n.6
  independent instrument of, 218 n.3
  nuclear weapons and, 194–95
  promotion of, 68
  struggle for autonomy in, 77–78
Alaska, 139
Aleutian Islands, 228 n.12
Analysis. *See also* Military analysis;
    *specific service*
  Air Force style of, 104–5, 109, 111
  Army style of, 159
  imagination and, 115–23
  Navy style of, 106–7, 110
Analytic techniques
  and defense analysts and toys of war,
    111–14
  parable of, 107–9
  of services, compared, 104–11
Andrews, Frank, 74–75
Antisubmarine warfare (ASW), 176.
    *See also* Submarines
Argentine Super Entendards, 227 n.6
Army
  ability of, to price commitments,
    155–59
  adjustment of, to nuclear era, 188
  balance of power among branches of,
    188–89
  ballistic missile defense and, 229 n.4

concept of war of, 138–42, 165–67
dependence of, on other services, 89–92
as "handyman" and good servant, 186–87, 190–91, 228 n.3
inadequacies of, 162–65
institutional interests of, 30, 191
intraservice distinctions in, 26–27
measuring size and composition in, 22, 210 n.17
national security and, 133–34
nuclear weapons and, 196–97
in Pacific theater, 168–70
patriotism and, 19–20
Pentagon corridor of, 35
pricing military commitments by, 152, 153
pride of, in skills, 33–34
pride of, in soldiering *vs.* equipment, 24
responsibility of, for strategy, 218 n.1
role of, in Central European war, 186, 187, 189–90, 228 n.2
role of, in nuclear era, 191–93
self-image of, 189–93
sense of identity and interests of, 37–38
Star Wars and, 199, 201
style of, in analysis, 105–6, 109, 110–11, 223 nn.1, 2
war as force for change in, 203–4
World War II and, 132, 186
Army strategy, 86–92
Arnold, Hap, 104
"Assured destruction" concept, 100, 222 n.10, 225 n.5
Atomic bomb, 77–78. *See also* Nuclear weapons
Australia, 177
AWG-9, 178

B-1 bomber, 43, 195, 222 n.12
B-1B bomber, 222 n.12
B-2 bomber, 22
B-29 bomber, 96–97
B-49 bomber, 212 n.9
B-35, flying wing, 212 n.9
B-52, 15, 195
B-58, 195
B-70, 195
Backfire bombers, 171, 172–73, 176
Badger bombers, 176, 227 n.4
Ballistic missiles. *See* Missiles
Barents Sea, 176
Belgium, 148
Berlin, 144

Blackjack bombers, 227 n.4
Boeing 707, 209 n.7,
Boldyreff, Alex, 221 n.4
Bombers. *See specific bomber*
Bradley fighting vehicle, 24
Budget constraints, 202–3, 229 n.2

Camranh Bay, 170, 177
Carrier battle groups (CVBGs), 172, 173, 176, 179
Central Europe
  Army's concept of war in, 138–42, 186, 187, 189–90, 224 n.8, 228 n.2
  Army forces in, 163–64, 166
  control of air space in, 137
  images of conflict in, 115–23
  probability of war in, 139–40
  role of U.S. forces in, 189–90
Cesar, Ed, 228 n.3
Chapels, academy, 34–35
Chennault's Flying Tigers, 23
China, 229 n.1
  and U.S. force posture in Pacific, 177
Churchill, Sir Winston, 51, 221 n.3
CINC. *See* Commanders in Chief
Coast Guard, 9, 208 n.6
Cold War, 64
Commanders in Chief (CINC)
  pricing military commitments by, 152, 153, 156
  strategy of, 57, 58
Commitments. *See* Military commitments
Communism, containment of, 52. *See also* Soviet Union
Concept of war. *See also* War
  Air Force, 129, 136–38
  Army, 138–42, 165–67
  future, 130–31
  importance of services', 127–29
  national security and services', 133–34
  Navy, 134–36
  sources of, 131–34
Conflict, images of, 115–23
Cruise missiles, 41–43
Cuba, 167, 227 n.6
Curtiss Jenny, 209 n.7
CVBGs. *See* Carrier battle groups

Defense strategy, 57, 58. *See also* Strategy; *specific service*

documents for, 217 n.3
examples of, 217 n.6
DeSeversky, Alexander P., 51, 69, 72,
    214 n.16, 218 n.6
  on air power, 76
Deterrence, 225 n.5
  in Central Europe, 187
  strategy of, 50, 64, 214 n.12
  U.S. forces and, 140–41
Doctrines, evolution of, 61, 63–64
Dominican Republic, 166
Douglas DC-3, 209 n.7
Douhet, Giulio, 64, 67, 214 n.16, 218
    nn.2, 6
  on air strategy, 67–68
Dulles, John Foster, 52

E-2, 178, 179
Eagle Squadron, 23
Eisenhower, Dwight, 40, 41
Equipment. *See* Technology; "Toys";
    *specific equipment; specific service*
Exocet missiles, 227 n.6

F-15, 178
F-16 aircraft, 175, 176, 178, 179
Falklands War, 113–14
Farragut, David, 224 n.4
FB-111, 15, 16, 195
FBM. *See* Fleet Ballistic Missile
Federal Republic of Germany (FRG),
    144, 225 n.2
  defense of, military objectives in,
    148–49, 226 nn.8, 9
  defense of, price for, 148–50
  invasion of, 138
  national security commitments of,
    147
  U.S. forces in, 141–42
Fighter pilots *vs.* bomber pilots, 138,
    224 n.7
Fiske, Bradley A., 32
Fleet Ballistic Missile (FBM), 199–200
Force postures, 180–81
Force structure, defined, 226 n.7
FORCEM model, 108, 223 n.4
Funding constraints, 202–3, 229 n.2

Geneva Conventions, 222 n.5
Great Britain, modernizing SLBMs,
    14–15
Greece, 143, 145
Grenada, 166

Hadley, Arthur, 8–9
Hawk missile, 179
Helicopters, 137
Harrington, Arthur, 210 n.15
Hokkaido, 228 n.12
Honduras, 144
Hoover, Herbert G., 15–16, 208 n.10,
    223 n.16
Horizontal escalation, 64, 218 n.23
Howard, Michael, 215 n.22
Huntington, Samuel P., 145, 186, 215
    n.18

ICBMs, 39–41
Identity, service, 36–39
Images of conflict, 115–23. *See also*
    Concept of war; *specific service*
Institutional legitimacy and relevance
  Air Force, 27–29
  Army, 30
  Navy, 29
Interservice conflicts, 65–66, 79, 159–62
Intraservice distinctions
  Air Force, 26
  Army, 26–27
  Navy, 25–26
Isolationism, 226 n.2

Japan, 144, 145
  LeMay's bombing campaign in,
    96–98, 221 n.4, 222 nn.5, 6, 7
  self-defense forces of, 213 n.19
  Soviet threat to, 173–74, 176–78
  U.S. force posture in Pacific and,
    177–78
  U.S. Navy and, 168–69
  Western trade and, 18–19
Joint Chiefs of Staff (JCS), pricing mili-
    tary commitments by, 151, 153,
    156, 158, 226 nn.11, 12
Jones, David, 31
Jones, William, 208 nn.3, 8, 210 n.17,
    222 n.7, 224 n.6

Kamchatka Peninsula, 176
Kennan, George, 52
Key West agreements, 91
Komer, Robert W., 81, 220 n.21
Korea, AirLand Battle of, 224 n.8. *See
    also* South Korea
Korean Peninsula, 164–65
  threat of invasion to, 171, 172

Korean War
  air power in, 134, 224 n.3
  Army difficulties in, 133, 186
  performance of services in, 129–30
  strategic bombardment in, 71, 219
    n.10
Krieger, Clifford, 210 n.19, 227 n.2
Kurils, 176


Lafayette Escadrille, 23
Latin America, 165, 166. *See also*
    *specific country*
Lebanon, 137
Lehman, John, 51, 214 n.17
LeMay, Curtis, 96–98, 221 n.4, 222 n.7
Long, Robert, 217


M-14, M-16 rifles, 24
MacArthur, Douglas, 51
McNamara, Robert S., 15, 51–52, 58,
    162, 225 n.5
  and Minuteman missiles, 223 n.17
  systems analysis and, 98, 99, 222 n.10
Mahan, Alfred Thayer, 61, 64, 74, 81,
    89
Manhattan Project, 97
Marine Corps, 9, 208 nn.6, 7
*The Maritime Strategy,* 81–82
Maritime strategy, 65, 81–85
  emergence of, 80–81
  Komer on, 81
  military force in, 84 t.1
  naval forces and, 83–84
  need for, by U.S., 220 n.20
  in Northeast Asia, 84, 220 n.21
Marshall Plan, 52
Medaris, John, 201
Mediterranean, 143
Mexico, 166–67
Middle East, 166
Midgetman missile, 195–96, 229 n.2
Military analysis, 95, 221 n.2. *See also*
    Operations analysis; Requirements
    analysis; Systems analysis; *specific
    service*
Military commitments. *See also*
    *specific country*
  nature of, 143–45
  pricing of, 146–53, 155–62, 225 n.4
  purposes of, 147, 225 n.5
Military institutions, resistance to
    change by, 202–6
Military planning, interservice interests
    and, 154–55. *See also* Strategy;
    *specific service*

Military postures, offensive *vs.* defen-
    sive, 178, 179–81
Mines, 131, 202
Minuteman missiles, 39, 102–3, 195,
    223 n.17
Misawa, 174, 176, 179
Missiles. *See also specific missile*
  Air Force and, 195–96
  effectiveness of, in Central Europe,
    115–19
  institutional behavior of services and,
    201–2
  service doctrine and, 63
Mitchell, Billy, 68, 74–75, 201, 214
    n.16, 218 n.6
Motivation, institutional *vs.* personal,
    10–12
Mottos of service academies, 34
MX missile, 39


National Guard, 209 n.8
National Security Council (NSC), 63
National security strategy, 57, 58. *See
    also* Strategy
NATO
  defense of, 150, 226 n.10
  deterrence of war in Central Europe
    and, 140–41
  flexible response by, 215 n.27
  U.S. commitment to FRG and,
    149–50
  U.S. interests and, 139, 225 n.9
Naval Academy Chapel, 35
Naval Institute, 81
Navy. *See also* Maritime strategy
  aircraft carriers of, and Soviet threat
    to Pacific, 172–73, 176
  concept of war of, 129, 134–36
  independent command at sea in,
    18–19, 209 n.6
  as independent institution, 31–32
  institutional legitimacy and relevance
    of, 29
  intraservice distinctions in, 25–26
  justification of forces by, 135–36
  loyalty of, to institution, 23–24
  measuring size and composition in,
    21, 210 n.15
  mine warfare and, 131
  nuclear warfare and, 134–35, 196
  Pacific as military theater of, 168–70
  Pentagon corridor of, 35
  reverence for tradition in, 18
  sea lanes threat in Pacific and,
    173–74

sense of identity and interests of, 36–37
style of, in analysis, 106–7, 110
war as force of change for, 203
World War II and, 133
Navy strategy. *See also* Maritime strategy
aircraft carriers and, 76–77
responsibility for, 218 n.1
search for, 74–81
New Zealand, 177
Nike air defense, 201
Nitze, Paul, 215 n.22
Northeast Asia, 166
maritime strategy in, 84, 220 n.21
U.S. military and threats to, 171–72
Norway, 144
Nuclear warfare
Navy and, 134–35, 196
seapower and, 79
Nuclear weapons, 222 n.10
Air Force and, 194–96
Army and, 191–93, 194, 196–97
FRG and, 149
in Pacific, 170
service doctrine and, 63
services' self-images and, 197–98
U.S. strategy and, 216 n.32

Office of Secretary of Defense, 151
Okhotsk Sea, 176
Operations analysis
defined, 99
examples of, 96–98
in World War II, 96, 221 n.3

P-3 aircraft, 179, 180
Pacific. *See also* Air Force; Navy
as military theater, 168–70
regional security interests in, 175–78
U.S. military posture in, 174–75
Packard Commission Report, 226 n.11
Patton, George S., 221 n.8
Peacekeeper missile, 39
Pearl Harbor, 221 n.3
Pentagon service corridors, 35–36
Perry, Matthew, 18–19
Perry, Robert L., 214 n.9
Persian Gulf, 133, 144
Philippines, 143, 144, 145 166–67, 180
Phoenix, 178
Planning. *See* Military planning; Strategy; *specific service*
Polaris Fleet Ballistic Missile program, 195
Polaris missile, 14

Poseidon missile, 14, 100, 101
Pricing military commitments, 146–53, 225 nn.4, 6
by Army, 152, 153, 155–59, 159–62
by Commanders in Chief, 152, 153, 156
by Joint Chiefs of Staff, 151, 153
by Office of Secretary of Defense, 151
Programming and Budgeting System, 110–11

Radar, early warning, 178
Rainbow war plans, 221 n.3
Reagan, Ronald, 51, 64, 198
Republic of Korea. *See* South Korea
Requirements analysis, 101–3
*Rex*, 75
Rickover, Hyman, 201, 211 n.26
Rogers, Bernard, 51, 217 n.5
Roosevelt, Franklin D., 51
Royal Canadian Air Force, 23
Ryan, Jack, 210 n.20

S-3, 179
Safeguard ABM, 201
Sakhalin, 174, 176
SAMs. *See* Surface-to-air missiles
Scowcroft Commission, 40, 196
Service doctrines, 61
Service strategy. *See also* Maritime strategy; Strategy; *specific service*
defined, 57, 59
example of, 217 n.4
purposes of, 59–60
uses of, 61–66
Silo spacing, 102–3
Single Integrated Operational Plan (SIOP), 102, 136, 217 n.2
SLBMs, modernizing British, 14–15
Smith, Perry McCoy, 73
Smuts, Jan C., 218 n.3
South Atlantic war, 227 n.6
South Korea (ROK), 144, 146, 170, 225 nn.2, 10
Army presence in, 141
threat of invasion to, 171
Southeast Asia, 165
Southwest Asia, 165, 166
AirLand Battle, 224 n.8
Soviet Union
future ground war with, 166
invasion by, of Central Europe, 167
long-range bombers of, 172–73
submarines of, 176

threat of, to Northeast Asia, 171,
    172–74
U.S. maritime strategy and, 83, 84,
    220 n.22
Spacecraft, service doctrine and, 63
Space defense, 139. *See also* Star Wars;
    Strategic Defense Initiative
Spain, 145
Spruance, Raymond A., 77
SSBNs, 135
Star Wars, 51, 140, 198–202
Stein, David J., 215 n.24
Stoner AR-15 rifle, 24
Strategic Air Command (SAC)
    concept of war of, 136, 137–38
    FB-111 and, 15–16
    nuclear weapons and, 196
    silo spacing and, 102–3
Strategic bombardment, 70–72, 219
    n.10
Strategic Defense Initiative, 51, 140,
    198–202
Strategy. *See also* Maritime strategy;
    Service strategy; *specific service*
    Army, 86–92
    of Commanders in Chief, 57, 58
    defense, 57, 58
    defined, 47, 48–50
    deterrence as, 50, 64, 214 n.12
    historical examples of, 51–52
    importance of knowing formulator
        of, 52–54
    inadequacies of, 56, 216 n.34
    national security and, 57, 58
    Navy search for, 74–81
    negative views of, 54–56
Submarines, 77, 135, 170, 199–200
Surface-to-air missiles (SAMs), 137,
    139, 180
Systems analysis, 98–101
    defined, 99
    and new bomber, 100–101


Tactical Air Command (TAC)
    concept of war of, 137–38
    nuclear weapons and, 196
Technology, airman's reverence for, 19,
    23, 32–33, 72, 209 n.7
TFX program, 15
Thailand, 145
"Toys"
    Air Force, 23

Army, 24
    defined, 210 n.18
    Navy, 23–24
Toys of war, defense analysis and,
    111–14
Tradition, importance of, to Navy,
    18–19
Trans-Polar theater, 227 n.2
Trenchard, Hugh Montague, 214 n.16,
    218 n.3
Trident, 14
Turkey, 143, 144


Vandiver, E. B., III, 212 n.10, 213 n.16
*Victory through Air Power,* 68
Vietnam War, 129–30, 133, 134, 186,
    224 n.3
von Clausewitz, Karl, 55


War. *See also* Concept of war; Nuclear
    war; *specific war*
    CINCSAC plan for, 217 n.2
    as force to change military institu-
        tions, 203–4
    future, and images of conflict,
        115–23
    importance of services' concepts of,
        127–29
    recent American experience with,
        129–31
*The War Game,* 223 n.1
War Gaming, 113–14
Warsaw Pact, 138, 148, 149
Watkins, James, 214 n.17
Weapons, influences on selection of,
    178. *See also* "Toys"; Nuclear
    weapons; *specific weapons*
Webb, James, 212 n.15
Wehrmacht, 213 n.19
Welch, Larry, 229 n.2
West, Bing, 214 n.17
West Point Chapel, 34
Winnefeld, James A., 209 n.3
Woodrum Committee hearing, 31
World War II, 132–33, 224 n.5
    air strategy in, 70–72
    naval strategy in, 75, 76, 77, 78
Wylie, J. C., on Army strategy, 88–90


Zumwalt, Elmo, 38

# SELECTED LIST OF RAND BOOKS

Alexiev, Alexander R., and S. Enders Wimbush (eds.). *Ethnic Minorities in the Red Army: Asset or Liability?* Boulder, Colo.: Westview Press, 1988.

Curry, Jane L. (trans. and ed.). *The Black Book of Polish Censorship.* New York: Random House, Inc., 1984.

Dorfman, Robert, Paul A. Samuelson, and Robert M. Solow. *Linear Programming and Economic Analysis.* New York: McGraw-Hill Book Company, 1958. Reprinted New York: Dover Publications, 1987.

Horelick, Arnold L. (ed.). *U.S.-Soviet Relations: The Next Phase.* Ithaca, N.Y.: Cornell University Press, 1986.

Hosmer, Stephen T. *Constraints on U.S. Strategy in Third World Conflicts.* New York: Taylor and Francis, 1987.

Hosmer, Stephen T., Konrad Kellen, and Brian M. Jenkins. *The Fall of South Vietnam: Statements by Vietnamese Military and Civilian Leaders.* New York: Crane, Russak & Company, 1980.

Hosmer, Stephen T., and Thomas W. Wolfe. *Soviet Policy and Practice toward Third World Conflicts.* Lexington, Mass.: Lexington Books, 1983.

Johnson, A. Ross, Robert W. Dean, and Alexander Alexiev. *East European Military Establishments: The Warsaw Pact Northern Tier.* New York: Crane, Russak & Company, 1982.

Korbonski, Andrzej, and Francis Fukuyama (eds.). *The Soviet Union and the Third World: The Last Three Decades.* Ithaca, N.Y.: Cornell University Press, 1987.

Leites, Nathan. *Soviet Style in Management.* New York: Crane, Russak & Company, Inc., 1985.

Leites, Nathan. *Soviet Style in War.* New York: Crane, Russak & Company, Inc., 1982.

Nerlich, Uwe, and James A. Thomson (eds.). *Conventional Arms Control and the Security of Europe.* Boulder, Colo.: Westview Press, 1988.

Nerlich, Uwe, and James A. Thomson (eds.). *The Soviet Problem in American-German Relations.* New York: Crane, Russak & Company, Inc., 1985.

Ross, Randy L. *Government and the Private Sector: Who Should Do What?* New York: Taylor & Francis, 1988.

Williams, J. D. *The Compleat Strategyst: Being a Primer on the Theory of Games of Strategy.* New York: McGraw-Hill Book Company, Inc., 1954. Revised 1966 edition reprinted. New York: Dover Publications, Inc., 1986.

Wolf, Charles, Jr. *Markets or Governments: Choosing between Imperfect Alternatives.* Cambridge, Mass.: The MIT Press, 1988.

Wolf, Charles, Jr., and Katharine Watkins Webb (eds.). *Developing Cooperative Forces in the Third World.* Lexington, Mass.: Lexington Books, 1987.

Made in the USA
Columbia, SC
22 November 2021

49523085R00155